New China Business Strategies

Chinese and American Companies as Global Partners

JOHN MILLIGAN-WHYTE
DAI MIN
MANNIE MANHONG LIU
HOWARD H. JIANG

SPECIALIST PRESS INTERNATIONAL

New York

Specialist Press International books can be purchased for educational, business or sales promotional use. For ordering details, please contact:
Special Markets Department
Specialist Press International – SPI Books
99 Spring Street • New York, NY 10012
(212) 431-5011 • sales@spibooks.com

For further information, contact:

New York

S.P.I. Books
99 Spring Street, 3rd Floor
New York, NY 10012
(212) 431-5011 • Fax: (212) 431-8646
E-mail: publicity@spibooks.com
www.spibooks.com

10 9 8 7 6 5 4 3 2 1

First Edition
Library of Congress cataloging-in-publication data available

ISBN(13): 978-1-56171-820-7
ISBN: 1-56171-820-3

———≈◈≈———

Also by John Milligan-Whyte and Dai Min

CHINA AND AMERICA'S EMERGING PARTNERSHIP:
A REALISTIC NEW PERSPECTIVE
(Specialist Press International Books — S.P.I. Books)

Table of Contents

NEW CHINA BUSINESS STRATEGIES: CHINESE AND AMERICAN COMPANIES AS GLOBAL PARTNERS

Acknowledgements

This book about partnerships of human beings in countries and companies could not have been created without the wisdom, courage, and support, for a quarter of a century, of Orlando Smith, the Managing Partner of Milligan-Whyte & Smith.

The tireless support of Lei Valli Thompson, Amani Flood, Dora Baker and the staff of Milligan-Whyte & Smith, Doris Goodman of Reporting and Transcription Services, and David McCormick of the University of Toronto were also essential. As were the contributions of Robert Levin of Transclick, Ian Shapolsky of SPI Books, and Wilder Knight and Robert Stein of Pryor Cashman.

We are grateful for the encouragement of U.S. Ambassador Richard Swett of APCO Worldwide; the late U.S. Representative Tom Lantos, former Chair of the House Foreign Affairs Committee; U.S. Representative John Conyers, Jr., Chair of the House Committee on the Judiciary; U.S. Representative Carolyn Maloney, Chair of the House Financial Services Committee's Financial Institutions Subcommittee; U.S. Representative Lester Wolff (Retired), former Chair of the House Asian Affairs Subcommittee; former UN Under-Secretary General Maurice Strong; Seymour Topping, former Managing Editor and Editorial Director of the New York Times; Maurice Johnson, Editor of Business Wire China; Cyril Rance of XL Capital; Mary Grace of e-Smart Technologies; The Honorable Judge Melvin Schweitzer; Jytte Marstrand; Zhang Liyong, President of China General Chamber of Commerce in U.S.A.; Dr. Chen Wenshen; Jin Juanping; Dr. Deng Ya; Hu Jun; Prof. Li Shixin; Xie Na and Dr. Geng Xiefeng of Peking University; Chen Xialou; Ji Sanmeg; Liu Fan; and Dr. Zhao Gangzhu of Renmin University.

Jerry de St. Paer, the former CFO of XL Capital and Honorary Chairman of the China Bermuda Society, and Virginia Kampsky, of Kampsky & Associates and the China Institute, provided significant impetus for the book.

We also thank the over 1.6 billion Americans and Chinese who inspired and for whom the book was written.

Foreword

by **Capt. Wei Jiafu**

It is my great pleasure, as President & CEO of COSCO Group and a representative of the Chinese business community, to provide this forward to *New China Business Strategies: Chinese and American Companies As Global Partners*. I look forward to having candid and practical discussions on matters relating to the win-win cooperation between the Chinese and American business communities which this book champions.

American political and business leaders, and American and Chinese companies, must play a successful leadership role in guaranteeing the sound development of bilateral business and trade relationship between our two nations. It is our wish that the U.S. policies on commerce and trade will encourage more Chinese companies to invest in the U.S. and will allow more U.S. companies to enhance their business ties with China. I know this book will be of assistance to American and Chinese political and business leaders in the advancement of win-win based business relationships between China and America and between Chinese and American companies.

COSCO is a China-based international shipping company that operates the world's second largest ocean-going commercial fleet with a total deadweight tonnage of 41 million tons. It is the mission of COSCO that we provide refined, efficient, secure and reliant shipping and logistics services to contribute to the sustainable growth of global trade.

As a key trans-Pacific carrier, COSCO has always played a vital role in China-U.S. trade, which has experienced a sharp increase of over 80-fold from 2.4 billion USD in 1979 to 211.6 billion USD in 2005. In fact, it was COSCO that re-opened the China-US maritime trade in April 1979 by sending the first-ever PRC commercial ship, *M.V. Liu Lin Hai* from China to Seattle. The historical visit by *Liu Lin Hai* to a U.S. port after 30 years of absence of US-China trade marks the beginning of a new era of the world's most important trade relationship.

While rapidly growing our global competitiveness, COSCO, as a member of UN launched Global Compact, is making enormous efforts to realize sustainable development and to be a good corporate citizen. Recently, COSCO's annual report on sustainable development passed the joint audit of DNV and China Classification Society.

COSCO's case of sustainable development represents the strong commitment of the Chinese business community to contribute to the formation of an harmonious world, which is a goal set by President Hu Jintao towards the peaceful development of the world. The relationship between China and the United States is among the most important relationships in the world. As strong mutual interest and complementarities do exist between the business communities of China and the U.S., we believe that a win-win business cooperation between our two nations can greatly contribute to building an harmonious world.

COSCO has operated its business in the U.S. market for 28 years; and along the growth path of our U.S. business, we have benefited greatly from our long-term strategy to establish win-win relationships with our American business partners, clients, and suppliers. The outstanding partnership that COSCO built with the Massachusetts Port Authority sets a perfect example for Chinese businesses that are seeking growth in the U.S. market.

At the end of 2001, I received a letter from Governor Jane Swift of Massachusetts, telling me that the port of Boston was facing a serious challenge because of the departure of Maersk Lines container services, and thousands of workers with the port were about to lose their jobs. The governor was asking COSCO to set-up new container ship services from the far east to Boston to help promote trade and save jobs. After making careful considerations and evaluations, COSCO saw it as a good opportunity to re-establish a trade bridge between China and Boston by sending container liner ships to Boston. As a good corporate citizen, we also felt it was our mission to help save 9,000 port-related jobs in Massachusetts and to seek a win-win-win solution among local shippers, Massport and COSCO. Since COSCO sent the container ship *M.V. Zhen He* to the port of Boston in March 2002, the port's container throughputs have grown sharply. The volume of import containers in our first year of operation at Boston registered a growth of four times, and export container two times. Because of COSCO's presence, the trade between the six states in New England and China was stimulated, local jobs were saved, shippers benefited tremendously from the convenience brought by direct liner service, and COSCO also benefited from rising profits from our liner operations.

COSCO's collaboration with Massport has also set-up a strong model for Chinese and U.S. companies that are searching for win-win relationships. Statistics have proved that the mutual business presence of China and the U.S. have greatly benefited both countries. COSCO is one of the more than 800 Chinese companies that have invested in the United States, and the healthy growth of all China-invested business in the U.S. is undoubtedly contributing to the growth of the U.S. economy and employment.

Meanwhile, the rapid growing investments from the U.S. multi-nationals in China have also benefited both countries. By doing business with China, U.S. companies have made good profits, enhanced their global competitiveness and strengthened their positions in the U.S. market. According to the American Chamber of Commerce in China, the 2005 total revenue of U.S.-invested companies in China reached 107.6 billion USD, and 42% of these companies registered higher profit returns than their global average. Through a bullish and well-regulated capital market, these U.S. companies can generate dividends to millions of U.S. public investors who can indirectly benefit from the success of U.S. companies in China.

The rising bilateral trade between China and the U.S. has also created huge benefits for the people of both countries. According to Morgan Stanley, in 2004 alone, quality yet inexpensive Chinese goods saved U.S. consumers 100 billion USD, and trading with China created over four million jobs in the United States.

China's economy is now in a new period of growth. China's development goal for the next 15 years is to increase its GDP to about four trillion US dollars, or, 3,000 USD per capita, in nominal terms (at 2005 exchange rates), or roughly $12,000 per capita on a puchasing-power-parity basis. China's development will present enormous business opportunities to the United States, because China has a huge market and big demand for America's advanced technologies and management expertise.

Given the rapid growth, sheer size and wide scope of American and Chinese business ties, it is hardly avoidable that some problems have occurred. It is our common hope that these problems can be properly addressed through consultation and dialogue on an equal footing as we work to expand our business ties.

Capt. Wei Jiafu,
President & CEO COSCO Group
China Ocean Shipping Company

Readers' Guide

A new win-win mindset regarding China is presented in *China & America's Emerging Partnership: A Realistic New Perspective* and *New China Business Strategies: Chinese and American Companies as Global Partners*. These interrelated public policy and business strategy books examine what we term "The China Game" and the case for elite accommodation and a committed, genuine economic and geopolitical partnership between America and China, and a new mindset about China's nation-building and "Socialist Market Economy Capitalism."

This book examines the mindset changes and new Genuine Global Joint Venture Model, and advanced "win-win" strategies and structures, and the structures, strategies and best practices that foreign companies have used with China.

The advantages of the new Genuine Global Joint Venture Model and of American companies aligning their China strategies with the goals of China's economic development, and Chinese companies going global, are examined.

In the real world, politics and economics are played-out in business, and vice versa. Resolving political and business problems requires the successful interaction and alignment of political and business strategies. Readers interested in geopolitics, political economy, macro economic growth or competitiveness may focus on the first book; but the second will help in understanding the business dynamics, combining zero-sum-game and win-win strategies that drive or damage the relationship of America and China. Business-oriented readers may focus on the second book, but the first book will help in understanding the mindset changes about doing business with China and win-win structures and strategies required for them to have powerful competitive advantages in the 21st century.

China & America's Emerging Partnership: A Realistic New Perspective is presented in 17 chapters and *New China Business strategies: Chinese and American Companies As Global Partners* is presented in 13 chapters. The overviews at the beginning of each chapter are designed to provide a concise summary and enable readers to find the discussions of topics of interest to them. Our thesis and key themes are reiterated frequently to facilitate both mindset change and selective reading.

Detailed information that is presented in the 30 chapters examining our thesis and key themes is excessive for some readers' needs, but useful for others new to or very familiar with China's development. These books were written in 2005-2007. Details change over time, but our thesis and key themes remain compelling and unchanged by such changing details in recent years. The overview that begins each chapter will enable readers that wish to skim or skip its subject, or the detailed information in it, to see what each chapter's focus and main points are. The italicized headings throughout each chapter are also designed to facilitate selective reading.

In *China & America's Emerging Partnership: A Realistic New Perspective*, Chapter 1 examines the need for elite accommodation between America and China. Chapter 2 examines why they will fail or succeed together. Chapter 3 examines the American policy choices of containment or collaboration and five key questions facing America's political and business leaders. Chapter 4 examines China's capitalism which is redefining the competitiveness and wealth of nations in the 21st century. Chapter 5 examines China's success as a "Permission Society", a "Consensus Democracy" and "Pre-Rule of Law Society" in which 22% of humanity is increasingly thriving. It had been assumed before

China's participation in the global economy that economic competitiveness required an American style "Rights Society," "Majority Rule Democracy" and "Rule of Law" system. Chapter 6 examines the genius of the Chinese government, people and culture in so rapidly emerging from the economic wreckage of the Cultural Revolution.

Chapter 7 examines whether America can peacefully accept China's peaceful rise. Chapter 8 examines leadership failure and American resentment and fear of China. Chapter 9 examines conflict or collaboration between America and China. Chapters 10 and 11 examine how America and China are currently economic partners and how a committed, genuine global partnership between America and China would ameliorate the trade deficit, job losses and other issues confronting America and China that the current relationship based on ad hoc, zero-sum-game strategies will fail to do. Chapter 12 examines win-win and zero-sum-game approaches to the relationship of America and China and game theory relevant to their interaction's success. Chapter 13 examines China's past and future scientific and technology contributions to America. Chapter 14 examines the very similar evolution of the concept of intellectual property rights and their piracy and enforcement in America in the 19th and 20th centuries and in China in the 21st century.

Chapter 15 examines how America and China's partnership can be established and sustained in the 21st century. Chapter 16 examines whether America and China will choose together to succeed or fail as civilizations. Chapter 17 examines why a committed, genuine partnership of the world's current and emerging superpowers is essential for America and China to both consistently produce leaders in the 21st century able to sustain their shared peace and prosperity.

In Part 1 of our companion business strategy book twenty illustrations provide a visual synopsis of both books and of an American executive's China mindset change.

Part 2's chapters 1, 2, 3, 4, 5 and 6 examine best practices in traditional China business strategies and a new win-win mindset, strategies and structures designed to align American companies' strategies with the Chinese government's strategies for economic development and the needs of Chinese state-owned and private companies "going global." Chapter 1 examines the competitive advantages for American companies of a win-win mindset, value propositions, strategies and rewards.

Chapter 2 examines how American companies seeking profits in doing business with China's "Permission Society," "Consensus Democracy" and Pre-Rule of Law system can sustainably profit from China's economic growth and what we refer to as the "IBM+Legend=Lenovo deal" template of a Genuine Global Joint Venture Model pioneered in late 2004. The IBM+Legend=Lenovo deal itself is unfortunately viewed in 2006 as a failure in China because it was not executed in what to date is seen in China as a really win-win deal. However, the IBM+Legend=Lenovo deal template points the way towards greater win-win success for American and Chinese companies and therefore America and China.

The IBM+Legend=Lenovo deal template is contrasted with the template for failure in the relationships between America and China, and American and Chinese companies, seen in the profoundly significant battle in 2005 between China National Offshore Oil Corporation (CNOOC) and Chevron over the acquisition of Unocal, an American oil company.

Chapter 3 examines advanced strategies aligning American companies with Chinese companies going global. Chapter 4 examines an advanced structure for American and Chinese companies as Global Partners. Chapter 5 examines case studies of traditional structures, strategies and best practices used by American companies joint venturing or investing in China. Chapter 6 examines further case studies of traditional structures and strategies and the advantages of the Genuine Global Joint Venture Model.

In Part 3, Chapter 7 examines China's commitments as a member of the World Trade Organization and some observers' expectations about them in the context of the evolution of China's Permission Society. Chapters 8, 9, 10, 11, and 12 examine alignment opportunities for American companies with China's evolving financial services sector. Chapter 8 examines the current mindset among many Americans that unrealistically assumes China's evolving financial services sector must copy foreign models. Chapters 9, 10, 11, and 12 then examine in more detail China's evolving banking, insurance and reinsurance, stock market, and venture capital industries and alignment opportunities for American companies. Chapter 13 examines China's education and regional disparity challenges and alignment opportunities for American companies.

John Milligan-Whyte
America-China Partnership Foundation
New York
May, 2008

PART 1

An American Executive's China Mindset Change

"It's big ... everyone says it's important."
"Yes ... but what is it?"
"I don't know, but it's capitalism ... with Chinese characteristics."

Stupid people think they are smart, because they can satisfactorily answer any question they can think of. Smart people think they are stupid, because they cannot satisfactorily answer any question they can think of.

Jack Welch says if you want to be the world leader in your industry, you have to be the leader in China. But how can you be...if you are not Chinese?

"The laws of economics are clear. China can only be successful if it is like America."
"Are you sure? The laws of economics are enabling China's economy to grow three times faster and at least four times longer ... than America's."

The World Economic Forum's Global Competitiveness Report ranked America # 1 and China ranked 33rd in macroeconomic and 38th in growth competitiveness of 80 nations in 2002 and in 34th in competitiveness in 2006. So how can China have attracted over US$650 billion in foreign investment since 1978? Why does America have a $233 billion a year trade deficit with China in 2006?

"When the President of China wakes up in the morning, his biggest concern is how he will feed 1.3 billion people."
"So what...How is that relevant to my company's China Strategy?"
"It is the key to your company's China Strategy. He sees China differently than we do. China is a "Permission Society," not a "Rights Society"; a "Consensus Democracy," not a "Majority Rule Democracy"; and a Pre-Rule of Law Society."

The wealth and competitiveness of nations has changed. I need a new China Strategy and a new model of globalization and of Chinese capitalism.

"Do you know about yin and yang? They are very influential in China, Mr. Chairman."

"Are they a law firm?"

"No…but you see…"

"If not, exactly how are yin and yang relevant to my China Strategy?"

"Think of it this way…What is in it for the Chinese to want your China Strategy to work and keep working? That is yin. What are you going to do when your China Strategy does not work? That is yang."

"Why is our joint venture partner in China going in that direction rather than with us?"

"Well...it's their way of indicating that we have passed the apex of their curve of gratitude."

"What strategies and structures work in your company's China Strategy?"
"Good question...but many foreign companies are making money in China.
I have to compete with them and Chinese companies going global."

(continued on next page)

"*Why don't the Chinese do things the American way? It's the only way they can be as successful as we are...tell them that again...*"
"*I will sir...but they like doing things their way too...and they had a $ 233 billion trade surplus with us last year...so they are hard to convince.*"
"*Try again. Try that "win-win" stuff, appeal to fairness, and threaten them...*"

Legend buys Microsoft? How are the starving Chinese suddenly such rich capitalists?

How can I explain, in terms his American mindset can comprehend, that the Chinese will not accept losing? He knows Americans will not accept losing, but it is beyond his zero-sum mindset to understand the Chinese won't accept losing either.

I need "Nash Equilibrium"…with China…whatever that is…

If you cannot change what you perceive, change how you perceive it.

My company needs its critical China Strategy to work! So what are the Chinese government's problems and goals? How can I help them get what they want? How can they help me get what I want? How do my company and Chinese companies make money on a continuing basis in a sustainable, aligned "win-win" strategy?

"We are going to try that Genuine Global Joint Venture Strategy."
"It won't work! We don't understand the Chinese! They won't let us win or play the game by our rules," said Mr. Mindset Problem.
"How can we make it work,-sir?" said Ms. Mindset Change.

"What do you think about America and China and American and Chinese companies becoming global partners?"
"It's nonsense. But we have to make that work somehow."

"How can we make our Chinese and American companies successfully work together?"

"I don't know…but tell me what you need and I'll tell you what I need."

"Ok…I need lunch…every day."

"Good…I do too."

"Great….let's go eat someone else's lunch together."

"Hey…let's buy a restaurant…have some M&A, an IPO on NASDAQ… then lots of people will have to pay us for their lunch."

"Will they pay us in US dollars?"

"Sure…every day…"

"Perfect…by the way, I need to send my kids to school in America."

"They can stay with my family. I need to send my kids to school in China."

"My biggest successes in China were in my imagination. When I thought I was winning, I was losing. Zero-sum strategies that work in a 'Rights Society' were self-defeating with China's 'Permission Society'. So I tried 'win-win' strategies and aligned my China Strategy with China's Strategy. That's how I won in the China Game."

PART 2

American and Chinese Companies as Global Partners

1

Mindset Change as a Competitive Advantage for American Companies

Overview

This chapter examines the different business management and cultural styles in America and China and the need to integrate the strengths and ameliorate the weaknesses of each.

How Can We Respect People Who Are Different and Do Not Understand Us?

How can we understand or respect people who are different from us, who could be threats, allies, or both? American political and business leaders at the cutting or "melding" edge of the emerging partnership and elite accommodation between America and China, and American and emerging Chinese companies, must recognize and respect the genius of the Chinese government, people and culture in transforming China so quickly from a failing planned economy into a "Socialist Market Economy Capitalism" system of social and economic organization that is redefining the world.

Negotiating and Carrying Out Contracts: A Meeting of Minds?

In American contract theory, a contract is made when there is an offer and acceptance in a context in which both parties intend to create a contract. This is also referred as "a meeting of the minds." American contract theory also relies on the assumption that contracts can be enforced. What happens when the parties to a contract have an offer and acceptance but not a meeting of the minds and no means of enforcing the contract? In the China Mindset, a contract is not a contract; it is simply a stage in the negotiations.

By "China Mindset," we are referring to their mindset of Mainland Chinese origin. This is, of course, an amorphous and an ambiguous term; but it can be defined or at least recognized by the differences it has to the "American Mindset," which is also an amorphous and ambiguous term, but has commonly recognized features.

The China Mindset has fundamentally not been changed by interaction with foreigners. The China Mindset is absorbing Western technology and work processes, but is not changing as rapidly, if at all. Foreigners doing business with Mainland Chinese must deal with not only an unfamiliar set of rules of the game, but also an unfamiliar set of habits of thought and behavior. Since Mainland China's economic evolution is the dominant economic force in the 21st Century global economy, it is likely that the Chinese Mindset will be more able to resist change than the American Mindset.

The Chinese and American Mindsets are shaped by different backgrounds, experiences, expectations, and perceptions of self-interest. Two ways of responding to this "disconnect" are either not successfully responding to the disconnect or shifting mindsets. The second is a more promising approach than the first, but the second requires the American Mindset to understand the Chinese Mindset.

It is tempting to ignore the differences in the Chinese and American mindsets and rely on an unreliable assumption that people behave according to "self-interest," but that contains the fallacy that people often do not understand others' perception of self-interest. The second fallacy it contains is that people often do not understand their own self-interest.

We will refer to China's culture and traditions as being "a Permission Society" rather than a "Rights Society," a "Consensus Democracy" rather than a "Majority-Rule Democracy," and a Pre-Rule-of-Law rather than a Rule-of-Law Society. These important differences are examined in detail in *China & America's Emerging Partnership: A New Realistic Perspective.*

The Chinese View of Outsiders

Americans have struggled to understand the Chinese since their interaction began. One Western observer has framed the problem thus:

> There is ... a certain schizophrenia involved in the Chinese view of Westerners, senses of inferiority and superiority that may curiously exist side by side...On the one hand, the Chinese see Western society as highly advanced in many ways. They view its achievements in the development of science and technology, manufacturing, transportation, and agriculture, and its significant economic accomplishments, as worthy of emulation, envy and respect. On the other hand, however, China has a profound, five-thousand-year history, and a civilization and culture the Chinese consider second to none. The Western world may well be more advanced materially, but many Chinese see it as clearly lacking in moral fiber; how else to explain the preponderance of drugs, illicit sex, and other degenerate conduct they read and hear about in the United States and elsewhere? By this reckoning, Westerners cannot possibly be the moral equals of Chinese. As far as many Chinese are concerned, Westerners are ultimately not much better than barbarians. They don't understand the finer points of etiquette and can't necessarily be counted on to behave properly. What this underscores is

the propensity of the Chinese to judge Westerners and their behavior according to Chinese standards. For Chinese, there are relatively few choices as to what constitutes proper and improper behavior; they grow up imbued with very clear ideas of what is right and what is wrong. Lacking another set of standards, they can hardly be faulted for using this yardstick to judge others, even those who were not reared in their culture.

A Mindset of Fallacies

In the next 25 years, any analysis of China's strategy and the China strategies of American companies based on fallacies is unlikely to be successful. The root causes of American cognitive dissonance about China's emergence from poverty often are xenophobia, hostility, selfishness, and arrogance. The foreign press is rife with the spirit and detail of these approaches. Here is a classic illustration: *The Economist,* after citing China's government and people's miraculous accomplishments, opined in 2004:

> This survey will cut through all the hyperbole currently enveloping China. Progress there is as real as it is dramatic, but the country is still in transition from *one political and economic system to another.* The constraints imposed by the communist leaders (not least on themselves) have produced "a darker reality" behind the impressive statistics and soaring skylines, in the words of Orville Shell, a professor at Berkeley who knows the country well.[1] (Emphasis Added)

Cognitive dissonance or denial and ill will are not where the solution to America's challenges in "The China Game" will be found. Capitalist nations are being challenged at their own capitalist game by China's emergence from poverty. A radical re-think and shift in mindsets is required for American political and business leaders and American companies to succeed in the new dynamics of the competition of American capitalism and China's "Socialist Market Economy Capitalism."

There is a second, deeper problem of cognition in the relationship of Americans who dominated the world in the 20th century and Mainland Chinese now "going global" with such awesome success so far in the 21st century. It is the lack of overlap of America and China's experiences and, therefore, mindsets in the past fifty centuries. A nation that a thousand of years ago built a wall to keep foreigners out[2] is now interacting with a nation built by immigrants. America and China are strangers who are building their relationship day by day.

Americans are proud and understand American ways of doing things. Mainland Chinese are proud and understand the Mainland Chinese way of doing things. Each sees the other through what may usefully be compared to binoculars through which they are looking the wrong way. The key challenge is somehow finding an effective way to get Americans and Mainland Chinese to look through their binoculars in the way that enables them to see what is far away, but not that far away, if looked at properly.

Americans consciously and unconsciously project that China is like or should be like America. Mainland Chinese see America through their fifty centuries of experience. It is hard for one mindset to understand a different mindset if they do not overlap sufficiently.

American Majority-Rule Democracy may facilitate an aggressive zero-sum-game attitude and behavior in its leaders. The current American administration is very aggressive and sees the world with zero-sum-game perceptions and attitudes. Unfortunately the competition of nations seems like a sporting event in which hometown jingoism is deemed normal and appropriate. But, the relationship of the leading developed and developing superpowers is a potentially species lethal "game" with the highest possible stakes and risk factors for mankind.

There is a third, even deeper problem: some people like or need to dominate others. Such persons are more likely to have a zero-sum-game mindset than a win-win mindset. Persons or nations which like or need to dominate others are more likely to see the world as a zero-sum-game competition than people and nations that are less aggressive and more interested in consensus and avoiding loss of face.

There is a fourth problem in human cognition. Recent neurological research is beginning to be able to predict attitudes, i.e., conservative or liberal for example, by studying the different brain areas that are affected differently by the same information.[3] Our behavior may be "hard wired" in our brain functions. We are a species currently merely beginning to understand the important drivers of human perceptions, attitudes, and behavior. Having looked briefly at "nature" and noted these four of many cognitive problems, let's briefly now look at "nurture." Nature and nurture may ultimately be different aspects of the same phenomena. But, for the moment, we will ignore that, and assume that history and the nature of human beings are distinguishable.

Americans have been experimenting with their way of government, under their Constitution and other related and ancillary documents (a set of written rules interpreted by men with checks and balances) that has had its interpretation incrementally evolve, for three centuries. Contemporary Americans see the world through the binoculars of American Majority-Rule Democracy, which has produced the world's current only superpower. The Chinese see the world through the results of fifty centuries of experimenting with different rulers, known in the past as dynasties and today as a political party in a one-party-rule state. China also has a constitution; but China is carrying out a Chinese experiment with Socialist Market Economy Capitalism, not the "American Experiment." America is at a different stage of nation building than China. America is late in what we will refer to as the "modern technological nation building process." China is early in that process, and is nation-building in the context of China's historical experience, culture, need, and goals. In relative terms, America is a finished work, and China is a work in progress.

In 1978, a new experiment began in China's long history with what we refer to as "Socialist Market Economy Capitalism." That experiment involved an incremental but massive mindset change in China that is changing the world and, therefore, America. It is America's turn now to make a similarly massive mindset change.

The Chinese Government Has Displayed a Striking Mindset Change

The mindset change of the Chinese Communist Party and Chinese government from a planned economy to "Socialist Market Economy Capitalism" after Mao Zedong's death, under the leadership Deng Xiaoping, Jiang Zemin, Zhu Rongji, Hu Jintao, and Wen Jiabao and their colleagues, is unusual and impressive.

Kishore Mahbubani asserts:

> To China's good fortune, a great leader emerged to take over the helm after the traumatic years of the Cultural Revolution: Deng Xiaoping. History will eventually recognize him as one of the world's greatest leaders, delivering greater improvement to more lives than virtually any other leader....
>
> How did Deng Xiaoping decide to move more than a billion people? Change begins in the minds of men and women. After two traumatic centuries and a rich reservoir of feudal culture (which Mao had diminished but not eliminated), keeping China together would have been an achievement. But Deng wanted to catapult his billion people into the modern world, despite China's enormous historical disadvantages. He wanted to take the quickest short cut in history. He found his road map in America.
>
> When Deng visited America in January 1979, he could have decided to use the absolute control he had over the Chinese media to carefully control the flow of information on his visit. Similarly, he could have chosen to restrict the flow of

information on American society Indeed, until Deng's visit, the Chinese had been fed a distorted view of American society through the state-controlled media...

Nevertheless, Deng decided to take a huge political risk and instructed the Chinese media to show (without any propagandistic overlay) how the American people actually lived. He allowed Chinese TV to show scenes of ordinary American homes, filled with items that were then way beyond Chinese dreams: refrigerators, washing machines, cars. In so doing, Deng shattered the Communist Party myth that the ordinary American people toiled in poverty and misery. He also made the Chinese acutely aware how backward their conditions were.

Deng knew exactly what he was doing. The Chinese Communist Party had had many achievements but one of its biggest achievements was to transform the industrious Chinese people into a non-industrious race. With the 'iron rice bowl' provided by the Chinese Communist Party rule, there was no incentive to work hard....

Deng decided to use the American dream to smash the "iron rice bowl." He told the Chinese people that they could prosper if they sought to work as hard as the Americans and accumulated individual wealth. He could have made these arguments logically and rationally. But it would have taken decades to work. Instead, he just showed the Chinese people how ordinary Americans lived. The sharing of the American dream provided the Chinese people with their critical ingredients for success: hope and motivation.

The TV exposure Deng allowed was not a one-off event. Throughout the 1980s and 1990s, one of the most popular programs on Chinese TV was a program entitled "One World," which was produced by a beautiful American Chinese woman, She showed many different aspects of American society to the Chinese.

Deng decided to share the American dream with the Chinese people through a big-bang approach. This appears to have worked.[4]

For American capitalism to prosper with China's "Socialist Market Economy Capitalism," rather than to seek unsuccessfully to contain it, an unusual and impressive mindset change in American political and business leaders will be required, and through them, in American domestic and foreign policy and Americans' business strategies with China.

Mindset Change as a Competitive Advantage for American Companies

Many companies' "China strategies" are narrowly focused on "getting a piece of China's huge market" and exhibit a zero-sum-game mindset and strategies which do not provide the strategic and tactical insights required to collaborate profitably short- or long-term with "China's strategies" of economic development. An American company that goes to China with a "Rights Society" mindset focused only on taking market share or on taking advantage of Chinese companies or China's low labor and material costs may find instead that it is taken advantage of by the Chinese government and Chinese trading partners.

Many foreign companies feel that dealing with the Chinese government and trading partners should be and will become like dealing with a "Rights Society." China's strategy's rapid success and China's "Permission Society" context is not the "Rights Society" context they are geared to compete in. Some foreign companies may unnecessarily[5] accept that they will not be profitable in China for a long time. Some seem to believe that China will "open up" and become a "Rights Society" and that then they will be in position to be profitable. But what if China remains a "Permission Society" longer than these companies can afford to be unprofitable in China? How are they going to compete successfully with competitors that are profitable in China while they are unprofitable?

A "win-win mindset"[6] can be a competitive advantage in a "Permission Society." Foreign companies that align their value propositions and strategies to the context of a rapidly evolving "Permission Society" with arbitrary, changeable rules can have a

competitive advantage over foreign companies that rely on their
non-Chinese notion of their "rights." But, a foreign company
needs to be able to understand why its China strategy should be
aligned with "China's strategy," have win-win value propositions,
and use creative strategies and structures.

Some companies are not able to shift from a zero-sum-game
mindset that is successful in a "Rights Society." Some can only call
upon their ingrained zero-sum-game mindset in even trying to
perceive the need or possibility of a "win-win mindset." If a
foreign company is able to shift out of a "Rights Society" and
"zero-sum-game" mindset, it can be in the same mindset as its Chinese
trading partners. That is increasingly important because "China's
strategies" and economic development are entering a new "go-
global" phase.

The Mindset of Corporate Imperialism[7]

There are signs of the beginning of mindset change. C.K. Prahalad
and Kenneth Lieberthal in a 2003 *Harvard Business Review* article:
"The End Of Corporate Imperialism" noted that:

> During the first wave of market entry in the 1980s, MNCs
> [multinational corporations] operated with what might be
> termed an imperialist mind set. They assumed that the big
> emerging markets were new markets for their old products.
> They foresaw a bonanza in incremental sales for their existing
> products or the chance to squeeze profits out of their sunset
> technologies. Further, the corporate center was seen as the
> sole locus of product and process innovation. Many multi-
> nationals did not consciously look at emerging markets as
> sources of technical and management talent for their global
> operations. As a result of this imperialist mind-set, multi-
> nationals have achieved only limited success in those markets.
>   Many corporations, however, are beginning to see that the
> opportunity big emerging markets represent will demand a
> new way of thinking. Success will require more than simply
> developing greater cultural sensitivity. The more we

understand the nature of these markets, the more we believe that multinationals will have to rethink and reconfigure every element of their business models.

So while it is still common today to question how corporations like General Motors and MacDonald's will change life in the big emerging markets, Western executives would be smart to turn the question around. Success in the emerging markets will require innovation and resource shifts on such a scale that life within the multinationals themselves will inevitably be transformed. In short, as MNCs achieve success in those markets, they will also bring corporate imperialism to an end.

...For years, executives have assumed they could export their current business models around the globe. That assumption has to change. ... The end of corporate imperialism suggests more than a new relationship between the developed and the emerging economies. It also suggests an end to the era of centralized corporate power—embodied in the attitude that headquarters knows best—and a shift to a much more dispersed base of power and influence. ... In order to participate effectively in the big emerging markets, multinationals will increasingly have to reconfigure their resources, rethink their cost structures, redesign their product development processes, and challenge their assumptions about the cultural mix of their top managers. In short, they will have to develop a new mindset and adopt new business models to achieve global competitiveness...[8]

Research in this area is accelerating, as the rapid success of new Chinese companies is increasingly not only a competitive challenge to American companies in China, but in America and other markets.

Chinese Companies Going Global Are Absorbing Non-Chinese Business Mindsets and Skills

As Chinese companies absorb non-mainland Chinese business mindsets, skills, and competitive practices, the rate of China's economic growth and macro-economic competitiveness will accelerate. Chinese companies are absorbing non-Chinese-origin knowledge and business management skills at what will be a steadily increasing rate. American corporations must develop a mindset better suited to understanding China's one-party government system and China's capitalism's successes and business culture. Genuine global joint ventures between American and Chinese companies can be the learning model in which the necessary integration occurs. Such global joint ventures' profitability and sustainability will depend upon the success of American and Chinese shareholders, management, and staff collaborating to achieve the integration of attitudes and skills required.

As is discussed next in Chapter 2, the other alternative is that the emerging Chinese companies "going global" will acquire or displace leading foreign companies without collaborating with American companies in genuine global joint ventures or other business combinations. As Chinese companies "go global," individual American companies must choose one or other approach, i.e., a zero-sum or win-win approach. Whichever approach is chosen, the rate of progress of Chinese companies and thus of China will accelerate.

Mainland Chinese Are Studying American Management Skills

Enhanced management skills in Chinese companies are being developed through hiring foreign executives, and mainland Chinese attending business schools in China as well as abroad and through foreign business experience and the acquisition of foreign companies.

In December 2004, there were 89 Chinese educational institutions authorized to provide Masters of Business Administration ("MBA") programs in Mainland China. Since 1991, there have been 50,000 recipients of MBA and Executive MBA ("EMBA") degrees. The Chinese government initiated EMBA programs in China, and in 2004 there were approximately 30 EMBA programs.

As of June 2004, there were 31 MBA and EMBA programs that were joint ventures between foreign and Chinese institutions. In addition, at least 10 MBA or EMBA programs provide foreign institutions' degrees.[9]

The unmet needs in China for business education programs present major alignment opportunities for supporting MBA and EMBA programs in China for American companies with funding capabilities, expertise, and the "right spirit" which also need better-trained Chinese executives.

Accepting the Need for New Strategic Planning Methods and The Integration of Chinese and American Strategic Planning Methods

Haley, Haley, and Tan point out[10] that Michael Porter's and other Western strategic planning approaches, such as those of Charles Hofer, Dan Schendel, C.K. Prahalad & Gary Hamel, and Henry Mintzberg, require that a rich information environment is present where corporations compete:

> ...When they cannot obtain reliable hard data or information (as in China), they [Western corporate strategic planners] must make use of alternatives including experience, their line managers' strength. Hence, the type of information companies use in decision-making should range from the hard data that staff analysts require to the subjective data that line managers develop through experience. ...Western planning generally utilizes a staff-intensive approach to analysis and decision-making. The personnel involved may have expertise in various technologies of data analysis and manipulation that transform raw data into usable information. However, as a result of their duties, they rarely develop the intimate contact and knowledge of corporate operations, products, and markets that line managers have. Similarly, line

managers generally lack the time to develop or to maintain specialized knowledge of analytical technologies. Yet, effective strategic planning, especially in volatile environments, requires drawing on both data and experience, on both staff and line managers.[11]

Several strategic management textbooks cover the basic model of Western strategic planning. ... The model provides a clear indication of the complexity and the linear analytic approach that serves as the ideal of Western planning. For example, corporations would have a strategic planning staff charged with supporting both top management and the business units in the strategic planning process. The staff's primary responsibilities should be to identify and to analyze company-wide strategic issues, and to suggest corporate strategic alternatives to top management; and to work as facilitators with business units to guide them through strategic planning.

Thus, strategic planning at most Western corporations centers on the activities of staff who have been trained using the planning technologies currently in vogue. Yet, few of these staff has had substantial experience in line management or in the corporation's operational functions. Consequently, Robert Kuok, the Asian sugar, property, hotel and media tycoon said, 'When I hear somebody's got an MBA, I have a feeling of dread, because normally they come to me with an over-pompous sense of their own importance. And no way are you going to prick that bubble, with the result one day there will be a cave-in in their department. So, they learn painful lessons at my expense.

Additionally, line managers, and personnel who deal with day-to-day problems of generating corporate profits, do not have primary responsibility for planning, and may actually be the last to know about corporate plans.

Western strategic-planning technologies reflect the environment in which they originated and in which they have been used. These technologies incorporate abundant, easily available data on companies, industries, markets, and environments; and significant investments in staff to collect, to collate, and to analyze that data. The staff then interprets the information and recommends alternative strategies for senior managers to accept, to reject, or to modify for implementation by line managers.

> Western strategic planning methods differ from those
> employed in Asia in the amounts of hard data that planners
> require and the intensity of involvement of staff and line
> managers."[12]

The inappropriateness of the Western style of strategic planning, which relies on an abundance of data and experience information that is available in America but not in China, plays a role in the design and deployment of traditional China Strategies of American corporations use to operating in a "Rights Society" context that find themselves having to operate in a "Permission Society" context in China and in dealing with Chinese companies. The type of mindset change or improvement that Haley, Haley & Tan highlight as needed in Western strategic planning, and therefore business management, is part of the larger mindset shift that can give American companies a competitive advantage if they can change mindsets.

Haley, Haley & Tan point out the need for a "convergence" or integration of the strengths of Western style and Chinese-style strategic planning and business methods. This integration, while combining American and Chinese strategic planning and business methods' respective strengths, also uses each to ameliorate the others' weakness.

What American Managers Can Learn from Successful Chinese Companies

In 2006 Boston Consulting Group released a study that indicated that a group of high-growth companies from emerging markets is likely to outpace rivals for the main industrial nations and create an increasingly potent cause of takeover deals. One hundred companies were identified, that had out-performed their main competitions from America, Europe, and Japan in stock market terms in the past six years. Of the 100, 44 are from China and 21 from India. The study estimated that by 2010 the

100 companies are likely to have doubled their revenues from outside their home nations and twenty or more of them will be in the top five companies in their categories globally, up from only a few in 2006. The newcomers have low costs, ambitious leaders, appealing products, and modern facilities. Incumbents from the developed world will need to learn how to compete head on, partner, and/or create their own challenges to these emerging businesses.[13]

David N. Sull, an American who worked at McKinsey & Co, taught at Harvard Business School, and now teaches at the London Business School, published in 2005 *Made In China: What Western Managers Can Learn From Trailblazing Chinese Entrepreneurs*[14]. On the cover of the book, Bob Higgins comments:

> There is no economy in the world as important and yet as poorly understood as China's. In his penetrating book, Sull helps us understand what really happens in some of China's most important companies. Packed with both startling and reassuring stories, this book can help any entrepreneur seize the opportunities and manage the risk of trying something new.

Sull profiles eight formidable Chinese companies: Legend, Sina, Haier, Guangdong Galanz, Utstarcom, AsiaInfo Holdings, Hangzhou Wahaha Group, and Ting Hsin Group, which developed rapidly while their Chinese and foreign competitors failed to see opportunities and dangers as well or react swiftly and correctly in China's highly competitive, dynamic, and unpredictable market. In markets such as China, where multiple, uncertain variables interact, managers enjoy limited visibility into the future. Abandoning the fiction of prediction requires that they change their thinking about strategic planning. Traditional American strategic planning sees the objective of strategy as being first to build and then to protect a sustainable competitive advantage. Sull contrasts the traditional approach to the winning strategies of eight champion Chinese companies. Sull summarizes his approach to formulating and executing strategy in an unpredictable dynamic market as:

1. Acknowledge that in a dynamic competitive environment your perception of the future is foggy and often inaccurate;

2. Conduct constant reconnaissance into the future;

3. Replace long-term planning with strategies that can change in real time;

4. Be better and faster than all competitors at using a constant process of sensing, anticipating, prioritizing, and executing in response to emerging threats and opportunities;

5. Manage relationships dynamically and opportunistically;

6. Rapidly changing markets like China's periodically present golden opportunities to create and capture significant value in short periods of time;

7. Develop a flexible hierarchy able to balance top-down priority setting with decentralized execution;

8. Get big right: scale effectively when pursuing a major opportunity; and

9. Lead in an uncertain world.

But what does this list mean and how can it be operationalized in the real world?

Towards the Convergence of Chinese and American Business Management Styles

Haley, Haley & Tan[15] present research into the contrasting Chinese and Western cognitive styles, and emphasize the need for and provide evidence of the beginning of a convergence of Chinese and American business management styles in Western companies doing business in China and Chinese companies doing business outside of China:

> When Chinese or Western managers confront alien and unfavorable data environments, their traditional cognitive styles may fail them. However, Western companies must improve their information-processing capabilities to compete more effectively in high-potential, data-poor markets such as China, and with competitors from these markets. ... On the other hand, Chinese companies seeking success in overseas markets must cultivate their strategic long-term perspectives, especially investments in brand—names, and in technological and institutional capacities, to compete more effectively against Western and Japanese companies in mature, information-rich markets...
>
> Applying standard operating procedures derived from headquarters overseas has rarely served Western companies well in China. In Western markets, Chinese companies lose the government networks, experience, and insider information that give them an edge at home.
>
> In the new inter-dependent, global economy, the disparate Chinese and Western management styles must converge to create an effective, more comprehensive and adaptable strategic-management system. ...
>
> In managerial convergence, companies from the weaker business cultures adopt and adapt the perceived strengths of the stronger cultures to strengthen their competitive positions. With successful adaptations, the weaker companies will show resurgence. ... companies such as Legend demonstrate that managerial convergence has already begun between Chinese and Western companies.

Cultural Sensitivity and "Win-Win" Value Propositions, Strategies, Training, and Rewards

Many commentators have emphasized the different cultures' perceptions, attitudes, and negotiating procedures of Chinese and Westerners, and the need for Westerners to understand and respect

Key differences in attitudes of Western and Chinese   16

Chinese view of Westerners	Westerners' view of Chinese
– too direct and can give offence	– unwilling to express open disagreement
– use colloquial, unfamiliar language	– opinions are not expressed strongly
– dominant in meetings (which shows that they think the Chinese are not competent)	– don't want to share information
– difficult to tell if they are serious or joking	– difficult to tell if silence and nodding mean 'Yes' or 'No'
– tend to be culturally arrogant	– don't show physical signs of urgency or excitement
– expect a quick, simplistic response to complex questions	

Different perceptions and negotiation procedures   17

	Chinese	Western
Negotiation focuses on:	Process	Content
	Means	End
	Generalities	Specifics
The outcome is:	Trust	A legal contract
A contract is:	A summary of discussion A 'snapshot of the relationship'	The point of it all
	Mutable	Binding
Fairness is assessed by:	Procedure	Outcomes

Adapted from Chen, *Inside Chinese Business*.

Chinese sensibilities and culture in negotiations and doing business. For example, the tables on the previous page present a spectrum of such Chinese and Western stereotypes.

Common Stereotypes of American and Chinese Cultural Differences

Against that background, for the purpose of comparison only, we will recite the following well-known generalizations or stereotypes[18] and the contrasts that emerge which challenge the successful interactions of Americans and mainland Chinese. Our goal in doing so is to better understand and find a basis for mutual respect or at least the mutual respect of some shared principles that empower respect and collaboration rather than hostility and frustration.

Mutual respect is essential, because underlying the cultural stereotypes is a profound and fundamental historic difference: China is *ruled by law* and America is ruled by *the rule of law*. Law is administrative and customary in nature in China and administrative, adjudicative, and codified in America.

In considering the generalizations and stereotypes, we must focus on how Americans and Mainland Chinese, who are subject to the same laws of physics but have such different cultural, historical, and political experiences, can successfully interact in a 21st century genuine global geopolitical partnership of their two nations and in Genuine Global Joint Ventures among American and Chinese companies.

Americans are quintessentially individual oriented. The Chinese focus on the group instead of the individual. Americans value individual recognition, and feel group membership to be ephemeral. The Chinese focus on the group instead of the individual, and do not like to be singled-out as having unique qualities and do not accept individual responsibility. Chinese people gain their identity from the family, the group, or the company. There is no word in Mandarin for "privacy." Individuals in China seek the opinion and support of their group.

Americans expect people to express their opinions openly; and in matters of public policy or group decision making, the majority rules. It is more acceptable to question authority figures. For the Chinese, areas of responsibility and delegation of authority must be clear. The Chinese want to know exactly who is responsible for what and who has exactly what kind of authority. Those in authority cannot admit lack of knowledge or mistakes, or they will lose face. Questioning authority figures is not acceptable. Americans like debate, but Chinese dislike confrontation. They do not separate issues from persons.

Americans see power as more important than status or maturity. One's position in life is determined through individual effort. For the Chinese, one's position in life is achieved through family and connections. An ambitious Chinese strives to be an energetic and intelligent conformist. Americans can deal with criticism more readily than Chinese. Chinese do not want to stand out, and criticism is to be avoided rather than embraced as productive. Americans prefer people to say what they mean, and are uncomfortable with ambiguity. They like direct questions. Americans are generally frank and open; and they feel direct answers, even if they are negative, are most efficient. The Chinese avoid negative answers because they cause loss of face, disharmony, and are rude. Politeness is more important than frankness. For Americans, frankness is more important than politeness. Since the Chinese are afraid of losing face, they will not admit when they do not understand. Frankness is not appreciated. Direct questioning is seen as rude. They dislike confronting problems directly, and tend to go around the issues, which can be frustrating to Americans.

Americans do not see business as personal, and believe time should not be wasted on unnecessary conversation and social niceties. For the Chinese, friendships are formed slowly and last a lifetime. Human relationships and person-to-person communication is critical to the Chinese. Time should be taken to build solid relationships before doing business. A person's reputation and status is very important. Unless they know you personally and have acknowledged your existence, you do not exist.

Compared to America, where relationships may be more short term and ephemeral, in most instances relationships in China are lifelong and critical to personal worth and success. The Chinese distrust strangers. Strangers can be treated with indifference or contempt. Americans have fewer problems meeting strangers and are inclined to trust others until proven wrong. In every encounter, the Chinese study strangers' and friends' temperament and sincerity. If they decide they do not like you, they will not do business with you. Americans are diverse and there are fewer real norms for behavior as there are in Chinese culture. Chinese tend to find Americans puzzling, and don't know what to expect.

Face-saving is very important to Chinese, and less important to Americans. Americans believe that candor and action are virtues and anger is an acceptable emotion which when properly channeled, can get to the heart of problems and thus allow a solution to be found. To Americans accuracy is important, but errors are tolerated. Admitting mistakes is seen as a sign of maturity. They believe you can learn from failure, and therefore encourage risk taking. The Chinese feel it is very important never to put a person in a position of having to admit they do not understand or admit a mistake or failure and never to criticize or ridicule what a person is doing. To save face, a Chinese might withhold information, color information, avoid commitments and responsibility, cover up, or just do nothing.

Anger is unacceptable behavior to the Chinese. They dislike being challenged and having answers demanded of them. Americans like to talk, and believe it is all right to exaggerate. The Chinese believe it is better to listen and it is important to be consistent in what you say.

For the Chinese, telling another what they believe that person wants to hear instead of the absolute truth is considered part of hospitality. Nothing must be allowed to disrupt surface harmony, and it is permissible to give an answer just to please the listener. Americans will do the same thing, but perhaps to a lesser degree.

Americans are egotistical (as are Chinese), but the Chinese do not, for practical cultural reasons (i.e., Feudalism and the Cultural Revolution) like to be singled-out for unique qualities. Americans value individual recognition. The Chinese do not value individual accomplishment or privacy as Americans do. Individuals in China avoid doing things on their own. Having recited the stereotypes, now let's dig deeper.

Epistemologically and Emotionally, How Different Are Chinese and Americans?

How different are Americans and Mainland Chinese? The same laws of physics govern both. Isn't "business" "business"? Our answer is "yes" and "no." But, that said, fundamentally...our answer is "yes." We believe the differences of Mainland Chinese and Americans can be reconciled through mutual respect and collaboration.

Mark Daniell has perceptively noted:

> The history, culture, and nature of the two systems—Chinese and Western—are so fundamentally different that the perspectives held by each often share little in common [but] ... Ultimately, the Chinese system is essentially rational, seeking to find the most effective relation or means to its own shifting ends, but only pursuing those ends on a uniquely Chinese rationality. These means, ends, and the

logical and historical structures linking them together cannot be fully comprehended from a Western perspective—any more than a Chinese perspective can fully comprehend a Western system. There is a shared need to reconsider policy and action to bring the two nations together, on a foundation of clearer understanding.[19]

China has internal tensions of an old, feudal, centrally-controlled economic and political system in the midst of a fundamental and daring reformist determination to modernize China in order to enter and thrive in the 21st century global economy. Against this complex background, so different from America's, China is a mosaic united by its shared historical experience in which China's collective memory and commitment to economic growth operate. There is a constant struggle between reform and preservation of the old order.[20]

In many ways, it is simplistic to view China as if it were a single entity. It has economic, cultural and political differences, that vary among the richer coastal provinces and underdeveloped interior provinces.[21] China is also composed of many different ethnic groups. But China has a common history and comprehensive set of cultural attributes that have survived the test of time in a 5000-year civilization, which has shared recent memories of being force-fed opium by the British, been brutally colonized by the Japanese, and cast into economic exile by the capitalist countries for nearly 50 years, in which a communist, then socialist, and now capitalist ideology were added to an insular feudal society.

China's diversity is managed by the members of the current Central Committee of the Communist Party of China, which has an overwhelming dominance of persons of Han ancestry.[22]

> Underlying these modern tensions is a four thousand-year history of the Han civilization. Attitudes towards money, religion, fate, diet, medicine, family, language, central authority, the state, and even life and death are colored by a rich and deep vein of history and collective experience stretching back over

millennia. The concept of the Middle Kingdom, a vision of a China suspended between heaven and earth, is also an enduring part of the Chinese view for the future. Yet, also, memories of past losses and humiliations remain close to the surface. This mix of confidence and insecurity will require deeper understanding and more thoughtful engagement by the West to move forward together on a balanced path of peaceful progress.[23]

...The increasing globalization of China's trade patterns, investment sources, and political influence is perhaps the most salient characteristic of the systemic development of the world's most populous country. The increasing complexity of China is equally evident—its evolving languages, political structures, religions, beliefs, collective memory, and fundamental worldview are but a few of the elements making up the essence of the Chinese civilization.

The apparent contradictions are not, by Chinese standards, inconsistent. A unique blend of feelings of strength and powerlessness can only be understood in Chinese terms. The dynamic and accelerating pace of change is reflected in a century of dramatic swings in political and economic structures from a feudal base 100 years ago through agrarian communism and the tribulations of the Maoist era, to a modern reforming Communistic structure ... against that cultural background let's return to the "convergence" of American and Chinese management styles.

...Throughout waves of war, colonial oppression, rebellion, occupation, starvation, uprising and growth, the Chinese system has demonstrated a pattern of obsolescence and reinvention, constantly reinventing itself and recasting the structures of modern society on a foundation of millennia of old values and beliefs. Over time, the Chinese system is converging toward a more international set of economic principles, discarding inefficient doctrines of state intervention in the economy, and using the resulting growth to consolidate the country's disparate regions and industries to the fullest extent possible.[24]

Convergence of Strengths of Chinese and American Business Styles

Haley, Haley & Tan describe the current situation:

The first steps to convergence have been taken. As Legend's managers indicated … major Sino-Asian companies are building Western Skills and adapting their managerial practices for perceived benefit. Until recently, former Chinese prime minister Zhu Rongji served as dean of China's most prestigious business school, Tsinghu University's Business School, and significant factions within the government endorse Western management systems and practices. Other trends indicate further convergence:

Top Western business schools have provided training for many of the PRC's first generation and Greater China's second and third generation business leaders.

Many of these business leaders also have significant experience working in Western companies.

Local economic and political elites have invested heavily in founding and building their own top business schools, which are now increasingly comparable to the best in the West.

Overseas Chinese and PRC Chinese companies are making successful forays into Western markets, and will continue to expand their Western subsidiaries and investment.

Pressure from stakeholders for better governance, increased disclosure and transparency from Chinese companies is mounting.

China's WTO membership, and the international trade it fosters, should contribute to closer contact and competition between different managerial cultures.

In addition, globalization and rates of environmental, social and technological change will contribute to increasing managerial convergence between Chinese and Western companies.[25]

Haley, Haley & Tan offer one new model of what they term an "Adaptive-action Road Map" (ARM) of the convergence of American and Chinese business styles, which meld the strengths while ameliorating the weaknesses of each approach. ARM is composed of a system of adaptable strategic rules for success.[26] This area of research, and of mindset change, by Americans seeking to benefit from China's growing economic power and

Mainland Chinese seeking to "go global," urgently needs a great deal of research and adaptive experimentation.

Joint Ventures of American and Chinese Companies

The Legend + IBM = Lenovo deal in 2004, examined in detail in the next chapter, is an unfolding case study regarding the combining of American and Chinese management approaches and cultures in business. The IBM + Legend = Lenovo deal and the Genuine Global Joint Venture Model for American and Chinese companies examined in this book can facilitate Chinese companies being able to rapidly and safely orient themselves to multinational business practices and provide a model for how American companies can work, profit, and grow with Chinese companies that are responding to President Hu's call for them to "go global."

Unfortunately, in 2006, Chinese observers view the IBM + Legend = Lenovo deal as a failure. That is, in part, because Lenovo did not really maintain either the permanent benefits of retaining key IBM executives, and the IBM brand, or all of the revenue that IBM's PC business had from the American government and American customers. It is also, in part, because of cultural tensions. An example of cultural friction that a top Chinese executive (not involved in the IBM + Legend = Lenovo deal) gave was the different cultural reactions of Chinese and American executives to the death of one of their colleagues. The American executives offered light-hearted remembrances of the deceased in attempts to comfort their Chinese colleagues, who took offence because the Chinese approach is very solemn behavior. This illustration of real world workplace differences in culture must be kept in mind when Americans formulate management theories seeking to define a successful convergence model of American and Chinese business styles.

The America-China Partnership

The America-China Partnership Foundation, created by CORE Capital Ltd and China International Strategies Ltd., is a forum for leaders of Chinese and American companies considering, or involved in, working effectively together in joint ventures. The Foundation will publish updates presenting the successes and failures of the win-win business strategies and Genuine Global Joint Venture model discussed in detail in Chapters 4, 5, and 6 and the results of the Foundation's win-win oriented executive forums, education programs, and research seeking advanced strategies to successfully integrate the wisdom of Chinese and American management and conflict resolution traditions.

There is a science of business management and an art of feeling and understanding the thought processes and emotional responses of people with whom you are trying to successfully interact. It is wise, as David Sull does, to study successful and unsuccessful companies, and prepare lists of processes and check lists. We will refer to these as the "science" or "how's" of successful businesses. But it is also wise to study the "why's" of how people think, feel, learn, and make decisions. We refer to this as the "art" of business management. It is wise to ponder the certainties and mysteries of American and Chinese business management (in the Socratic tradition that American business schools use) in studying the innate mysteries, foibles, and realities of human nature. What may not be wise is to assume, consciously or unconsciously, that there is a "one model that fits all cultures" or even a convergence of a science of business management.

There is more required to understanding how Chinese companies view and operate in the world than merely seeking to translate their management success secrets into traditional American business management thought processes. Translating Chinese business management secrets into a science is essential but not sufficient for American companies to learn how to compete with and work with champion Chinese companies. They must also learn to collaborate with champion Chinese companies, which will have overwhelming competitive advantages in the 21st century.

Another competitive insight that American business people and companies need is to see themselves through the eyes of another civilization that has led the world for all but 200 of the past 5,000 years and is re-emerging in that leadership role now. To understand another culture's mindset, one must either intellectually (by thinking) or empathetically (emotionally) be able to understand yourself and your world through the other culture's mindset. In other words, there is a science of business management and an art of understanding the thought processes and emotional responses of Mainland Chinese people with whom Americans are trying to interact successfully . Both are instructive and essential for success.

What Will Happen When a Very Profitable Chinese Business Culture Encounters a Less Profitable American Business Culture?

As we explain in *China & America's Emerging Partnership: A Realistic New Perspective* and in this book, the success of China's nascent Socialist Market Economy Capitalism from 1979 to 2006 in sustaining the highest rate of economic development in the world was achieved while economic reforms were merely being introduced in a "Permission Society" rather than a "Rights Society." Before China's capitalist business culture's undeniable recent economic success, Americans believed that productivity, competitiveness, and profitability could only thrive in a Rights Society with a Majority-Rule Democracy and Rule of Law.

Here in blunt terms for American readers with zero-sum-game, or win-win mindsets, are challenges for American companies that have been created by China's successful capitalism:

1. Put in zero-sum-game terms: What will I do when Chinese champion companies buy or put out of business American champion and weakling companies?

2. Put in win-win game terms: Will I do whatever it takes for Chinese and American champion companies to successfully collaborate and prosper together?

3. Put in zero-sum-game terms: Will I benefit if there is trade war, Cold War, and armed conflict between America and China?

4. Put in win-win game terms: Will I benefit if America and China prosper peacefully together?

Your answers to those questions, we submit, prove the validity of our win-win game theory based thesis. The question is: *what does it take* to make champion Chinese and American companies successfully collaborate and prosper together? Our public policy and business strategy books' new realistic perspective on China respond in detail to that question about the *cost of success* in the 21st century.

Socrates in China

Some American business executives may not see the relevance of the following discussion of Chinese philosophic history to their company's 21st century business model, value propositions, strategies, sales, or financial results. Those who find mindset change difficult or impossible will find the next six pages a complete waste of time. Ironically, they are the readers that most need to think "out of the box" of their cultural background and mindset about doing business with China. The next six pages are a mindset litmus test.

Those who see the relevance or enjoy the discussion presented in them should consider the application of the ideas and facts in them, by analogy, to how American and Chinese management attitudes, traditions, and techniques may converge or conflict. Let's, as an experiment in the subtleties of mindset change, examine the impact some foreign ideas about epistemology, metaphysics, and the meaning of life have had in China.

It has been said that figures paralleling Socrates and Christ did not emerge and influence China's rich philosophic history as they did in Western philosophy.[27] It can be claimed that Western Civilization and American democracy evolved from, amongst other things, the combination of the success of the teachings of Socrates and Christ. Both were executed by their indigenous societies, so by one measure, their new ideas were initially forcefully resisted. Although Socrates and Christ were brilliant communicators, others sought to silence them. But their ideas became immortal. Why? Part of any answer has to be that Socrates and Christ, as brilliant communicators, had "the right spirit" in their innovative teachings that touched something fundamental in the spirit of human beings.

China's recent economic achievements, while being a "Permission Society" rather than a "Rights Society," suggest the question: Would Socrates "succeed" in negotiating a business deal in China today? Let's leave aside the fact that Socrates did not, as far as we know, focus on negotiating business deals. Americans often use Socrates' style of analytic, logical reasoning, and blunt, penetrating questioning. Would Socrates succeed in convincing modern Mainland Chinese to enter into a business deal with his "Socratic Method" of questioning every answer… often in an intellectual confrontation? It is unlikely. The style of confrontation does not work well in China. Yet we believe that candor is a critical component of successful elite accommodation and partnerships between American and Chinese companies.

Christ found ways to communicate with and persuade people who initially disagreed with him. He used parables often as communicative tools in encounters with people who challenged him emotionally, intellectually, or culturally. Christ's style enabled him to communicate so effectively that Americans measure time from the date of his birth. Christ is a leading example of a person who has "the right spirit," i.e., thinks deeply about values and therefore can communicate with people at the level of feelings rather than merely using reason and logical argument. A person who is genuinely concerned about other persons' or nations' needs has a major advantage in communicating with them.

Was Christ a more persuasive communicator *in some ways* than Socrates? In this question might lie part of the solution to the great solitude or cultural divide between China and America. Perhaps Christ is more effective as a communicator because Christ *empathized* with others whom he sought to persuade to do things his way. Socrates, however empathetic he may have been, analyzed and *judged* people, and most people were inadequate.

China's 5,000-year history and culture is very different from America's 500-year Western history and culture. Now, American and Chinese capitalism are bringing these two great societies into contact, conflict, and ultimately, of necessity in our view, into collaboration.

In China's "Permission Society," relationships define obligations. If a person had no relationship with another, if they were strangers, the Chinese view and morality is that one has no obligations to a stranger. Moreover, treating a stranger fairly might well entail being disloyal and unfair to those in your group to whom obligations were owed, and as relationships ebb and flow, obligations change. In America's "Rights Society," the Rule of Law defines obligations. How are the interaction of China's

Permission Society and America's Rule of Law in the crucible of capitalism going to influence each other?

In China's "Permission Society" history and culture:

> Chinese philosophers have always argued that society serves to extend the families and the families' pre-eminence has profoundly affected the evolution of Chinese Society. Families comprise a collection of very personal relationships that elicit specific duties and behaviors; but they, generally, also tend to forgive transgressions. Hence, Chinese society transmits highly personal perspectives and interpretations of events. As many Western managers know, doing business in China requires developing strong personal relationships with Chinese business associates; indeed, personal relationships indicate business relationships which often appear as mutations of familial relationships.[28]

Case Study: Chinese Thought Melds with and Transmutes A Foreign Philosophy

Buddhism is one of the few foreign cultural traditions absorbed in China.[29] Fritjof Capra, in *The Tao Of Physics*, explores the parallels between modern Western physics and Eastern Mysticism. Fritjof's discussion of the interaction of Indian and Chinese philosophy is thought provoking when considering how American capitalism and China's "Socialist Market Economic Capitalism" may meld and be transmuted by China's reemergence as a leading trading nation in the global economy.

Fritjof notes:

> When Buddhism arrived in China, around the first century A.D., it encountered a culture which was more than two thousand years old. In this ancient culture, philosophical thought had reached its culmination during the late Chou period (500–201 B.C.), the golden age of Chinese philosophy, and from then on had always been held in the highest esteem.

From the beginning, this philosophy had two complementary aspects. The Chinese being practical people with a
highly developed social consciousness, all their philosophical
schools were concerned, in one way or the other, with life in
society, with human relations, moral values and government.
This, however, is only one aspect of Chinese thought.
Complementary to it is that corresponding to the mystical side
of the Chinese character, which demanded that the highest aim
of philosophy should be to transcend the world of society and
everyday life, and to reach a higher plane of consciousness. This
is the plain of the sage, the Chinese ideal of the enlightened
man who has achieved mystical union with the universe.

The Chinese sage, however, does not dwell exclusively on
this high spiritual plain, but is equally concerned with worldly
affairs. He unifies in himself the two complementary sides of
human nature—intuitive wisdom and practical knowledge,
contemplation and social action—which the Chinese have
associated with images of the sage and of the king. Fully
realized human beings, in the worlds of Chuang Tzu, 'by their
stillness become sages, but by their movement kings.'

During the sixth century B.C., the two sides of Chinese
philosophy developed into two distinct philosophical schools,
Confucianism and Taoism. Confucianism was the philosophy of
social organization, of common sense, and practical knowledge.
It provided Chinese society with a system of education and with
strict conventions of social etiquette. One of its main purposes
was to form an ethical basis for the traditional Chinese family
system with its complex structure and its rituals of ancestor
worship. Taoism, on the other hand, was concerned primarily
with the observation of nature and the discovery of its Way, or
Tao. Human happiness, according to the Taoists, is achieved
when one follows the natural order, acting spontaneously and
trusting one's intuitive knowledge.

The two trends of thought represent opposite poles in
Chinese philosophy, but in China they were always seen as poles
of one and the same human nature, and thus as complementary.
Confucianism was generally emphasized in the education of
children who had to learn the rules and conventions necessary
for life in society, whereas Taoism used to be pursued by older

people in order to regain and develop the original spontaneity which had been destroyed by social conventions.

In the eleventh and twelfth centuries, the Neo-Confucian school attempted a synthesis of Confucianism, Buddhism and Taoism, which culminated in the philosophy of Chu Hsi, one of the greatest of all Chinese thinkers. Chu Hsi was an outstanding philosopher who combined Confucian scholarship with a deep understanding of Buddhism and Taoism, and incorporated elements of all three traditions in this philosophical syntheses.[30]

Fritjof continues:

The Chinese believe that whenever a situation develops to its extreme, it is bound to turn around and become its opposite. This basic belief has given them courage and perseverance in times of distress and has made them cautious and modest in times of success. It has led to the doctrine of the golden mean in which both Taoists and Confucianist believe "the sage", says Lao Tzu, "avoids excess, extravagance, and indulgence."

In the Chinese view, it is better to have too little than to have too much, and better to leave things undone than to overdo them, because although one may not get very far this way one is certain to go in the right direction. Just as the man who wants to go farther and farther East will end up in the West, those who accumulate more and more money in order to increase their wealth will end up being poor. Modern industrial society which is continuously trying to increase the 'standard of living' and thereby decreases the quality of life for all its members, is an eloquent illustration of this ancient Chinese wisdom."[31]

Fritjoh comments:

When the Chinese mind came in contact with Indian thought in the form of Buddhism, around the first century A.D., two parallel developments took place. On the one hand, the translation of the Buddhist sutras stimulated Chinese thinkers and led them to interpret the teaching of the Indian Buddha in light of their own philosophies. Thus arose an immensely fruitful exchange of ideas, which culminated... in the Hua-yen

(Sanskrit: Avatamsaka) school of Buddhism in China and in the Kegon school in Japan.

On the other hand, the pragmatic side of the Chinese mentality responded to the impact of Indian Buddhism by concentrating on its practical aspects and developing them into a special kind of spiritual discipline which was given the name Ch'an, a word usually translated as meditation. This Ch'an philosophy was eventually adopted by Japan, around A.D. 1200, and has been cultivated there, under the name Zen, as a living tradition up to the present day.

Zen is thus a unique blend of the philosophies and idiosyncrasies of three different cultures. It is a way of life which is typically Japanese, and yet it reflects the mysticism of India and the Taoist love of naturalness and spontaneity and through pragmatism of the Confucian mind.[32]

What's the Bottom Line?

This interaction of Indian and Chinese philosophic traditions is an example of how ideas developed in a foreign culture were absorbed yet mutated in Chinese philosophy and culture. It is an example that suggests that capitalism in China will retain a Chinese character. Observers who assume that China's adoption of a market economy inevitably means that China's Permission Society culture will inevitably change into an American Style Rights Society culture will find that Chinese and American capitalism are not identical in the short, medium, or perhaps even the long term. They will also find that Chinese business culture increasingly validates its prowess with enormous profits and innovation, which American companies that compete with champion Chinese "mega multinationals" cannot obtain in many instances.

2

Creating Successful Genuine Global Joint Ventures Between American and Chinese Companies

Overview

This chapter examines the challenges and opportunities for America and American companies from China and Chinese companies' integration into the global economy. It examines case studies of the Legend + IBM PC = Lenovo deal, American companies' responses to the Chinese government's need to preserve China's economic sovereignty and the needs of Chinese companies to develop global brands and advertising and market research expertise, and the competitive advantages of global joint ventures between American and Chinese companies.

China's Emerging Mega Multinationals

In 2002, Hu Jintao, the then-new President of China, instituted a "go-global" campaign, that urged Chinese companies to explore other markets and develop new brands. This now is bringing a number of Chinese companies onto the world stage as potential "Mega Multinational" companies. American corporations may not be able to compete successfully with them in the future. For American companies the answer to the challenge of the competitive advantages that China has is to collaborate with Chinese companies now going global.

China Is "A Real Game Change"

Jack Welch, former head of GE, assessed the challenges facing non-Chinese companies from China's embrace of Capitalism since 1978:

> ...I don't want to sound like a Pollyanna about China. Its presence is a real game-changer in business today. And even if trade restrictions get enacted, its currency is allowed to fluctuate, and intellectual property laws are passed, no political solution in the world is going to make it go away.[1]

Welch summarized the challenges and opportunities arising from China's competitive advantages in his book *Winning*[2] in his answer to the CEO of a Mexican company who asked:

> "We spent the last ten years bringing our company up to speed with training and process improvement, and with our low-cost labor, we were extremely competitive. But now we're getting killed by China. How can we stay alive?"

Jack Welch said:

> I have heard this question everywhere—except China, of course. When I visited Dublin in 2001, for instance, a couple of months after Gateway announced it was closing up shop, an Irish technology executive anxiously asked, "Does this mean the end of the long boom for us?" In Milan in 2004, I spoke with a German manager who wondered if his company's only hope was to sell out to an Asian company that wanted his European distribution capability. At a conference in Chicago the same year, a machine parts manufacturer based in Cleveland described in agonizing detail how the Chinese kept lowering and lowering the price of their competing products. "Will there be any manufacturing jobs left in Ohio?" he asked.

There is no easy answer to the China question. Yes, you heard about China's problems—its scarcity of middle managers, for instance, and the massive number of poor farming families moving into unprepared cities with not enough jobs to support them. Lumbering, bureaucratic, state-owned enterprises still make up most of its economy. And the country's banks are saddled with bad loans.

But for China these aren't mountains to be scaled, they are blips to be flattened by the giant, high-speed bulldozer that is its economy. Increasing prosperity from spectacular economic growth over the past twenty years has given the Chinese enormous self-confidence. But, China has so much more: a massive pool of low-cost, hardworking laborers and a rapidly expanding number of well-educated engineers.

And then there is its work ethic, which may be its single biggest strength. Entrepreneurship and competition are baked into the Chinese culture. Consider the executive who hosted me during a weeklong visit to Shanghai and Beijing last year. She said she's at the office from 7:00 am. until 6:00 pm., goes home for dinner to join her husband and son until 8:00 pm., and then returns to work until midnight. "This is very typical here," she said, "six days a week." And she works for a U.S. multinational.

So faced with the inevitability of China, what do you do?

First and foremost, get out of the tank. The sense of bleakness that I heard from Mexico to Milan and across the United States is perhaps understandable, but it doesn't get you anywhere.

…At the very least, a can-do-attitude is the place to start… Low-cost competitors are not new. Hong Kong and Taiwan have been in the game for over forty years, and Mexico, the Philippines, India, and Eastern Europe have been a factor for some time …change is what China demands of us now.

How …cost, quality and service…drive them to new levels, making every person in the organization see them for what they are, a matter of survival…. Don't think about reducing costs by 5 to 10 percent. You have to find the ways to take out 30 to 40 percent. In most cases, that's what it will take to be competitive in the China world. On quality … get rid of [all] defects…. Service is the easiest advantage to exploit. China is thousands of miles away from most developed markets…. Again, your challenge is not just to improve. It is to break the service paradigm in your industry or market so that customers aren't just satisfied, they're so shocked that they tell strangers on the street how good you are. FedEx and Dell come to mind as examples of this.... Take a new, hard look at your market. Search out untapped opportunities; find new niches. ...

...Think of China as a market, an outsourcing option, and a potential partner...China's huge market is relatively open to direct investment. Many can go it alone there, ideally selling their product in the Chinese market while sourcing products for their home market.

Alternately, you can join forces with a local business. Needless to say, Chinese joint ventures aren't easy. In my experience, to make them happen *you have to make sure the Chinese partner feels as if it has gained a lot, perhaps more than you. But, there are ways to craft win-win deals.* When GE Medical formed a joint venture in 1991, its Chinese partner brought great local market know-how. That was a big factor in the new company achieving the No. 1 market share in imported GE high-end imaging products. At the same time, the joint venture's Chinese engineers designed and built low cost, high-quality products that were exported through GE's global distribution network.[3] (*Emphasis added*)

This chapter presents a new, advanced template for win-win deals designed to ensure that the Chinese and American companies as global partners gain a lot on an ongoing basis. Traditional templates in which American companies merely invest or do business in China and even the win-win deals cited as examples by Mr. Welch may in the future have less and less sustainable value for Chinese companies and therefore for American companies.

A New Template for Win-Win Deals for America Companies' China Strategies and Chinese Companies' Going Global Strategies

The most advanced win-win deal template is for astutely matched, advised, and managed American and Chinese companies to create exceptional profits and shareholder value in well managed, successful, sustained genuine global joint ventures that are able to be number 1 or 2 in the industries they operate in and the global and Chinese markets, combining successful China strategies for American companies with "going global" strategies for Chinese companies. Such business combinations will be in part financed, and subsequently valued and given liquidity, by the international capital markets. We refer to such deals as "Genuine Global Joint Ventures." Our key focus is to facilitate Genuine Global Joint Ventures because their proliferation is essential for America and China being successful global partners.

Chinese Companies Going Global Have China's Advantages and Goals

Many of China's major companies are wholly or partly Chinese government owned or controlled. Other "champion" Chinese companies are completely private, such as Baidu, Sina, Sohu, Netease, Geely, SVT, Little Swan, and Fosun. China's "capitalism with Chinese characteristics" means that foreign companies face both "champion" non-state-owned Chinese companies[4] and wholly or partly state-owned companies that are well positioned in the huge emerging Chinese market. Privately-owned Chinese companies that have emerged in spite of great obstacles in China's ultra competitive market, and demonstrated great success, are often then "championed" by the Chinese government. State-owned companies also have the resources and support of the Chinese government, which is overseeing the fastest growing economy in the world.

If state-owned and private Chinese companies retain major positions in China's rapidly expanding domestic market, they can leverage the formidable 21st century combination of China's economic competitive advantages, their own competitive advantages in China, the Chinese government's rule-making power in China's Permission Society, the Chinese government's vast financial and intellectual capital resources, and the accelerating advantages China has in the "Knowledge Revolution." Champion Chinese companies have the same and additional advantages.

China's Economic Sovereignty

It would be surprising if the Chinese government were to voluntarily permit foreign companies to dominate and control China's domestic economy. The Mainland Chinese people would not tolerate that. However, the Chinese government today is more openminded about free market competition than many observers recognize or give it credit for.[5] Foreign companies are making significant inroads in China's domestic economy. For example, Proctor & Gamble currently dominates the personal hygiene market in China, General Motors is one of the dominant participants in China's burgeoning auto industry, and Yum! is by far the largest fast food company in China. Control of the development of China's domestic economy and economic sovereignty is being gradually affected by China's opening up since 1978 and China's WTO commitments and benefits. Nevertheless, economic nationalism among the Chinese government and people[6] and the need to preserve China's economic sovereignty are naturally vital lasting realities in China's economic development and integration into the global economy.

A key point in American companies' competitiveness is that their success or failure depends on using the cost savings and developing a market position in China's already huge and growing domestic economy. The need for American companies to achieve both competitive advantages in China and in trade with China are increasingly important as China's domestic economy grows. American companies without the cost advantages manufacturing in China provides, and significant market positions in China's economy, will be less competitive in the global markets than American or other foreign companies that are successful in doing business inside and outside China with Chinese companies.

There are two ways for American companies to look at this issue when they seek to use the competitive advantages China provides. Each of the two ways has different issues imbedded in them. One perspective, the Chinese perspective, is that in order for Chinese companies to compete inside China with highly capitalized and well established multinational companies, Chinese companies need to operate internationally and gain marketing and management expertise. The other, the American companies' perspective, is that it is essential for American companies to achieve the competitive advantages and economic rewards of successful "China Strategies."

These Chinese and American perspectives raise interrelated issues. On the one hand, how can the Chinese government fulfill its internal stability and economic development needs by permitting American companies to participate in, but not dominate, China's domestic economy? On the other hand, how can non-Chinese companies continue to dominate international markets if they do not dominate China's domestic market as it grows into such a huge part of the international markets?

How can these questions be answered to both America and China's satisfaction? The Genuine Global Joint Venture Model between Chinese and American companies discussed here and in further detail in Chapters 3, 4, 5, and 6 offers a template to deal in a "win-win" way with these different perspectives and interrelated questions. The traditional investment and joint venture structures used discussed in Chapters 5 and 6 are not optimum strategies aligning these Chinese and American perspectives and solving these interrelated issues.

Between 1978 and 2006, Chinese companies' lack of experience in the global economy and in "for profit" business made it especially challenging to align in a "win-win" template the different

Chinese and American perspectives and goals. In that initial stage of China's economic development, the Chinese government was struggling to establish the economic growth and reform foundations of what it refers to as "China's Socialist Market Economy," which we term "China's Socialist Market Capitalism." Chinese companies were not focused on competing in, let alone dominating, the international markets in 1979 to 2002. Between 2002 and 2030 in the era of emerging global operations, acquisitions, investments, and development of Chinese multinationals, a new window of opportunity for successful and sustainable collaboration and Genuine Global Joint Ventures is developing. It is very important that American companies recognize and take advantage of that new window of opportunity. If they do not, it will close and they will be on the outside looking in on China's enormous economic growth.

The Positive Aspects of Chinese Companies Competing Internationally

Terry Barnett, head of Novartis' China operations, summarized the multi-faceted positive impact of Chinese companies becoming successful multinational corporations:

> We all need to appreciate where China is coming from and that it is going through the most dramatic and massive economic transformation ever attempted in history, in any country. In a country of this size, which has been closed to the outside world for decades, as foreigners we should be sympathetic to Chinese concerns. They fear that we will enter the [Chinese] market and exploit the economy, using our business skills, which at this point are greater than those of Chinese enterprises. It will take some time before the Chinese are confident that their companies, the first big Chinese multinationals, succeed locally and then on the world stage. All of us would benefit because the

Chinese would gain a much better understanding of the issues multinationals face doing business [in China].[7]

Case Study: Legend and IBM Deal: A Global Joint Venture Precedent That Must Be Improved Upon

Fortunately, there is an example of a global joint venture strategy between major Chinese and American companies. Each company was a leader in its field, which was recently experiencing challenges after tremendous success in their respective existing markets. Legend wanted and got IBM's Personal Computer brand in the acquisition of access to IBM's faltering PC Division. IBM's failing PC business had not made a profit in three years[8] before it was acquired by Legend.

This first major acquisition by a Chinese company of a major American company and brand is the initial example of a "Global Joint Venture Strategy Model." We are using "joint venture" in this context to describe the collaboration of two companies. A traditional joint venture legal structure can be, but is not necessarily, the legal structure used to achieve such collaboration. The Legend and IBM deal was not structured as a traditional joint venture, but functionally Legend's successful China strategy and IBM's global network and experience complemented each other and were combined, and IBM acquired part of Legend, which changed its name to "Lenovo" to brand the new global business.

Unfortunately, as mentioned, the Legend + IBM = Lenovo deal is viewed as a disappointment among Chinese political and business leaders because of the loss of parts of IBM's business by Lenovo to Dell after the acquisition, the loss of key IBM staff to Dell, and restrictions on the use of the IBM brand in the deal. This reaction in 2006 is an important one within the decision makers in China, which indicates that future deals modeled on the Legend

+ IBM = Lenovo deal should be careful to seek to ameliorate Chinese decision-makers' perceptions of success and failure in such a deal, so that future deals in the view of Chinese government and business leaders do achieve the level of successful *genuine* global joint ventures.

Subject to careful attention being given in future deals to that caveat, the Legend + IBM's PC Division = Lenovo template does provide a precedent-making case study for other American and Chinese companies to study and emulate. China's economic competitive advantages in the second 25 years of China "opening up" and the "for profit" development of successful Chinese companies may increasingly enable them to buy leading American companies or to compete successfully with them and perhaps put them out of business. Collaboration with emerging major Chinese companies, rather than competition, is the better strategy for American companies that are capable of collaborating.

It is useful to look at the mindset change that Legend's Chairman had in initially rejecting IBM's unsolicited offer to sell IBM's personal computer business to Legend and subsequently accepting the deal. Haley, Haley & Tan wrote, before the Legend IBM deal:

> Legend Group, founded in 1984, is China's largest desktop-PC maker, with a 28% market share in 2002. After enjoying years of astounding growth, the company now faces the same problems as Western computer manufacturers: slowing growth, heightened price competition and narrowing margins.
>
> "Our earliest and best teacher was Hewlett-Packard (HP)" said Liu Chuanzhi, Legend's chairman. For more than a decade, Legend served as HP's distributor in China. Liu studied and adapted HP's way for China's market. In the 1990s, Legend introduced its own brand of PCs.
>
> While Legend had lower costs than Western companies, its biggest advantage lay in its distribution network. The Chinese government owns 65% of the company, and Liu used

his government network to sell computers to SOEs. He could not match Western companies in R&D spending, but adapted for the local market. For example, Legend introduced a new keyboard for Chinese characters. In 1997 it beat Western companies to become China's top-selling brand by offering lower prices and comparable quality the company tailored for the Chinese market.

However, by 2003, price wars were raging at the high end of the Chinese PC market, an echo of the battles that started in the West in the late 1990s. In late May 2003, Legend reported a 2% drop in profits and a disappointing 5% rise in revenues. To recapture growth, Legend has moved into new markets in China, such as notebook computers, servers, mobile phones, MP3 music players, and digital cameras. It is laying the ground for further new products, including IT services and network products. It is also turning out a new line of application-based desktop computers. Most ambitiously, like HP and Dell before it, Legend has longer-term plans to take its business overseas to recapture growth. In April, the company changed its English brand name to the sleeker 'Lenovo.'

In the new competitive environment, Liu said he worried more about Western companies, especially Dell, than domestic competitors.[9]

IBM was a world leader in developing the computer business globally. However, by 2001 IBM's personal computer (PC) business was faltering. Legend was the first company to introduce the home computer concept in China. Legend has been the leading PC brand in China since 1997 and was traded on the NYSE. But by 2004, Legend's China strategy was facing increasing competition in the Chinese market, which was putting pressure on its share price.

In 2004 the Chairman of Legend said he would not dream of competing against IBM in the American market.[10] "If you can't beat them, join them" is an American expression. On December 7, 2004, IBM announced that it was selling its entire Personal Computing Division for US$1.25 billion to Legend to create a new worldwide PC company, making the combined businesses the world's third largest computer hardware company, with approximately US$12 billion in annual revenues. Simultaneously, IBM was taking an 18.9% equity stake in Lenovo, creating a global strategic alliance between IBM and Lenovo in PC sales, financing, and worldwide service. The new combined company's worldwide headquarters would be in New York, but its principal manufacturing operations would be in Beijing and Raleigh, North Carolina, and research centers would be in China, America, and Japan. Sales offices would be worldwide. The new Lenovo would be the preferred supplier of PCs to IBM, and IBM would be the new Lenovo's preferred supplier of

Samuel J. Palmisano[12]

services and financing. About 10,000 employees would move from IBM to Lenovo.[11]

Sam Palmisano, IBM's Chairman, approached Legend's Chairman in 2003, proposing Legend acquire IBM's loss-making personal computer manufacturing business. Legend founder and Chairman Yang Yuanqing initially declined, worrying about losing IBM customers after the acquisition and its ability to continue to use the IBM brand and keep IBM's salespeople and keep CEO.[13]

Clyde Prestowstiz describes the IBM Legend deal's genesis:

> ...U.S. CEOs are accustomed both to telling the U.S. government what they want and often getting it. Their

dealings abroad, however, are quite different. In China there is no rule of law, no democratic congress or parliament, and no such thing as an independent regulatory body. But there are industrial policies and bureaucrats and communist party leaders with enormous discretionary authority. American CEOs need to accommodate the bureaucrats and the party leaders if they want to do business.

A good example is the ... IBM sale of its PC division to China's Lenovo. Although the sale was announced in December 2004, it got underway in July 2003, when IBM chairman Sam Palmisano made a special trip to Beijing. Palmisano later told the New York Times he was not traveling primarily to initiate talks with Lenovo's chairman. Instead, his first meetings were with top-level Chinese government officials from whom he sought permission to sell to a Chinese company. Palmisano explained that he wanted to help build a modern and truly international Chinese owned company. The Chinese responded, as he hoped they would, by saying, "That is the future model for where we see China headed." With that green light, he proceeded to negotiate the deal with Lenovo's top executives. Under the agreement, the Chinese government will be a major shareholder along with IBM in China's fifth largest company. *According to Palmisano, IBM wants to support China's industrial policies with the expectation that this will pay off big in new business for IBM down the road. The IBM strategy, he says, is 'a subtle, sophisticated approach. It is that if you become ingrained in their agenda and become truly local and help them advance, then your opportunities are enlarged. You become part of their strategy.*

...In a good example of insourcing, Lenovo quickly announced it was moving its headquarters to Armonk, New York, where IBM is based. Furthermore, it will put a group of senior IBM executives in charge of what will become the world's third largest computer company after Dell and Hewlett-Packard, and adopt English as the company language. Here is a case of China outsourcing management to the United States. Said Lenovo chairman Liu Chuanzhi, "The most valuable asset we have acquired through IBM's PC business is its world-class management team and their extensive international experience." This deal could turn out to be a brilliant stroke for IBM, Lenovo, and China.

Perhaps it is also a brilliant stroke for the United States, but no one is analyzing whether it is or not.[14] (*Emphasis added*)

Is Lenovo an American or a Chinese company? The CEO of Legend became Chairman of Lenovo. Lenovo's CEO was IBM's senior vice president and general manager of IBM's Personal Systems Group. Lenovo's COO was general manager of IBM's PC Division. Lenovo's CFO was the CFO of Legend. Lenovo is listed on the Hong Kong Stock Exchange as well as the New York Stock Exchange. The press release announcing the new company stated: "As a global business, the new Lenovo will be geographically dispersed, with people and physical assets located worldwide."

Lenovo became not only China's largest computer manufacturer but the world's third-largest PC maker by shipments, behind Dell and Hewlett-Packard, by acquiring IBM's PC making operations. Lenovo has been transformed into a global PC titan in terms of sales. The former IBM operations in 2005 account for about 70% of Lenovo's revenue. IBM's PC business had four times the revenue of Lenovo before the acquisition.

Capital market analysts wondered how IBM's three years of losses in its PC unit would affect Lenovo after the acquisition.[15] Lenovo announced a 6% increase in its profits in the first quarter of the new arrangement.[16] IBM's PC business was marginally profitable in the period that Lenovo has owned it, since May 2005, because Lenovo separated it from IBM's high cost platform.[17] Lenovo appeared to have turned around IBM's old PC division "faster than a computer can reboot".[18] In April 2005, the IBM PC division had a pre-tax loss of US$149 million. After its acquisition by Lenovo, it posted an operating profit of about US$33 million for May and June 2005.[19] Lenovo attributed the turnaround to freedom from IBM expenses, the new ability to sell PCs to other units of IBM above cost and the shedding of warranty liabilities that were kept by IBM.[20]

Legend was one of the most advanced of the emerging Chinese multinational companies. It's acquisition of IBM's PC business is path breaking for several reasons:

1. The acquisition was needed to help Legend deal with competition from foreign and Chinese firms in China.

2. The acquisition helped Legend "go global" and become the first Chinese company to acquire an icon American company.

3. The acquisition addressed Legend's need for American brand recognition, marketing skills, and distribution channels in an acquisition of a major American icon company.

4. Legend, facing increased competition in China from foreign and Chinese firms, needed to become more competitive and as a publicly listed company (NYSE), needed to get more benefits for its shareholders.[21]

5. Legend had 25% of the revenues of IBM's PC division and expanded its revenue base 75%, and in the acquisition became the third largest player in the global PC market.

6. Legend changed its name to Lenovo and moved its headquarters from China to America.

7. Lenovo had a management team combining senior Chinese and American talent: a Chinese Chairman, American CEO, and Chinese CFO and other resources, i.e., brand, marketing and distribution network.

8. The deal combines the respective strengths and ameliorates the competitive weaknesses respectively of leading American and Chinese companies.

9. IBM's PC business had been unprofitable for three years and had become unable to compete profitably.[22]

10. IBM was unable to return its PC business to profitability.

11. Legend was able to make the IBM PC division profitable to the surprise of observers.[23]

12. Legend applied a different management philosophy and approach than IBM did.

13. IBM obtained an 18.9% equity participation in Lenovo.

14. Lenovo immediately added 25% to the revenue and market share that IBM's PC division had prior to the acquisition.

15. IBM got rid of a problem it could not manage, acquired 19% of a leading Chinese company, and forged a very valuable alliance.

16. The integration of the American and the Chinese company in Lenovo was significantly more competitive than either Legend or IBM's PC Division by themselves.

17. Lenovo's first new, improved IBM Think Pad portable computers were, according to *Fortune,* "perhaps the best Think Pad yet" with wider screens, a better DVD, built in wireless broadband card and antenna allowing connection to the Internet without needing to be near a WI-FI hot spot, a better keyboard, fingerprint security scanner, and a blue Think Vantage key that safeguards important business data.[24]

18. Then Lenovo's new CEO, Bill Amelio, announced Lenovo had missed profit expectations in the third quarter of 2005 after Lenovo had to slash prices to meet sale goals of the former PC operations of IBM. But revenue was up from Legend's revenue of HK $6.31 billion, before the acquisition, to HK $31.1 billion. Lenovo's gross profit margin was 13.2% in the third quarter of 2005, down from 14% in the second quarter because of the price cuts.

Lenovo's net profit was US$ 47 million in the third quarter. Lenovo's unit shipments grew 13% in the third quarter, compared to the overall PC industries' growth rate of 17%.[25]

19. Dell slashed PC prices in the wake of the Legend acquisition of IBM's PC business.

20. Lenovo lost IBM contracts with the U.S. Government to Dell because of American government concern about Lenovo's Chinese links.[26]

21. Lenovo's new CEO indicated that Lenovo will get past various transition problems and build off the successes generated in China, and regain some of the prominence the IBM brands had over time.[27]

22. Lenovo's new CEO previously led the Asia Pacific operations of Dell, Lenovo's largest competitor in personal computers in the last 5 years.[28]

23. Mr. Amelio said he decided to take the Lenovo CEO position because he was impressed by the opportunities ahead for the company and its success in China, which is now the world's second-largest personal computer market. He saw more opportunity to learn to grow as a business leader, because there is so much more action in our industry than in China and Asia.

24. Mr. Amelio stated: "The other thing that is fascinating is this is a groundbreaking opportunity between a Chinese and American company."[29]

25. Lenovo's CEO stated in late 2005 that Lenovo's China operation does a better job of understanding its sales in China than IBM did.[30]

26. Lenovo is now the world's third largest maker of personal computers.[31]

27. Lenovo's Chairman, Yang Yuanqing indicated in May 2006 that its profitability would not improve until 2007 as it continued to restructure the IBM PC business.[32]

As we have seen, while Chinese companies are struggling to be competitive in China and globally with foreign and other Chinese companies, American companies have a window of opportunity to participate by assisting in the process of Chinese companies "going global." American or other foreign companies with win-win rather than zero-sum strategies can align with the Chinese government's needs and goals for Chinese companies to "go global." Such collaboration is an important way for many American companies to compete effectively and profitably with their current non-Chinese competitors, while forging genuine global joint ventures with emerging Chinese "mega multinationals" which leverage their competitive advantages in China and globally.

Legend was not a Chinese state-owned company and it only received a US$25,000 investment from China's Academy of Science, which helped launch Legend. Lenovo is not a Chinese government-owned company.[33]

Case Study: Maytag, Whirlpool, and Haier—Brand Recognition and American Market Access

Business Week examined four ways, in 2006, that American companies have responded to emerging multinationals:[34]

1. "Know your challengers" and anticipate how they will change your industry; "compete head on" by investing heavily in research and development and allying with its competitors;

2. "Tap their resources," i.e., make better uses of Chinese and Indian engineers, factories, and suppliers than companies based in China and India;

3. "Know when to fold" by exiting a business where the competitor has overwhelming advantages; or

4. "Join 'em" by forming a joint venture, licensing intellectual property, or selling services to them.

Business Week commented: "Leading companies in developing nations can be great partners. They know the terrain and real market needs at home and in other key emerging growth markets. By collaborating on product development, you can leverage their low cost advantages."[35]

Whirlpool is using a strategy of refusing to cede market share to Chinese competitors. Whirlpool paid a "surprisingly high $2.8 billion to buy Maytag Corp. It wanted to keep Maytag out of the hands of China's Haier, which is ramping up in the U.S. and made a rival bid."[36] Haier is China's largest home appliance maker, with 30% of the Chinese market, the most valuable China brand, and self-reported revenues of US$9.7 billion in 2005. Since the mid 1980s, it has expanded its products and exports to over 150 countries and has 22 production facilities and 18 design centers outside of China. It is a "champion" Chinese company that is a leader in Chinese companies going global.[37] Haier wanted the Maytag and Hoover brands and their distribution channels because Haier's own brands did not sell as well in America. Haier believes that the 21st century will be "the Warring Multinationals Era."[38]

Haier has entered the American market and adopted a strategy of selling their best range of products against the medium-range American fridges and has quickly gained market share. In June 2005, Haier and two leading American private-equity firms, Blackstone

Group and Bain Capital, informed Maytag they were prepared to make a US$1.28 billion bid for the American appliance producer. An American competitor, Whirlpool, indicated it was prepared to make a higher offer, which increased Maytag's publicly traded share price. Haier dropped its offer.

Haier's fundamental problem was its poor capital structure affecting its financing capabilities. Haier was not listed until recently through a reverse merger on the Hong Kong Stock Exchange. It used debt instead of shareholders' equity in its growth. Whirlpool had been unable in the 1990s to make its "China Strategy" work, and withdrew from China. It may be worthwhile for Whirlpool and Haier to consider a "Genuine Global Joint Venture."

The graphs below show the inexperience with market research and advertising of most Chinese companies. They developed in the transition from China's planned economy, where market research and advertising were not important.

Advertising Expenditures Per Capita In 2001 39

Market Research Expenditures Per Capita In 2001 40

However, the combination of savvy Internet marketers and companies like Haier can revolutionize the lack of Chinese brands reflected in the graphs below.

Oded Shenkar notes that even now however:

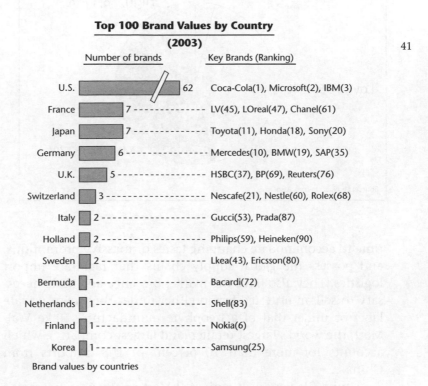

Top 100 Brand Values by Country

(2003)

41

Country	Number of brands	Key Brands (Ranking)
U.S.	62	Coca-Cola(1), Microsoft(2), IBM(3)
France	7	LV(45), LOreal(47), Chanel(61)
Japan	7	Toyota(11), Honda(18), Sony(20)
Germany	6	Mercedes(10), BMW(19), SAP(35)
U.K.	5	HSBC(37), BP(69), Reuters(76)
Switzerland	3	Nescafe(21), Nestle(60), Rolex(68)
Italy	2	Gucci(53), Prada(87)
Holland	2	Philips(59), Heineken(90)
Sweden	2	Lkea(43), Ericsson(80)
Bermuda	1	Bacardi(72)
Netherlands	1	Shell(83)
Finland	1	Nokia(6)
Korea	1	Samsung(25)

Brand values by countries

The preponderance of Chinese products, from clothing and furniture to electronics and appliances, on the world's retail shelves, illustrates how fast Chinese imports are capturing market share from domestic products as well as from third-country producers. The trend has been especially pronounced in the U.S., where China's share of U.S. imports has been growing steadily...

A key reason behind the remarkably fast penetration of Chinese products into the U.S. retail market is it's increasing domination by large retailers. These retailers are more price sensitive, require massive production capacity and short lead-

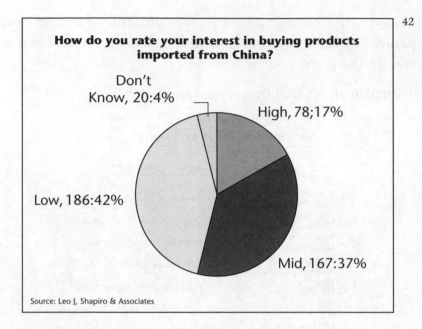

42

How do you rate your interest in buying products imported from China?

Don't Know, 20:4%

High, 78;17%

Low, 186:42%

Mid, 167:37%

Source: Leo J, Shapiro & Associates

time to accommodate changing tastes or massive promotions, and possess the global supply chains that facilitate import logistics. They also have the market presence and scale necessary to sell an untested brand either under their own private label or under that of a neophyte manufacturer. Take Wal-Mart, the world's largest retailer (and largest company), which accounts for more than 10 percent of U.S. imports from China. ...

China fits very well with Wal-Mart strategy of "everyday low prices," coupled with huge promotions, which bring masses of shoppers into its store for one-time events...

The increasing share of large retailers like Wal-Mart, and the increasingly prominent role China plays in their plans, suggests continuous pressure on manufacturers throughout the world and a growing presence of Chinese goods on retail shelves. With Chinese dominance of apparel, toys, and consumer electronic markets, fewer and fewer non-Chinese firms will be able to provide the scale, product scope, lead time, and price that the large retailers seek. The Chinese, on their side, need the large retailers to take their growing production capacity—at least until they are able to develop their own distribution and establish their brands.[43]

Case Study: ACI/MyFactoryDirectInternational Limited

Internet retailing is making the need to use other existing distribution channels less critical by marketing high quality items manufactured in China to direct online customers. For example, ACI/MyFactoryDirectInternational Limited is a Bermuda company in Globalization 3.0.

Austin Kirk established a traditional China-America trading firm in 1997. In 2000, he founded American Catalyst Incorporated ("ACI") and began an Internet retail effort, including fiber-optic Christmas trees, golf swing trainers, leisure furniture, and goose down comforters. Realizing the online market would grow exponentially, ACI dedicated its efforts increasingly to online retail marketing. Austin Kirk sees the future of global marketing:

> It is our vision that in the 21st century economy, Chinese manufacturers will seek to gain market share by controlling prices, increasing the quality of product produced, and by using expanding global integrated information systems to bypass conventional wholesale markups and sell directly to the end users in every market in the developed world. By doing so Chinese suppliers will be in the position to command the majority of profit margin per unit sold. Further, they will enjoy the greatest degree of control over their market share ever possible by suppliers of finished goods. We recognize this inevitability. We further recognize that those who first act to implement direct distribution of finished goods on a global scale will dominate the 21st century economy.

Case Study: Chinese Companies Need Enhanced Design, Engineering, and Marketing Expertise

Many foreign companies resist allowing Chinese joint venture partners or customers access to non-Chinese developed technology. Some, such as Motorola, are rejecting that strategy. The issue is more than who owns the intellectual property. The issue is how the owner of the intellectual property can best utilize it for its market positioning. Many companies are moving beyond the approach of withholding and thereby strangling the further development of their technologies.

The out-sourced development in India and the research and development centers in China point to a higher level of commercial thinking emerging, emphasizing market positioning and time to market. The withholding intellectual property and cutting-edge technology approach will not win in the 21st century. If an American company is not in a major market, substituting technologies will be developed by other competitors and occupy the Chinese market and eventually the American company's home and global markets, taking leading market positions.

Globalization 3.0 for China's major companies is like Globalization 2.0 for American multinational companies. In the hallowed traditions of capitalism, of which America is the leading proponent, there are stronger and weaker competitors. The stronger competitors leverage their competitive advantages. In the second 25 years of the design and deployment of the Chinese government's "China strategy" of economic development, the competitive advantages of China are being leveraged. The strategic focus of that leveraging was a primary focus of the Chinese government in the last 25 years. In that period, China became the "Factory Floor Of The World". The focus of the Chinese government in the next 25 years is making China: "The Innovative Economy Of The World".

Case Study: Swiss Companies' Zero-Sum-Game China Strategies: Too Little, Too Late

Some foreign companies are aligning their "China strategy" with "China's strategy" and some are not. Which are likely to remain profitable? The 2005 Julius Bar survey[44] of Swiss companies doing business in China stated:

> Swiss suppliers are confronted with a shift of large parts of their existing European, American and sometimes Asian customer base to China, and are under increasing pressure to gain a foothold there themselves.[45]

The survey stated that the biggest problem, cited by 63 of the technology companies surveyed, is the protection of intellectual property. This is one likely reason why technology companies that import semi-finished goods into China generally report an above-average share of semi-finished goods in the total product value. Between 20% and 50% of the final value are fed into the Chinese value chain in the shape of semi-finished goods. The more critical the know-how, the higher the share. Characteristically, only few of the technology companies that participated in the survey said they pursue research and development activities in China. In semiconductor production, R&D capacities are primarily being used to satisfy the needs of local customers.

The Swiss study stated:

> The investments the Swiss technology companies have made in China are relatively small. To date, they have been below CHF 5 million per company, i.e. less than 5% of these companies' total capital expenditure of the last five years. Only one company has invested between CHF 5 million and 30 million, or between 6% and 10% of total capex [capital expenditures] used in the last five years. Half of the companies active in China have already passed break-even on an

operational level. Generally, companies plan to reach the operational break-even one to three years after making the initial investments. All Swiss technology players surveyed said they planned to step up investments in China in the next three years, with the investments either on a par with or above those made so far.[46]

In an effort to protect intellectual property, some companies have chosen not to manufacture sensitive products in China. Some even prevent local staff from gaining access to sensitive information about processes and procedures. None of the companies said it trusts protection through lawful measures.[47]

The Reality That China Needs Semiconductors and Is Strategically Focusing on Them

It has been America's policy to seek to contain the export of high technology in general and semiconductor technology in particular to China and other communist countries. America's attempt at containment in this area is not succeeding. In 2005, China's computer product exports exceeded $100 billion for the first time, reaching $140.85 billion.[48] The graph below shows China Georgia Tech Technology Standing Index growth from 1993 and 2003 relative to Japan and America. The other graphs below shows China's research and gross domestic expenditure in 2003 relative to America, the European Union and Japan.

The Chinese government and companies are using China's economic, scientific, and technical competitive advantages in both China's and the global markets in strategic sectors, such as semiconductors, which are key to leading edge technology for Fortune 1000 firms. It is increasingly important for American companies in such sectors to have profitable and sustainable

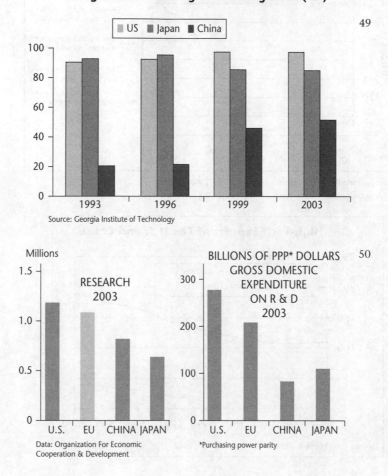

Is FDI Enabling Technological catch-up?
Georgia Tech Technological Standing Index (TSI)

Source: Georgia Institute of Technology

RESEARCH
2003

Data: Organization For Economic
Cooperation & Development

BILLIONS OF PPP* DOLLARS
GROSS DOMESTIC
EXPENDITURE
ON R & D
2003

*Purchasing power parity

"China strategies" in order to be profitable at all. China's labor costs for technology companies are 40% to 80% lower.[51] China is also the key emerging, huge market in the world. The failure of an American company's "China strategy" can quickly destroy its future global competitiveness.

A chart below shows the royalty and license fee payments and receipts for America and China between 1970 and 2000. The

52

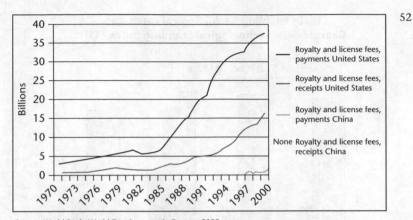

Source: World Bank, World Development Indicators, 2002
Royalty And License Fee Payments and Receipts For The U.S. and China.

53

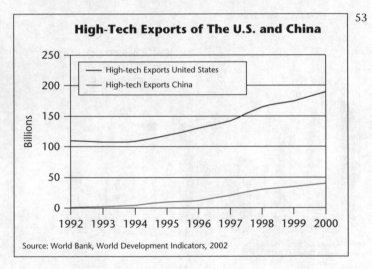

other chart above shows the high technology exports of America and China from 1992 and 2000.

The Chinese government is building on China's compelling cost advantages in creating and operating "fabs," which manufacture semiconductors. Semiconductors constitute a huge and growing market that is strategically important in global economic development in which the Chinese government is focused on self-sufficiency and global leadership.

Case Study: Intel's Zero-Sum-Game and A.M.D's Win-Win China Strategies

The Chinese government is positioning China to enhance its competitive advantages by investing heavily in building China's own semiconductor industry. Companies with China strategies that compete rather than collaborate with China's strategy may be in for a lose-lose result.

Intel's "China strategy" generated US$3.7 billion in revenue in China, which was 12% of Intel's global revenue in 2003. American sales generated $7.4 billion, but demand in America barely grew in recent years and is expected to grow by about 5% a year. But China is developing its own chip industry and Intel's stock price was down by 45%. China could be Intel's number one market and fix Intel's problems for the next five years as demand for chips in China is projected to expand at double-digit rates for the foreseeable future. But

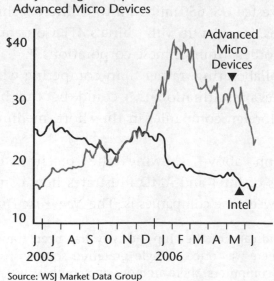

Two Brands of Chips   54

Daily closing share price for Intel and Advanced Micro Devices

Source: WSJ Market Data Group

Chinese companies are partnering with Intel's competitor, Advanced Micro Devices ("AMD"), a foreign company, which is assisting them.

Chinese companies like Shanghai's Semiconductor Manufacturing International Corp. have gone from nothing to almost US $1 billion in revenue in 4 years. Many of its top 1,000 managers are foreigners; and it has built a US$1 billion fab, acquired another in Tianjin, and is opening a third in Beijing. Intel may underestimate the accelerating rate of progress of Chinese companies in China and globally.[55] The Chinese government, Chinese companies, and companies such as Motorola are investing heavily in R&D and other facilities in China.

Motorola faced the dilemma of not providing its most advanced technology secrets and not having them used as the platforms for China's domestic market, or providing them and having Chinese companies become lethal competitors. Motorola decided to make money and keep market share now and take the risk that Chinese competitors will take both later. Motorola, like AMD, is assisting the Chinese government's strategy of transforming China into "the innovative economy of the world." Cisco has invested US$650 million into Chinese technology company start-ups, forged a tie with China's ZTE Corp, and continues to win large orders from Chinese corporations.[56]

Again, collaborating, rather than competing with emerging Chinese "mega multinationals," could be the better China strategy for foreign companies in the short, medium, and long terms.

The graph above showing the recent stock market performances of Intel and AMD illustrates how competitive the dynamic between the companies is. The *New York Times* reported:

> ...the landscape of the chip industry has been transformed. Where there was once a single preferred source of chips for personal computers, there are now two competitive suppliers: Intel and Advanced Micro Devices. Before this, A.M.D. was a

wannabe, with inconsistent quality and enhancements ... but they've changed the dynamics of the industry.[57]

The Reality That in Future Semiconductor Competition: America Loses/China Wins

As we have seen, the Chinese government and Chinese companies are focused on self-sufficiency and global leadership in the semi-conductor industry. The Chinese government is adding to China's compelling cost advantages in creating and operating fabs[58] because semiconductors constitute a huge and growing market and a hugely important market in China's and in global economic development.

The cost of acquiring new fabs does not differ between America, Taiwan, and China, if potential government subsidies are excluded from consideration. But due to lower labor costs alone, China has at least a 14% competitive cost advantage as a location for new fabs compared to America.[59]

The Swiss study presented the following data:

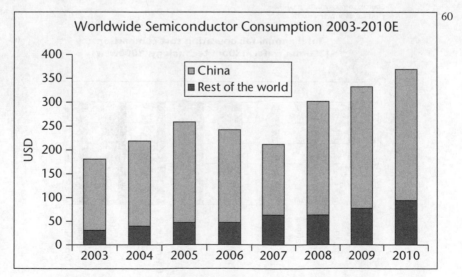

Source: Gartner Dataquest, SIA, Julius Bar

61

Comparison of total annual wafer manufacturing cost

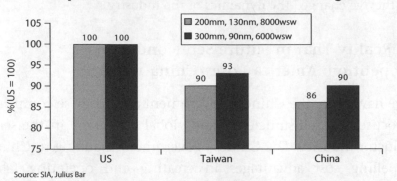

Source: SIA, Julius Bar

62

Labor Costs in China
(main production locations outside of china = 100%)

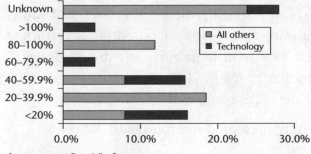

Source: company Data, Julius Baer
(Total of all answer = 100%)

63

Total annual fab operating cost comparison
(200mm wafer, 130nm technology, 8000wsw)

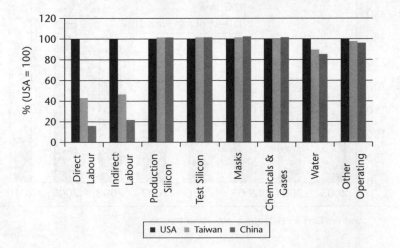

The Swiss study estimated in 2005 that by 2010, 25% of all semiconductors would be sold in China. It estimated that worldwide demand growth will be 11% per year in that period, but would be 17% in China and only 9% in other markets. It identified one driving force behind the increasing demand in China to be the outsourcing of the production of electronic products from America, Europe, and other parts of Asia to China.

It estimated that in 2004, 66% of the semiconductors that are used in consumer electronics, communications, and data processing applications in China were exported as part of finished products. These applications accounted for 96% of the 2004 demand for semiconductors in China. China's demand for the use of semiconductors domestically only accounted for 5% of global semiconductor demand. It found that outside of China, the highest annual rate of semiconductor growth is in industrial application, but in China this is currently only 1%. Producers of data processing devices, i.e., personal computers and notebooks are the biggest buyers of semiconductors globally. But China's domestic demand for semiconductors used in data processing, the study stated, is currently growing at a rate below the global average. Communications applications are growing at 22% per year and were estimated to reach 36% by 2010.

The study noted that the increasing purchasing power of China's population should boost domestic demand in the years ahead in personal computers and laptops, and consumer electronics, particularly cell phones. Cell phone use and wireless data transmission technology enable China to achieve in a short period of time what took over 100 years in America.

The study produced the projections in the graph below of Chinese semiconductor demand in 2010.

What will happen if the Chinese government expands the industrial applications of semiconductors and all applications of semiconductors faster and more than the above graph predicts?

64

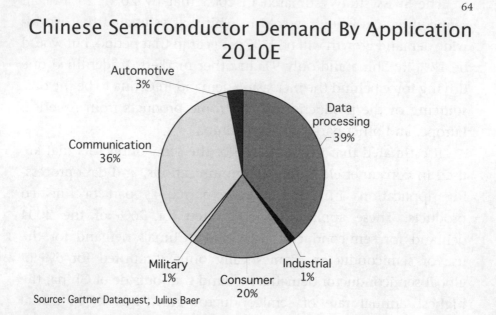

Chinese Semiconductor Demand By Application 2010E

Automotive 3%

Data processing 39%

Communication 36%

Military 1%

Consumer 20%

Industrial 1%

Source: Gartner Dataquest, Julius Baer

Oded Shenkar notes:

> In business, the rise of China will challenge basic assumptions regarding the nature of national and firm competitiveness, the value of geographic proximity, and the cost of market entry and exit. Location advantages that have underpinned company survival and prosperity for decades—sometimes for centuries—will be questioned, and the global mobility of production factors will accelerate under a global supply chain. As on prior occasions of dramatic economic shift, the coming changes will test both external and internal alliances. Players will be playing by new rules, with new winners and losers.
>
> How should businesses prepare for the Chinese century? Preparation begins by understanding the nature of the coming change and assessing its impact on one's industry, firm, and individual employees. Preparation continues with a willingness to re-evaluate the very *raison-d-étre* of the organization, questioning not only practices and routines but also the fundamental assumptions on which the business

model rests. The evaluation will often call into question the adequacy of responses that have worked well in the past but may not hold this time... As a whole, "business as usual" solutions will no longer work. Firms must rethink their entire value chain, which will likely lead to a new business model or to an outright exit.[65]

Business reaction to the China challenge has been mixed so far. Many industries and firms have been caught unprepared, failing to realize the threat to their current business model or the sudden acceleration of the structural shifts that in the past took decades to consummate. Some have been blindsided by the promise of the China market to the point of neglecting the challenge in their own backyard; others have given up all too easily on the burgeoning Chinese economy, forfeiting opportunities to more aggressive players. Still others have been sidetracked by the tired and by now obsolete responses of U.S. unions that have been focusing on China's admittedly dismal human rights record while failing to offer much in a way of solutions besides ... protectionism.

Some industry groups pin their hopes on political pressure, buoyed by the interest politicians have taken of late in the job issue, but they will be, at best, buying time.... Others believe that currency adjustment will take care of the problem, but they need to look no further than the mid 1980s, when the appreciation of the Yen in the aftermath of the Plaza Accord brought, at best, a temporary halt in the *growth* of the deficit. Even under a radical scenario of a 30%–40% increase in the value of the Yuan, China's labor intensive products would continue to enjoy an enormous price advantage. ... In short, business should not count on the government to bail them out but prepare for the new reality that is about to dawn.[66]

China's economic miracle has just begun to surprise and change the world. China's economic growth rate and competitiveness will accelerate; and for many companies that will be unexpected, difficult, or impossible. An American policy of containment of

China will lead to American companies not having opportunities to participate in China's economic growth or collaborate with Chinese companies because of the American governments' choice of zero-sum-game strategies of containment.

3

Advanced Strategies Aligning American Companies and the Chinese Government and Chinese Companies' Goals

Overview

This chapter examines advanced strategies that seek to align American and Chinese companies' interests in designing and operating the genuine global joint venture template or traditional structures.

A Pragmatic Win-Win Approach to the Interaction of American and Chinese Capitalism

Several strategies may facilitate companies from a "Rights Society" and a "Permission Society's" collaboration in the real world of international business. In developing the concepts, we have been guided by the apparent requirements of successful collaboration, rather than by the traditional deal structures that have been used, sometimes successfully, sometimes less successfully, by American and Chinese companies. In some instances the traditional deal structures will better fit an American company's objectives, needs, and corporate culture than the new Genuine Global Joint Venture Model. But even in such cases, the concepts discussed below may be helpful to consider and sometimes use in the traditional and advanced deal structures and strategies examined in the case studies in this book.

Mediation and Arbitration in China

Arbitration is the dispute settlement mechanism of choice of most companies operating in China.[1] Chinese law and policy encourage arbitration rather than litigation. Arbitration is supported by a comprehensive Chinese and international legal framework. China's arbitration law adopts many of the key principles found in international legislation and practice, and provides a sound basis for domestic and foreign related arbitrations in China.[2] China acceded to the New York Convention in 1987 which permits the recognition and enforcement of Chinese arbitration awards in over 120 member states. Arbitration receives significant support from the practices of SOEs conducting international business. Virtually all of the foreign trade corporations require that business be conducted pursuant to a standard contract form that usually requires the arbitration of disputes. Arbitration provisions are also found in the model contracts developed by China's state-owned oil and gas companies and in the model joint venture contract developed by China's Ministry of Foreign Trade and Economic Cooperation (MOFTEC). Arbitration provides, particularly in the context of China's "Pre-Rule of Law" system, greater party autonomy, more flexible procedures, cost effectiveness, finality, and confidentiality.

The Hong Kong Arbitration Ordinance contains a mediation procedure that enables a mediator selected by the parties to also serve as an arbitrator in the same dispute if mediation is not effective. Mediation and arbitration are encouraged. Litigation by foreign companies against Chinese parties is not encouraged in China, and usually is not a satisfactory dispute resolution mechanism for foreign companies.[3]

Never Beyond the Apex of "The Curve of Gratitude" Strategy

Avoiding mediation and arbitration saves time, energy, money, and morale. Strategies often succeed or fail for unforeseen reasons. It is important for an American company to rely on attractive and sustained value propositions when doing business with the Chinese government or dealing with Chinese companies. It must use profitable structures and meaningful financial rewards. Creativity in designing a genuine global joint venture is an extremely important competitive advantage.

Since China's evolving legal system and regulatory system have features of a "Permission Society" rather than of a "Rights Society", it is vital for a foreign company not to get "beyond the apex of the curve of gratitude" of the Chinese government entities whose approval is required for the success of its China Strategy and the Chinese trading partners that it relies upon. The rules of the game in China change to fit the needs of the Chinese government and people's evolving economic development. The ongoing attractiveness of the value propositions a foreign company offers for the Chinese government and its Chinese trading partners will influence their actions more than contractual rights and obligations.

In order to "never get beyond the apex of the curve of gratitude," a company must carefully use structures of activities in China that contain and maintain a "Generous Tit For Tat Strategy"[4] in responding to changes in the rules of the game by the Chinese government and by its Chinese trading partners. The concept of "never beyond the apex of the curve of gratitude" refers to the sustainability of the foreign company's value proposition from the

Chinese way of looking at things. Once the Chinese players in the China Game have obtained what they value, the reasons for the agreements to be performed degrade. It is at that point that the foreign company has put itself in a position that it is "past the apex of the curve of gratitude," without the Rule of Law to create a shared expectation among non-Chinese and Chinese persons of the enforceability of contractual agreements.

Generous Tit-for-Tat Strategy

The success of China's economic development, and problems encountered in the China strategies of foreign companies and the relentless foreign demand to participate in China's low costs and other advantages, economic development and huge emerging market, has created an attitude that foreigners are ignorant about China and have to pay to learn. Foreigners, as "outsiders" in China's moral culture, are not owed obligations of fair behavior. In addition, the Chinese often feel that because the foreign companies are rich, they therefore have an obligation to benefit China.

A Genuine Global Joint Venture can contain many useful features of a "China strategy" based on Generous Tit For Tat and "never getting beyond the apex of the curve of gratitude" strategies.

A Generous Tit-for-Tat Strategy involves the American and Chinese partner being sure in advance that if one of them makes positive moves, the other partner will make positive moves. And if one of them makes negative moves, the other partner will react with a positive move and then copy the negative or positive character of the other partner's moves subsequently in an absolutely predictable way. For example, the Chinese partner knows that if it fails to carry out something it has agreed to, the American partner will first clarify whether the Chinese partner's

failure is deliberate or accidental. In doing so, the American partner will not automatically react to the failure of the Chinese partner to perform positively. But if the nonperformance is deliberate
or reiterated, then the non-Chinese partner will respond by not
performing as it agreed. This strategy in game theory is believed
to facilitate win-win sequences of behavior and to facilitate the
correction of deliberate or accidental win-lose behavior by participants in the game.

A Generous Tit-for-Tat Strategy is likely to be more effective,
all other things being equal, if it is used in a Genuine Global
Joint Venture, i.e., a joint venture owned by a holding company
outside of China. The joint venture being global rather than
just a joint venture inside China, allows the American company
to have contributions it can make, since it is contributing
resources and assets outside of China to the Chinese partner,
such as distribution channels, the confidence of and experience
in the international capital markets, and involving the Chinese
company as a *genuine global partner in the American company's
global operations.* Chinese companies "going global" need the
experience, expertise, and relationships only obtained by
experience in operating in foreign markets. The American
partner contributes the skills and relationships the Chinese
partner needs outside of China. The Chinese partner contributes
the experience, expertise, and relationships it has in the
Chinese market. Each adds what the other needs and cannot
itself create easily, nor in a way that creates loyalty and
sustainable profits. The loyalty component, hopefully, along
with the rewards used to support loyalty, contributes the
loyalty that holds the genuine global joint venture together,
with neither partner getting beyond the apex of the curve of
gratitude of the other.

Game theory is based on the premise that players are behaving
"rationally." Human beings' behavior is not as rational as mathe-

matics. So there are real limitations in applying game theory to human affairs. But, if game theory is used as a base, and motivators like money, success, and other coveted things are aligned with the Generous Tit-for-Tat Strategy, then a genuine global joint venture can be more sustainably valuable to both the American and Chinese company.

Genuine Global Joint Venture Strategy Mindset

It is also critical that the particular American and Chinese companies selected for genuine global joint ventures each have the capabilities in their executive teams to be suitable candidates for them. The partners must have the win-win mindsets required as well as the aligned structures, strategies, and rewards to make a genuine global joint venture work. This will require specialized external ongoing advice in the design and coaching of the American and Chinese partners' executive teams in the implementation of a genuine global joint venture.

In the real world there are many complications. The first example of a global joint venture, the 2004 IBM + Legend = Lenovo deal was not seen by the Chinese as a *genuine* global joint venture for the reasons we have seen. The complications in the real world are where advanced expertise, research, and collaboration between American and Chinese executives in genuine global joint ventures must focus. This is a new and critically important area of cross-cultural "know how" and "know who" that must be quickly developed and reiterated successfully. As discussed in Chapter 1, this is the specialized focus of the work of China International Strategies Ltd and the Milligan-Whyte Foundation, which is an executive education forum for selected American and Chinese executives working on designing and implementing genuine global joint ventures. As discussed in Chapters 4 and 10, the China Bermuda Society's special focus is also on genuine global joint ventures and executive education programs.

A foreign company that is able to understand the "Permission Society" mindset in China, is, all other things being equal, better able to align its China strategy with China's economic development strategy and its Chinese partners' goals and mindset and to collaborate with Chinese companies that are currently early in the process of learning to operate internationally.

With the tools of better understanding, motivating, and rewarding Chinese partners, an American company is, to some degree, better able to carefully select a Chinese company with which to partner and to influence the better operation of such genuine global joint ventures. The Chinese company is less likely to falter in its learning and expansion process; and the non-Chinese company is, to some degree, better positioned to profit from assisting the Chinese company to reach its goals.

As discussed in Chapter 4, corporate structures using a joint venture company in Bermuda are useful to accumulate shares, assets and US dollar cash in a holding company outside of China, which can be later publicly listed. The American company can also assist the Chinese company to become a powerful multinational company earning foreign currency and training its management talent internationally by involving the Chinese company in the foreign company's business outside of China. The American company's China strategy can also benefit from astutely choosing Chinese joint venture partners that are profitable and have a young management team with foreign educational and employment backgrounds.

Attracting and Rewarding a Good Chinese Management Team Strategies

The intellectual capital, compatibility, and compensation incentives of the Chinese management team a foreign company selects arguably is the greatest asset in its China strategy. With the right choices, all other problems can be addressed; with the wrong choice, none can be solved. The best choice is Mainland Chinese-born executives that have been educated and worked outside of China, who want to return to China. These talented people are in short supply and intense demand.

The commercial value and rewards offered by the American company to executives and staff with such attributes can be more important to the success of a company's China strategy than the current size, stature, and power of potential Chinese partners. But the rewards offered by the American company must be understood by and actually motivate its Chinese joint venture's shareholders, management, and staff. Earnings in cash, particularly foreign currency, are understood and motivate effort in China. Stock options currently are not as well-understood or effective motivators. But the concept of an IPO is understood as an event that can produce a lot of cash, like winning a lottery.

Never-Finished Contractual Negotiations

As we have seen, the negotiation and signing of a contract is often understood or treated by the Chinese parties as merely the beginning of negotiations, which continue and reflect the changing positions of power of the parties. In a "Rights Society", where contracts are respected or enforced as a necessary part of sustaining the "rights" based nature of the economy, a contract is a contract, and its terms can be enforced. In a "Permission Society", a "contract" is sometimes the equivalent of a non-binding Memorandum of Agreement in a "Rights Society."

Therefore, a foreign company's value proposition and strategy's compelling nature must "never get beyond the apex of the curve of gratitude" of the Chinese parties if the non-Chinese parties wish a contract to be performed. It is often the ongoing strength of a foreign company's value propositions, rather than its acumen at implementing its strategy, that is outcome determinative in China.

Using incremental share swaps with Chinese companies listed on the Singapore or other international stock exchanges generating US dollar cash and capital appreciation, can be useful sometimes in rewarding Chinese trading partners that are incrementally adding value to the American company.

Even without a genuine global joint venture strategy, using a Bermuda holding company in a joint venture in China to earn US dollars and meet the Chinese partners' goals can help.

Business Ethics in China

Chinese business ethics are not situational; they are relationship driven, and depend upon how long the relationship is reciprocally valuable to them. American business ethics are transactional, rather than situational. The binding relationship in American business ethics is established by the rule of law. In China's Pre-Rule-of-Law culture, it is important that American companies build a relationship as insider with and never get past the apex of their Chinese partner's curve of gratitude.

Mutual respect and mutually beneficial collaboration, which are vital in a company's China strategy, are not possible without intellectually understanding and emotionally accepting the differences between these two types of societies.[5] In managing moral hazard risks, it is necessary to factor in the attitudes, which may surprisingly and then understandably and obviously pertain in a "Permission Society." Some behavior that is "natural" and "expected" in a Permission Society is "dishonest" and "outrageous" in a "Rights Society." People from a "Rights Society" may be outraged that officials and trading partners in China behave in a manner they see as "dishonest."

A recent Chinese study asserted that 10% of American and 40% of Chinese entrepreneurs receiving venture capital funding turn out to be dishonest and noted that it may have been virtually impossible or difficult in many instances to lawfully make money or succeed in private enterprise in China.[6] However, reportedly, 9.8% in 1990 and 33% by 1999 of all economic sectors in China consisted of mixed-ownership, which permit the accumulation of private property and wealth outside the SOE system.[7] Chinese newspapers, television programs, and web discussions in recent years have focused on "trust issues" among Chinese business people and the Chinese generally. There is recognition in these discussions that the Chinese do have trust problems, which may have arisen, in part, from past political influences which made people suspicious of others. Many argue that the Chinese people should acknowledge this weakness and improve their own image and interactions. The Chinese government has created programs to educate people by emphasizing successful business cases based on honesty demonstrating that only honesty can bring long-term and real wealth.

The failure of a company's "China strategy" is not acceptable to the foreign company. Allowing foreign companies to take over and dominate China's economy is not acceptable to China's leadership or Chinese companies. A non-Chinese company should deploy "never beyond the apex of the curve of gratitude" value propositions and win-win strategies that also produce compelling foreign currency earnings fulfilling China's strategy and its Chinese trading partners' aspirations. The Chinese government and Chinese companies want the intellectual and financial capital foreign companies have. China's leadership in deciding to sell control of SOEs to foreign and Chinese private interests adopted the proverb: "if you can't beat them, join them." It is a useful proverb also for a foreign company working-out sustainable win-win relationships with

Chinese companies. Fortunately, the Chinese have a proverb: "We cannot be friends until we have fought."

Helping Chinese Companies' "Go Global" Strategy

How does a Chinese company learn to be a successful multinational corporation and deal with competition in the global economy it is entering? While Chinese companies, like China's economy, will develop awesome competitive advantages in the next 25 years, there is the likelihood that mistakes will be made in the process. That process is where American companies that are masters at it can contribute very significantly and profit with emerging Chinese multinational companies outside, in addition, to inside China.

The Economist commented in the aftermath of the failure of the CNOOC bid for Unocal:

> Fears that Chinese firms are acting as the commercial arm of an expansionist state are thus belied by a more complicated and disorderly reality. The real reason to fear China's overseas expansion is quite different. Because Chinese firms have grown up in an irrational and chaotic business environment, they may export some very bad habits. ... when Japanese companies took over American ones, they mostly made them better. If the Chinese run foreign firms like they operate at home, driving prices down, misallocating capital and over-diversifying, that is genuinely something to fear.[8]

This illustrates the learning curve that Chinese companies have internationally, and highlights the dangers to existing multinationals of Chinese companies' success or failure being a danger. Chinese companies, some privately held such as Haier, have and will come out of nowhere to seize market share and undermine the business models of leading multinational companies. Other Chinese companies that falter will cause anguish at home and confuse international business in the short to medium term. The international capital markets will respond to well run, genuine global joint ventures between American companies and Chinese companies with business models that address both the requirements of success internationally and inside China.

Access to Know-how Problems of Chinese-Government-Owned and Private Companies

Chinese companies typically lack experience *outside* China, and need know-how and intermediaries they can trust and who will succeed in guiding them to their goals. This was lacking in CNOOC's disastrous bid for Unocal. Chinese companies going global also need distributors, and customers outside of China. As we have seen in Chapters 1 and 2, the Chinese companies going global, lack foreign know-how, expertise in using foreign marketing research and advertising, and a willingness to pay for services that American companies have. Chinese companies, executives, and the Chinese government urgently want such foreign capabilities to be available to and developed by Chinese companies.

Bartering Know-how Outside China for Know-how Inside China

For American companies' China strategies, a suitable Chinese partner, or partners, must have the talent and experience and education outside of Mainland China, "know how" and "know who" relationships in China, and, in some cases, Chinese currency to use *inside* China. Such Chinese partners can be compensated outside of China for deploying their expertise and resources successfully in carrying out the American company's China strategy. This may reduce the cash that the American company will deploy in China and take advantage of China's competitive advantages without the risks of being exposed to them.

The Profitability and Sustained Profitability Tests

The Genuine Global Joint Venture Model can be structured to pass the Profitability and Sustained Profitability tests more easily than some types of part-ownership or wholly-owned foreign enterprises ("WOFE") structures examined in Chapter 5. Assisting Chinese "champion" companies going global has a compelling and sustained value proposition for China's government, and the Chinese joint venture partner and its management and staff. The payment of revenue, profits, salaries, and bonuses in cash US dollars, tax free, outside of China as the Chinese joint venture partner faithfully carries out the foreign company's strategy in China increases the foreign currency earnings of China. The Chinese joint venture partner and its management and staff also gain from its development as a multinational corporation and from the IPO or reverse merger with a publicly traded company.

All that assists in ensuring the foreign company never gets beyond the apex of the curve of gratitude of the Chinese joint venture partner or China's leadership. It has a Generous Tit For Tat feature, because the foreign currency earning and the later stock price of the Bermuda-incorporated, publicly-traded joint venture vehicle will be negatively impacted by the Chinese joint venture partner not adequately performing the foreign company's China strategy which has been embedded in the Bermuda joint venture vehicle's income stream and valuation and other equity and debt issues.

US Money Outside and Chinese Money Inside Strategy

Money is an important motivator. But, money means "cash" now to Mainland Chinese. Cash paid in American dollars in the near term earned outside of China is a particularly strong motivator to the Chinese government and Chinese companies. Private

Chinese companies are usually short of cash. But privately and state-owned "champion" companies are supported by the Chinese government. Nonetheless, state-owned, partly-state-owned and private Chinese companies all want to earn cash in foreign currencies.

The US-Money-Outside-And-Chinese-Money-Inside Strategy is useful in traditional structures and genuine global joint ventures. It relies on four key concepts:

1. Wherever possible, Chinese capital should be used inside China for the reasons seen in the Artysen and other case studies examined in Chapters 5 and 6.

2. Where it is necessary for capital to be provided by the foreign multinational partner or the international capital markets, the Chinese partner may obtain access to the capital it wants as milestones are achieved in the Chinese partner carrying out the common enterprise.

3. Both the first and second concepts seek to create a relationship where the non-Chinese participant "never gets past the apex of the curve of gratitude" where the Chinese participants' motivation to carry out the agreed business plan deteriorates.

4. The foreign company doing business globally makes sure that it creates a system of agreed objectives, motivations, and rewards in which the Chinese partner earns more money in US dollars outside China by fulfilling their commitments in the foreign company's strategy inside China, than they would if they did not.

These four key concepts do not guarantee that business ventures combining American and Chinese companies' capabilities will succeed operationally and be profitable on a sustained basis. But they do better to align the expectations of the participants.

Solving Access to Capital Problems of Privately Owned Chinese Companies' Strategies

Chinese companies that are not wholly or partially-owned by the Chinese government or otherwise favored by it as "Champions" are typically denied access to debt or equity financing in China. Such privately-held companies, like Haier, which have demonstrated the ability to be highly competitive (even in a debt and equity capital starved environment and other restrictions on such companies in China's economic development strategy), need more sophisticated capital structures than they have to develop globally. A foreign multinational partner of such companies needs to find ways to provide such sophisticated capital structures in a manner that prevents it from getting past the apex of the curve of gratitude. A genuine global joint venture, set up through Bermuda holding and operating companies, can be used to provide, as agreed milestones in the genuine global joint venture's business plan, tranches of capital that the Chinese genuine global joint venture partner, working with the foreign multinational partner, needs to fulfill its aspects of the agreed business plan inside and outside China.

Using the Chinese Stock Exchanges to Source Capital Inside China Strategy

It has been very difficult to get permission to list companies that have received foreign investment on Mainland Chinese stock exchanges. But in the Kodak case study in the next chapter, we see how the concessions Kodak's George Fisher obtained from the Chinese government, motivated by its need to effect industrial development which had failed in the SOE context, enabled Kodak to purchase assets rather than the equity of Chinese companies, and use new corporate structures that could be listed on the Shanghai or Shenzhen stock exchanges and potentially attract investment capital within China. There are policy issues competing in the matter of allowing such public listings. On the one hand, the Chinese government is committed to creating "the innovative economy of the world." On the other, it needs to prevent powerful domestic companies from challenging the political stability that permits such economic development to occur in a planned way. American companies providing suitable value propositions meeting the needs of the Chinese government at the highest levels, as Gerald Fisher demonstrated, can achieve permission to list Chinese companies they invest in on Mainland Chinese stock exchanges.

The Strategy of Helping to Ameliorate Regional Disparity Challenges Facing the Chinese Government

The Chinese government's challenges in dealing with regional disparities involving at least 800 million of its 1.3 billion people ironically has similarities with the American government's problem with losing jobs to less developed economies. Part of the agenda for the partnership of America and China should be addressing enhanced amelioration of regional disparities in China and job loss in America. This could help reduce political unrest in both nations. Collaborating in this would also exhibit "the right spirit" to those that are suffering in America and China in spite or because of China's emergence from poverty.

The Chinese government must pull more people out of poverty. The unemployment rate nationally is 20% of 780 million workers and the Chinese government must ensure there are almost 15 million new jobs created a year to keep up with the demand for new jobs and prevent the unemployment rate from rising.[9] Success in doing so is critical to China's strategy.

The Chinese government has used the designation of "special economic zones" in Shanghai and Shenzhen with policies facilitating rapid economic development to stimulate China's economy, while not experimenting with new approaches to doing things across the entire nation and 1.3 billion-plus population. This "reform laboratory" approach has worked well, and is better understood by the Chinese government in 2006 than it was in its formative years.

Although China's economic development is accelerating, and shows no signs of needing more growth in the view of some non-Chinese observers in developed areas[10]. The Chinese government has created a "new engine of growth" to supplement the "dynamos" of Shanghai and Schenzhen, the two port cities at the forefront of China's economic transformation. A strip of "industrial sprawl and semi-wasteland 90 miles long on the northern coast" is being turned into a development zone far larger than Shanghai and Schenzhen. It is called the "Binhai New Area," and is intended to help northern China, including Beijing, and the provinces around the Bohai Gulf obtain the type of economic boom generated in Shanghai in the lower reaches of the Yangtze River and Shenzhen in the Pearl River delta. With tax incentives and far lower costs of land use, the Chinese government and local governments hope to make it a manufacturing powerhouse for aircraft, cars, microchips, and chemicals, and benefit from tourism and coastal recreation. Binhai's port is to double its size by 2010. The planners have been given the national government's blessing to experiment with a wide range of economic and streamlining bureaucracy reforms.[11] Local leaders established the zone in

1994, but in 2005 the Chinese government in Beijing gave the clear signal that this project was of national importance as an "experimental zone for comprehensive reform," not just a local venture. It is being focused on by President Hu Jintao and Premier Wen Jiabao.[12]

From 1994 through 2005, US$15.9 billion of foreign capital was attracted to the area, with the goal of attracting a further US$20 billion by 2010. The Tianjin Economic-Technological Development Area has companies already such as Motorola, Toyota, and Samsung with large factories. Binhai is targeting GDP growth of 17% annually during the next five years, and will spend US$15 billion on infrastructure. Experiments in privatizing of land ownership, venture capital, and investment banking are planned.[13]

Kenichi Ohmae's description of globalization today is illustrated in the strategy that the Chinese government adopted:

> The growth level of China averages around 9 percent per annum. But this is a figure for the whole country. It embraces vibrant region-states such as Dalian and Guangzhou, whose growth rates were between 13 and 15 percent per annum for 2003, and regions farther west such as Ningxia and Gansu, which are still enmeshed in poverty. There are China watchers who like to pour cold water on China's continued economic growth trends, stating that it is impossible for the country as a whole to maintain growth rates of 9 or even 7 percent. But such responses fail to take account [of] the reality that it is not China as a whole that is growing, but certain regions within it ...
>
> So, whether China continues to grow at a high pace depends on whether it can grow the number of megalopolises or region-states along with the growth rate of such regions. China produced 146 new cities with more than one million people in the 10 years between 1990 and 2000. There is no reason to believe that it cannot repeat this. There are, after all,

still 800 million people living in the Chinese countryside as farmers."[14]

The map below shows the principal cities and regions that have been developed to date and the specialization of each:

[15]

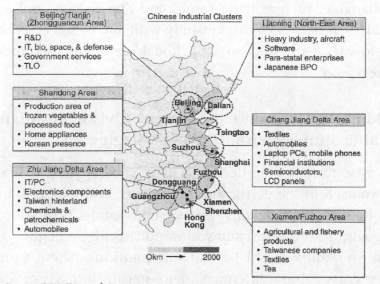

Beijing/Tianjin (Zhongguancun Area)
• R&D
• IT, bio, space, & defense
• Government services
• TLO

Shandong Area
• Production area of frozen vegetables & processed food
• Home appliances
• Korean presence

Zhu Jiang Delta Area
• IT/PC
• Electronics components
• Taiwan hinterland
• Chemicals & petrochemicals
• Automobiles

Chinese Industrial Clusters

Liaoning (North-East Area)
• Heavy industry, aircraft
• Software
• Para-statal enterprises
• Japanese BPO

Chang Jiang Delta Area
• Textiles
• Automobiles
• Laptop PCs, mobile phones
• Financial institutions
• Semiconductors, LCD panels

Xiamen/Fuzhou Area
• Agricultural and fishery products
• Taiwanese companies
• Textiles
• Tea

Source: BBT Research Institute.

The reforms of Deng Xiaoping began in 14 special economic zones along China's coast. The reforms of Zhu Rongji in 1998 focused on the problems of corruption, bureaucracy, and reengineering the SOEs, but also:

> ...were accompanied by a devolution of more and effective decision-making, down to regions of proven success. It is clear that places such as Dalian, Guangzho, and Qingtao were prospering and that nothing should be put in their way. They must be given their heads, and those on the ground who had power should be told to use it as they saw fit. The people who were granted this de facto autonomy were the provincial governors and city mayors ... Those mayors who have done

well in promoting economic development are kicked upstairs.
Both Jiang Zemin and former Premier Zhu Rongji were mayors
of Shanghai...[16]

The Kodak case study in Chapter 5 shows how an astute
American executive, Gerald Fisher, identified effective local leaders
in Shanghai, such as Jiang Zemin and Zhu Rongji, and aligned
Kodak's China strategy successfully with such leaders' economic
development strategy, so that Kodak's strategy became their
strategy, too.

Making the Decision-makers Your Advisors in Aligning a China Strategy with China's Strategies

It is wise to make the decision-maker your advisor. Attempt to
put yourself in the decision-maker's shoes, and look at the situation he sees and problems he has. Then ponder how your goals,
his goals, his problems, and your problems might align. Look for
what you think might be win-win solutions. Then, using the
wisest cross-cultural intermediaries you can find, *ask the decision
maker for his advice*. It is better to do so and, in the process,
identify his own problems, opportunities, and personal performance
expectations than to pitch, without listening first, a foreign-
developed business plan.

For example, regional disparities are a problem shared by
China's central government and many of the provincial, municipal,
and village governments. What solution to a regional development
problem can you provide in a mutually beneficial business deal?
If there is a potential to use your business plan to solve
government entities' problems, discuss their problems with the
most rational and cooperative government decision-makers you
meet in various regions requiring foreign investment.

Then reconsider your goals and the government decision-
makers' stated goals. Let's suppose that the decision-makers'

goals are "x". Then ask the decision-maker: If we did "y", would that help you obtain "x"? That dialogue, which may take time, is how you make the decision-maker your advisor. You have engaged him in a meaningful collaboration. Sometimes, the decision-makers will appreciate your consideration of their problems and goals. Sometimes, if the decision-makers help formulate your solution for aligning your resources and goals with theirs, they will support the recommendation that they give you regarding how you should proceed. That is what George Fisher of Kodak did.

Then you must repeat the process at every relevant level of decision-makers. It helps if you start at the top; but each group of decision-makers at the many levels of permission, licenses, etc. from which you will need support and approval must also become your advisors in the formulation of the aligned China strategy and China's strategy. Each level of decision-makers will have their own priorities and problems that must be aligned in your China strategy. China's strategy is diffuse.

By making all the decision-makers your advisors, you may have their assistance in implementing as well as designing your China strategy that is aligned with theirs. This approach is a win-win approach. Insist that your executive and advisor team use this win-win approach in designing, deploying, and amending your China strategies.

Often foreigners in China use a different approach. The foreign company looks at its goals and problems only through its eyes. It approaches the Chinese decision-makers involved with preset value propositions and plans. Let's call the foreign company's plans "y". The Chinese decision-makers listen to "y" and try to work out how "x", their problems, and goals, can be served by "y". There is a lower probability that they will be able to align "x" with "y" if you do not collaborate and make the decision-makers your advisors. You may find that "y" does not

align with their "x", but discover "z", "u", or "t", which you never seriously considered or identified, can align well with their goals and is alignable with your needs and goals.

The map above shows the relative per capita gross domestic products of various regions in China. It is also useful to identify local political leaders in China who are effective in attracting and satisfying foreign companies and who are competing with other provinces, cities, or villages for foreign direct investment and operations in order to enable their communities and themselves to distinguish themselves from others in China. Finding such talent and motivation may be possible where the foreign company's impact is more critical to the success of the decision-makers, i.e., in areas needing foreign investment the most. The

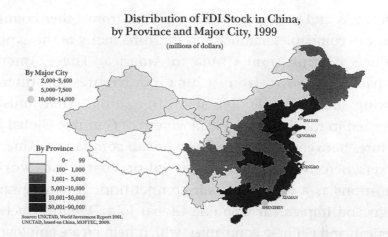

Distribution of FDI Stock in China,
by Province and Major City, 1999

18

(millions of dollars)

map above shows the distribution of FDI in China by province and major city as at 1999.

"The case studies presented in this book illustrate both the "make the decision-maker your advisor" strategy and the "align your China strategy with China's" strategy.

Genuine Global Joint Ventures' Roles in Creating Employment in America and China

The difficult issues in America and China's relationship include the loss of American jobs to China, the related issue of China's lower production costs, and America's growing trade deficit with China. These three problems will not be eliminated by the strategies American political leaders are using. These problems can be unsuccessfully addressed in an aggressive stepping up of America's containment strategy to China. But, ultimately, jobs will continue to leave America because other countries have lower production costs. Similarly, America's trade deficit might go down if it trades less with China, but America's economic problems likely will increase rather than decrease.

American companies move jobs to China not merely to enhance profits. They do so to lower their costs so they can stay in business and compete with companies from other countries. American companies manufacture in China many of the exported products coming from China to America. These American companies' exports from China contribute to America's growing annual trade deficits with China. That must be addressed in the design and deployment of Genuine Global Joint Ventures between Chinese and American companies. American workers perceive China's lower labor costs and working conditions as a form of unfair competition. It is necessary to design and implement Genuine Global Joint Ventures between American and Chinese companies, which help create employment in America in the cities and towns that are losing jobs to China.

Genuine Global Joint Venture of a Chinese Company with American Strategic Partner and Financial Investor Strategy

Americans are interested in buying cheaper, high-quality cars made in China. The Chinese government and car companies are ramping up production and seeking American distribution channels as the Chinese auto industry "goes global." Western and Chinese carmakers with Chinese operations (i.e., Volkswagen) are able to slash production costs (including materials, labor, and research and development costs) in China by 40% per car.[19] American companies are positioning themselves to profit from the changes in the automobile industry these new realities are creating. The graphs below show the interest levels of Americans in buying Chinese-made cars and China's growing capacity to produce them.

The 2004 joint venture proposed between Chery, one of China's top three among 120 automobile manufacturing companies, and Visionary Vehicles led by an American, Malcolm Bricklin, to build

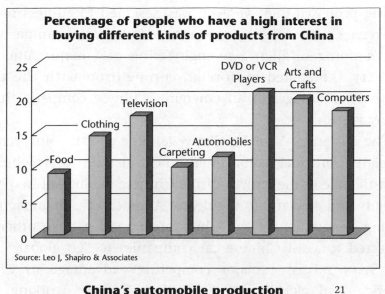

Percentage of people who have a high interest in buying different kinds of products from China

20

Food • Clothing • Television • Carpeting • Automobiles • DVD or VCR Players • Arts and Crafts • Computers

Source: Leo J, Shapiro & Associates

China's automobile production

21

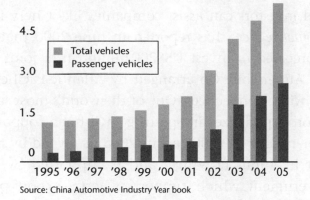

6.0 millions of units

- Total vehicles
- Passenger vehicles

4.5

3.0

1.5

0

1995 '96 '97 '98 '99 '00 '01 '02 '03 '04 '05

Source: China Automotive Industry Year book

luxury cars in China, with all the cost advantages China offers, is an example of Americans attempting to work with a Chinese company "going global." In the first stage of that proposed joint venture, Chery and Visionary Vehicles planned to distribute 1 million Chinese cars in America; and then in the second stage, build the second 1 million cars in America. Such joint ventures are at the melding edge of templates of genuine joint ventures between American and Chinese companies.

The proposed joint venture was designed to address several weaknesses in the business model of American car manufacturers and in doing so align a re-engineering of a major American industry threatened by foreign competition with the competitive advantages of an emerging Chinese company that is "going global."

The Visionary Vehicles-Chery genuine global joint venture template is one that major American car manufacturers who seek to participate in the growth of the Chinese car market may wish to study and emulate. To the degree American car manufacturers seeking penetration of the Chinese car market have otherwise neglected to assist Chinese car companies to "go global," they may have missed a major competitive advantage in China, America, and globally. In 2007 Chery is now working with Chrysler and Cerbeus.

Financial investors can assist companies like Chery in going global. *Automotive News* has reported in June 2006 that George Soros was prepared to invest US$200 million in a joint venture with Chery Automobile Co arranged by Atlantic-Pacific Capital Inc of Greenwich, Connecticut. One of the world's most successful investors, Soros specializes in spotting investment opportunities overseas. Chery sold 189,000 cars in 2005, is owned by the local government in Anhui Province, and is supported by China's central government which supports Chery's export plans. In 2005, Chery exported 18,000 cars to developing countries like Egypt and Malaysia, making it China's largest car exporter.[22]

What follows is an abridged version of an article by Darren Dahl that appeared in *Inc* magazine in July 2005. Note the approach Malcolm Bricklin used in negotiating with his desired Chinese partner.

> Arriving in Wuhu, China last July, after a 17-hour flight from New York, Malcolm Bricklin was so juiced up, so shot through

with adrenaline, that he couldn't sleep. All night, he paced back and forth in his hotel room, killing time before his meeting the next day with Yin Tongyao, president of the Chery Automobile Co, the eighth largest of the 120 carmakers in China. Since Chery's founding in 1997, Yin has made it known that his ultimate goal is to sell cars in the U.S. For Bricklin, the 66-year-old CEO of Visionary Vehicles, and the man who introduced Americans to both the Subaru and the Yugo, the meeting represented a thrilling opportunity. It was also a source of agitation. That's because Bricklin's advisors had warned him that he had to be uncharacteristically patient. In China, they had said, personal relationships must be developed before business can be done.

It was too much to ask. A few minutes into the breakfast with Yin and four other Chery executives, Bricklin shoved aside his PowerPoint presentation, as well as the handouts of his business plan. He then removed his tan suit jacket. The whole thing was captured on film by Bricklin's 28-year-old son, Jonathan, who is making a movie about his father's life and who tagged along on the trip.

In reality, Malcolm Bricklin was filming every moment of every meeting he had with his prospective Chinese partner. He understood ubiquitous note-taking and subsequent detailed and repeated pattern of questioning that Chinese often use in negotiating with potential foreign partners in a quest to get the most information and best possible terms.

As the older Bricklin began addressing the Chinese in English—without a translator—Jonathan zoomed in. "The word I hear about doing business in China is relationship,'"declared Bricklin, his face flushed. He then ratcheted down his red silk tie and punctuated his next works by unbuttoning his once-dry white shirt:

> 'The way I see it, [pop]
> We have two choices. [pop]
> We can either take our time [pop]
> And get to know each other. [pop]
> Or, we can get naked!'

With that, Bricklin tried to rip off his shirt—only to be foiled by a button snagged in his belt. As the Chinese execu-

tives smirked and exchanged sideways glances, he applied a
final burst and yanked the garment free, leaving his audience
to gawk at a chest overgrown with white hair. "I came here as
Malcolm Bricklin, but I'm leaving you as Visionary Vehicles,"
he declared, pulling on a baseball cap embroidered with his
company logo.

Either because of, or in spite of his theatrics, Bricklin had
his deal by December: exclusive North American distribution
rights for five new model lines from Chery starting in 2007.

There is little disputing that China, already producing
many high quality high-technology products for a fraction of
the price that they can be made in most other places, will
become a force in the U.S. car market. Of the many automakers
in China, Chery has one of the most modern manufacturing
facilities going—a state-of-the-art factory in Wuhu, a city of
one million. Chery also has substantial support from the local
and central government in China.

Bricklin is getting his seed money from Per Arneberg, a
shipping mogul who has invested with him in the past. Allen
& Co, the prominent investment-banking firm, has signed on
to help structure the financing for his dealership network.
William J. Vanden Heuvel, a permanent U.S. representative to
the United Nations, and Maurice Strong, the U.N.'s
Undersecretary-general and director of the World Economic
Forum Foundation, have joined the board of Visionary
Vehicles [and its advisory board respectively].

"Who wouldn't want to be part of this?" Bricklin asks,
adding that the Chery deal is the one he has been searching
for his whole life—his best opportunity to cause a sea
change in the kinds of cars people buy and the way they go
about buying them. "This is an industry in flux," he says.
"Can you believe that General Motors would be rated the
same as junk bonds"...

He hired Ron Harbour, a renowned automotive industry
expert and publisher of the Harbour Report, to begin
scouring potential factory sites in developing nations like
Poland, Romania, and India.... It wasn't until a chance
encounter with a casual acquaintance in April 2004 that
China came up. The man, a Russian who exported cars to
South America, offered to set Bricklin up with a company
called Chery, about which the Russian had heard great

things. "I thought I was going to find some factory in the middle of a rice paddy," Bricklin recalls. Instead, when he arrived in Wuhu, he thought he had landed in heaven. Not only did he find a modern facility staffed by a motivated work force, he also found a man he now describes as his entrepreneurial soul mate. It was Yin, Chery's 42-year-old president. Yin had spent the bulk of his career in the car business with companies like Volkswagen before being picked to head Chery in 1997. Bricklin says the two of them hit it off right from the start. Yin told Bricklin he planned to turn his 8,000-employee company into a Chinese Toyota. "His dreams were bigger than mine," says Bricklin.

He forecast that within five years, Americans will be buying one million Chinese-made cars from his dealers. The Chery product will be sheathed in Lexus-caliber luxury but will be priced 30% lower than its Japanese counterparts and carry a 10-year, 100,000 mile warranty. "We are going to produce better, prettier, and smarter cars for less money," says Bricklin. "We are not seeing how cheap we can do it, we're trying to see how good we can get it."

A Chery concept car—a convertible created by the Italian firm Pininfarina, designer of the Ferrari—won the top award at the Shanghai auto show in May. Bricklin intends to sell a version of that vehicle plus four other Chery models in the U.S.

Depending on the size of the sales territory, Bricklin is asking each potential dealer to invest $2 million to $4 million for a Visionary Vehicles franchise—an amount roughly equal to the going rate for Lexus or BMW.

Meanwhile, General Motors has a pending lawsuit asserting that the design for Chery's current bestseller, the QQ, is a knockoff of the Chevy Spark. GM has also warned Bricklin in a letter that, as far as its lawyers are concerned, the Chery name is too close to its Chevy brand to be sold in the U.S.[23]

Bricklin's business plan had compelling win-win value propositions for Chery, which was looking for a distribution network in America. The Visionary Vehicles deal was structured so that the Americans who buy dealerships would also be equity holders in the joint venture vehicle, which was to own part of Chery and part of the distribution company, have input into the design of the cars, and the opportunity to participate in the sale of Chinese cars in America. Visionary Vehicles' business case offers American car dealers an opportunity to benefit from the economic competitive advantages and impact Chinese cars can have in America. By buying a Visionary Vehicles dealership they could hedge the risk that the arrival of Chinese cars will supplant the business of the cars they are currently selling.

The feature in the Visionary Vehicles business plan providing for the second million cars to be built in America addresses Chery's desire to go global and responds somewhat to concerns about the impact Chinese cars could have on the American car makers. If a Chinese car company manufactures cars in America, are the results Chinese or American cars? One risk these joint ventures have is the potential for "CNOOC jingoism" or a deterioration of the relationship between America and China to affect the business model.

American political and business leaders chose a zero-sum-game lose-lose response in America's response to Japanese companies going global. Oded Shenkar notes:

> Nowhere was the Japanese threat more visible and threatening than in this most conspicuous symbol of the American economic might and way of life: the automobile. Japan, which designated automotive as a strategic industry already in the 1950s, restarted its car industry after the war by reverse engineering American models ... Less than two decades later, Japanese makers were already shipping product to the U.S., first at a few thousand units annually and by the early 1970s, hundreds of thousands of cars per year. During all those years, U.S. car exports to Japan remained at the same dismal level of a few thousand cars annually. Japan's initial success in exporting cars to America was first attributed in the public's mind to the oil crisis of October 1973 (in reality, the crisis merely accelerated an export surge that was already in full swing) which enabled many to argue that the Japanese were

merely lucky—they happened to have economy cars for sale just when the market needed them. When Japanese manufacturers extended their gains, another, unfounded argument came about: Japan was not playing fair, artificially lowering the value of the yen to boost exports while erecting barriers to American exports. The same criticism was directed decades later towards China.

In the late 1970s and early 1980s, another explanation for Japan's success gained ground: perhaps Japan was simply producing higher quality products at a more reasonable price, and to improve competitiveness, American firms needed to learn from Japan in such realms as quality control, productivity, and human resource management.[24]

...the Japan experience exposes the inefficiency of many of the responses undertaken by American industry and unions to counter foreign competition. After all, the trade deficit with Japan persisted in the face of "voluntary" quotas, dramatic realignment in exchange rates, and continuous U.S. government pressure to pry open Japanese markets. The deficit also survived the establishment of U.S. transplants by the major Japanese manufacturers (together with their suppliers), who were supposed to export back to Japan (but rarely did), and a dramatic restructuring, including marked improvement in quality and productivity by American makers. In fact, it now seems that the main factor curtailing the Japanese surplus has been the transfer of Japanese manufacturing capacity to China, which, by and large, shifted a portion of the deficit from one country to the other. Worse, it appears that some of the responses undertaken in the U.S. to fight the deficit with Japan may have backfired. For instance, limiting Japanese imports in unit amounts as part of the quotas only accelerated their up-market shift culminating in the establishment of luxury divisions by Honda (Acura), Toyota (Lexus) and Nissan (Infiniti), which targeted the Cadillac and Lincoln customer, along with German imports. Japanese firms have come full circle from low-cost producers to full-range competitors charging a premium for the perceived quality of their products. The U.S. manufacturing industry, on its part, discovered that the up-market was not protected from Asian competition either.[25]

This analysis, of course, rather than leading to the conclusion that containment of the Japanese car industry did not work, could be viewed as pointing out that more aggressive containment strategies to prevent the sale of Chinese cars in America should be used. Such a view, however, must convincingly explain how America can ultimately benefit from a selective or broad trade war with China.

"Vendor of Intellectual Property Rather than Victim of Piracy" Strategy

The fact that many in China do not respect intellectual property rights is outrageous to those brought up in a "Rights Society," who are taught from an early age to respect the concept of private property. But until recent reforms, there was no private property in China. In considering whether a person is "dishonest" or of "bad character," such cultural circumstances must be taken into account.[26] This example is cited to help a foreign company get past the debilitating emotion that Chinese who do not respect what the foreign company's mindset views as its "rights" are dishonest or of bad character.

The U.S. Money Outside And Chinese Money Inside Model alone or in combination with the Genuine Global Joint Venture Model can be used in corporate structures and Generous Tit for Tat value propositions and strategies designed to increase the likelihood that a non-Chinese company will be a profitable vendor of intellectual property rather than a victim of piracy. These models can be combined with the traditionally used model of manufacturing products in China, but having the critical intellectual property components manufactured outside of China, which we will call the "Foreign Secret Sauce Model." Another traditionally-used model is having several Chinese entities manufacture different components of a product with no one knowing about how the other components are made, we will call "The Divide and Conquer Model," which may not work on a sustainable basis and is a less attractive value proposition than what other companies, such as Motorola and Advanced Micro Devices, are using in China.

Singapore used to have a poor record of protecting intellectual property rights. But as it developed, that changed. It is expected that China will follow a similar path due to international pressure and the emergence of powerful Chinese companies with valuable intellectual property that will demand protection. In the meantime, Chinese companies are benefiting from copying foreign intellectual property.

The Alignment of an American Corporation and China's Goals Strategy

While many companies are worrying about intellectual property piracy and the competitive threat from Chinese companies, Microsoft is implementing what we term the "Alignment Of An American Corporation And China's Goals Strategy." Microsoft recognized the ramifications of China's high-tech development plans and the synergy of Microsoft and the Chinese government's goals. At the highest levels, Microsoft is collaborating with the Chinese government to achieve synergistic, multi-faceted, aligned competitive advantages immediately and in the future.

Microsoft has aligned its global strategy with China's global goals. Bill Gates, as Chairman of Microsoft, came to the view that the Chinese government is likely to make progress in creating intellectual property enforcement each year incrementally over the next ten years. Gates has aligned Microsoft's economic and intellectual capital success with the Chinese government's economic and intellectual capital goals. Gates made Microsoft's Beijing research and development lab the epicenter of Microsoft's intensifying battle against Google in the "search wars," Nokia in the "wireless wars," and Sony in "graphics and entertainment wars."[27] A great battle to be the "Microsoft" of the future is on.

In the emerging "Information Age Economy," the global economy is being changed by wireless technology, hugely powerful quantum computers,[28] Internet use for e-mails, blogs, photos, video games, movies, television, and a plethora of new applications not yet developed or commercialized. Microsoft has recognized that the software vending era will abate as "server farm technology" affects the current software delivery industry. Microsoft, Google, Yahoo, and others are spending billions of dollars to build "server farms" as fast as possible.[29] The melding of search technology, wireless communications, and entertainment is now being designed and deployed. Microsoft's Beijing research and development lab is using the talent in China's top universities and aligning Microsoft and China's goals to play key roles in the future of computing. Microsoft is using its synergy with China's huge intellectual capital resources, huge potential market, and the Chinese government's goal of making China the innovative economy of the world to benefit Microsoft and China.

The Alignment of an American Corporation and China's Goals Strategy meets the challenges foreign companies face in China and in the rapidly changing global economy by creating a win-win relationship, reciprocal competitive advantages, and sustainable payoffs for Microsoft and China. Microsoft is helping to provide a research and development training ground for China's computer science industry. One of the biggest rewards is Microsoft's stature as "friend of China" with the Chinese government.

4

An Advanced Structure for American and Chinese Global Joint Ventures

Overview

This chapter examines why leading Chinese and other multinational companies use Bermuda corporations to be competitive in their global growth. We will also examine Chinese public policy priorities that include whether the Chinese government wishes to make it a priority to facilitate Chinese companies going global in joint ventures with non-Chinese companies or to currently tax Chinese multinationals, making them less competitive globally.

Chinese State-Owned and Privatized Companies Are Being Positioned for Global Growth

American International Group (AIG) was a start-up company established in Shanghai in 1919, which set up operations in Bermuda in 1948. It has grown into a US$700 billion group of companies dominating the global insurance sector. The coming waves of Chinese companies have many competitive advantages, which AIG lacked in 1948.

Major state-owned and private Chinese companies preparing for private and public offers in the international capital markets and international acquisitions have begun, like American, European, and Asian companies becoming multinationals before them, to use offshore companies in neutral jurisdictions that offer competitive advantages that are necessary when companies compete for global growth opportunities and markets.

The number of Chinese M&A deals abroad increased from 40 involving US$2 billion in 2003, to 55 involving US$4 billion in 2004, to 23 involving US$22 billion in the first half of 2005.[1] Goldman Sachs has indicated, "The first people on any buy list will be Chinese."[2] China has established two U.S. $200 billion funds to assist Chinese companies.

Acquisitions and Equity and Debt Finance

Investments in and takeovers of privately-held or publicly-traded companies or their assets in or outside of Bermuda often benefit from the use of Bermuda companies, partnerships, or trusts to provide fiscal and regulatory advantages. Such vehicles may be used to assemble resources before a takeover bid or other transactions. Employing a Bermuda vehicle may simplify transactions by reducing or eliminating levels of fiscal, taxation, and other regulatory issues, particularly when financing sources or investors from multiple jurisdictions are involved. Leveraged buyouts also work better under the Bermuda system when forming a company or trust to acquire a target operation.

Bermuda holding companies or trusts are used in debt and equity finance, and often offer considerable advantages in cases of syndicated debt financings, equity capital, and bridge loans.

Bermuda entities are useful in reorganizations of companies or groups of companies. Court-approved Schemes of Arrangement are used with Chapter 11 cases and other foreign insolvency provisions.

Exempted limited partnerships are used in joint ventures, investment syndicates, and investment schemes when accumulating capital from multiple jurisdictions to acquire securities. General exempted partnerships are used to conduct business for a specific purpose or for a fixed period, particularly in joint ventures or syndicated investments involving multiple investors from several jurisdictions. Bermuda companies and partnerships are also used for arbitrage of all kinds, including trading in securities listed on the major exchanges. Interest rate and currency swaps are often accomplished through a Bermuda subsidiary of businesses with international operations.

Bermuda holding companies can be listed on the Bermuda Stock Exchange as part of an early-stage private placement with strategic or financial investors and then on NASDAQ rather than on the Hong Kong or Singapore stock exchanges.

Case Study: China Netcom

China needs telecommunications. The first and most successful international acquisition by a Chinese state-owned company was China Netcom's acquisition, through a Bermuda holding company, of assets of another Bermuda company. China Netcom paid US$270 million for assets of Asia Global Crossing with a book value of US$1.2 billion, which included 18,740 km of undersea fiber optic cable assets linking Hong Kong, Japan, Taiwan, South Korea, Singapore, and the Philippines. This was named the 2002 Asian M&A Deal of the Year from among 400. *The International Financial Law Review* selected this as the 2002 Asian Deal Of The Year because it involved a Chinese state-owned company going international and purchasing assets from a vendor in Chapter 11 Bankruptcy proceedings in America. Asia Netcom was later sold to British investors for US$400 million.

This was an example of the value Bermuda companies add in the globalization of Chinese companies. It could also have been a good pre-IPO structuring move for Chinese companies expanding internationally and using the American capital markets to fund domestic and international expansion.

China Needs Steel and Is Building Multinational Companies

China's growing need for steel being filled by partly Chinese government-owned and partly-privatized Chinese companies also exemplifies the go-global trend. Chinese steel companies intend to become "Mega Multinationals." It is critical to recognize that they will do so, whether or not America and American companies collaborate with them.

Case Study: Baosteel

Baosteel is an SOE with a minority stake held by private shareholders, which made a South American investment as a joint venture with the world's largest iron ore producer and investments in Australia. Baosteel ran the following two-page advertisement in the August 1, 2005 *Fortune* under the heading "Building Baosteel Ltd into the most competitive iron & steel enterprise in the world":

> China's most modernized steel maker, Shanghai Baosteel Group (Baosteel), is expanding rapidly by integrating its main lines of manufacturing—carbon steel, stainless steel, and specialty steel—and by diversifying into various industries including chemicals, engineering, equipment manufacturing, finance, information technology, and trading.
>
> Last year the Asian giant produced over 21.4 million tons of steel, a 7.8% increase in production over 2003. This boosted total revenues by 34.4% to RMB 161.8 billion. Profit growth

was even more impressive: it soared by 66.3% to reach RMB 21.9 billion. According to Standard & Poor's, as of 2004, Baosteel has a BBB+ credit rating, with a "stable" outlook.

The company follows the strategy of producing premium steel products for a wide variety of industries, including automobile manufacturing, ship-building, and transportation; oil and gas exploration, power generation, and the manufacture of boiler and pressure vessels; food and beverages; the manufacture of electrical appliances, stainless steel and metal products, and specialized materials; and high-level construction industries. Baosteel's long-term strategy is to create a predominant R & D base in China so that it can continue to develop new processes, new technologies, and new materials in the iron and steel industry.

The company is committed to clean production and pays great attention to environmental protections in order to build an ecologically friendly enterprise. Baosteel is the first among Chinese metallurgical players to receive ISO 14001 certification, and the air emissions from its plants meet the state-level standards for beauty spots.

The Chinese conglomerate is truly a global empire, with business in 86 countries and a far-flung sales network that consists of 20 trading companies. In addition, Baosteel has joint ventures with CVRD in Brazil and with Hamersley Iron in Australia that are already in operation.

The company's ultimate goal is to become a world-class enterprise focused on innovation. Baosteel remains highly committed to putting people first—both its staff and the communities in which it operates. As part of its corporate social responsibility charter it looks forward to creating a better life for society.[3]

Baosteel is one of nearly 48 listed companies chosen by the Chinese government to be the first to undergo the floating of their non-tradable shares. Baosteel and China Yangtze Power Co, one of China's largest power producers, have been given permission to do so. This will make China's Yuan-denominated shares that normally can only be traded by domestic Chinese investors and qualified foreign investors tradable. This is part of an experiment aimed at solving one of the structural problems plaguing the Chinese capital market: the huge overhang of restricted shares that put pressure on the Chinese capital market's attractiveness and trap wealth at the same time.

Case Study: Becoming a Multinational CEO: Mr. Han Jingyuan and China Oriental Group Company Limited

In 2000, China's third largest steel company, the state-owned Jinxi Steel, was privatized. In 2004, it set up a subsidiary in Bermuda, China Oriental Group Co Ltd, which JP Morgan and Merrill Lynch raised US$285 million for in an IPO on the Hong Kong Stock Exchange.

China Oriental Group Company Limited, incorporated in Bermuda, is a former SOE example of a company, which leading American companies with strategic and financial motivations to enter into a Genuine Global Joint Venture might wish to consider as a Chinese global joint venture partner.

Mr. Han Jingyuan's career is a fascinating case study of the potential synergy of an American company or foreign companies entering into a Genuine Global Joint Venture with leading Chinese

Mr. Han Jingyuan

steel interests. Mr. Han has in-depth industry knowledge and operational and managerial experience in China's iron and steel industry. Mr. Han began his career in the Chinese steel industry in 1984 when he was employed as a sub-division head of Han'erzhuang Iron Mine. He graduated from the People's University in 1994 with a degree in management. In 1992, he joined Jinxi Iron Factory and served as its deputy head until 1997, when he joined Tangshan Jinxi Group, one of China's leading steel companies as chairman of the board and general manager. When Jinxi Ltd, was incorporated in 1999, Mr. Han became chairman and general manager of Jinxi Ltd. In 2003, the Organizing Committee for Nominations of Celebrities named Mr. Han as one of the "Top Ten Celebrities for China's Reform Program in the New Century." Mr. Han led the establishment in 2004 of a Bermuda company named China Oriental Group Company Limited.

The combination, in a Bermuda company, of both leading Chinese and American steel interests could be a catalyst for an example of potentially compelling business cases globally. Such a Genuine Global Joint Venture could be a vehicle reciprocally achieving the goals of all participants inside and outside China.

The China Bermuda Society

Often the choice of jurisdiction made by Chinese businesses operating internationally is driven by minor incorporation cost differences which are not material in the overall costs of listing companies and on the assumption that the competitive advantages offered China related companies by the British Virgin Islands(BVI), Cayman and Bermuda are identical.

Bermuda, Cayman Island, and BVI holding companies are used in China-related corporate structures being prepared for IPOs. However, BVI holding companies are not accepted for

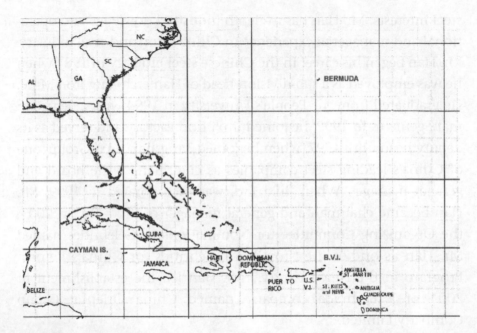

A century of Bermuda's success in attracting the world's leading corporations, and direct daily flights to New York, Washington, London, and many other cities, provide competitive advantages for American, European, Asian, and now Chinese businesses becoming multinationals.

listing by the Hong Kong or Singapore stock exchanges. Bermuda companies are and have enjoyed a high degree of acceptance and confidence in the international capital markets. Using Bermuda-incorporated companies is a competitive advantage that sophisticated major Chinese companies' being prepared for IPOs are using. Although sophisticated Chinese companies, such as China Netcom, are using Bermuda companies to "go global," other mainland Chinese are not yet aware of the competitive advantages, superior reputation, and success Bermuda enjoys in the capital markets.

The China Bermuda Society was founded in 2003 by Dai Min and John Milligan-Whyte, CORE Capital Ltd. and China International Strategies Ltd, to provide educational programs and exchanges, as a mutual forum for Chinese and Western political and businesses leaders, to provide research and advice to Chinese companies becoming multinationals, and to foster the implementation of successful Genuine Global Joint Ventures.

Competitive Advantages from Fiscal and Tax Neutrality

Bermuda has a taxation system that benefits start-up businesses and leading global corporations. Bermuda has no personal income taxes, corporate taxes, sales or export taxes, or exchange controls. Such taxes would simply be too expensive and difficult to calculate and collect in a small state like Bermuda. Ironically, that and the other competitive advantages Bermuda provides has led it to have the highest per capita income in the world.

International operations benefit from the fiscal and tax neutrality of a jurisdiction such as Bermuda. Bermuda companies are incorporated to carry on trade or business or to hold assets globally. Individuals, families, and global corporations that are approved by the Bermuda Monetary Authority can form companies to hold their worldwide assets and operate globally.

Bermuda holding or investment companies preserve, acquire, manage, and sell property of all kinds, including patents, trademarks and copyrights, personal and real property, and bonds issued by other companies, governments or public entities. They can manage trusts, and also control and coordinate a subsidiary or groups of subsidiaries. Bermuda companies are also used for the transfer of information technology, computer leasing, licensing of intellectual property, trans-border data flow and data protection. Bermuda entities, as well, are used for foreign sales, oil and commodity trading of all kinds, property transactions, commercial leasing of all kinds, and foreign investments. Bermuda has shipping and aircraft registries; and Bermuda companies are used for ship, aircraft chartering, leasing and financing, and commercial leases.

Genuine Global Joint Ventures by American and Chinese Companies in Bermuda

More than 10,000 major international companies have incorporated in Bermuda and do business globally. More than 750 of the Fortune 1,000 companies have subsidiaries in Bermuda. More than 52 percent of companies traded on the Hong Kong Stock Exchange are incorporated in Bermuda. Many leading European, Asian, and South American companies have subsidiaries or holding companies in Bermuda that do business on a global basis.

Bermuda is the innovative leader of the global insurance and reinsurance markets. Bermuda has become a base for 1,450 reinsurance companies. Bermuda is one of the world's most innovative and active financial centers, second, for example, in the insurance and reinsurance business only to New York. Two Bermuda reinsurance companies, which were start-up companies in 1985, purchased 25 percent of Lloyd's of London.

Bermuda has attracted $745 billion in mutual funds in more than 1,000 offerings. More than 200 of the mutual funds are listed on the Bermuda Stock Exchange along with many of Bermuda's major NYSE and NASDAQ traded companies. Bermuda is the preferred jurisdiction for capital formation. In the past three years alone, start-up companies in Bermuda have raised more than $20 billion in the capital markets. Established companies, moreover, raised another $20 billion in later-stage offerings.

How has Bermuda been so successful? Bermuda provides entrepreneurs and established businesses competitive advantages for carrying out global business plans and strategies. Nothing succeeds like success itself. Chinese executives marvel at and benefit from Bermuda's exceptional economic success. Bermuda has attracted innovative business people for more than 100 years by demonstrating an understanding of their competitive needs in a constantly changing marketplace.

The Bermuda dollar is pegged to the U.S. dollar. Bermuda is completely self-supporting, and has a positive balance of payments. Bermuda's 21-square-mile area contains no natural resources other than its strategic location, beautiful climate, and the ingenuity and prudence of its residents. Bermuda's 65,000 residents generate an annual gross domestic product of US$4 billion and a per capita income of US$63,973 in 2004. The Bermuda government has an annual budget in 2005 of US$738.5 million, and the national debt is limited by Bermuda's Constitution. Bermuda has universal healthcare, virtually no unemployment or illiteracy, and 70 percent of Bermuda's children go on to college or university.

Bermuda is a British Dependent Territory, and bases its legal system on English law; but has developed its laws to encourage businesses, instead of encumbering them with unnecessary restrictions. Bermuda constantly updates its laws to add value at the leading edge of clients' needs and to ensure that Bermuda is more advanced than competing jurisdictions.

Bermuda is approximately 700 miles off the east coast of North Carolina. It is easy to travel from Bermuda to New York in an hour and a half. In the 21st century, business can be done at the "speed of thought"[4] electronically. The development of e-commerce is a priority of the Government and Bermuda has attracted software companies and e-commerce entrepreneurs.

Bermuda's working day overlaps major business centers in North America, South America, Europe, and Asia. Bermuda time is four hours later than Los Angeles, one hour later than New York, four hours earlier than London, and twelve hours earlier than Hong Kong and Beijing. Bermuda has direct flights daily from major U.S. business centers and London. In addition, global telecommunications facilities and the Internet permit "instant" business through e-mail, and global voice and videoconferencing technologies.

Due to its proximity to U.S. financial centers, Bermuda has been at the leading edge of international business for over a century. As tourism developed early in the 20th century, Bermuda began to attract the rich and famous. Trust business developed in Bermuda from the 1920s. In the 1950s and 1960s, U.S. companies became multinational using Bermuda. Bermuda was quick to recognize the trend before other offshore jurisdictions, and Fortune 500 firms and oil-trading and shipping companies incorporated Bermuda companies to operate globally.

Due to a 400-year-old strong partnership between government and business, Bermuda developed an empowering regulatory system that makes it easier for businesses to operate. Many Bermuda companies, which elect to be taxable as U.S. corporations, operate from Bermuda because of its progressive regulatory system rather than Bermuda's tax planning and management advantages.

Bermuda is in a unique position to offer businesses:

1. Fewer, more efficient regulations.
2. Business-friendly tax plans.
3. A sophisticated infrastructure that welcomes business.
4. A worldwide reputation for honesty, integrity—and success.

Companies that do business from Bermuda are known as an elite group. Only the best applications to incorporate are accepted by the Bermuda Monetary Authority that regulates Bermuda's financial sector, which approves applications to incorporate and the share transfers of Bermuda companies. The Supervisor of Insurance regulates insurance companies. The Registrar of Companies regulates all other companies.

Bermuda "knows" its clients. The banking and regulatory systems ensure that only high-quality companies are permitted to do business. That level of excellence also gives Bermuda companies a competitive advantage that they can leverage. Bermuda is not attractive for money laundering or financing illegal operations.

A business vetted and approved by the Bermuda government signals quality, a competitive advantage not shared by businesses in some other tax neutral jurisdictions. Bermuda has a worldwide reputation for integrity and success. Other offshore jurisdictions do not have the century-old attraction of the highest quality clients or the reputation Bermuda has for vetting companies. This combination creates the powerful competitive advantages of unique prestige, global positioning, and enhanced investment returns for Chinese companies' management teams and investors.

5

Traditional Structures, Strategies and Best Practices Used by Companies Investing or Joint Venturing in China

Overview

This chapter examines traditional structures and strategies used by foreign companies joint venturing or investing in China in case studies focusing on best practices and how they can be improved, as foreign companies must adjust to Chinese companies going global and dominating China's own huge market.

Traditional Deal Structures in the 1979 to 2006 Stage of China's Economic Development

Four basic deal templates have been used in the 1979 to 2006 phase of the Chinese government's economic development program:

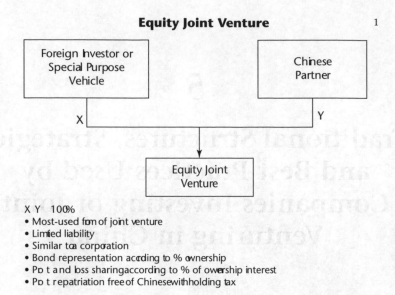

Equity Joint Venture   1

Foreign Investor or Special Purpose Vehicle

Chinese Partner

X

Y

Equity Joint Venture

X Y 100%
- Most-used form of joint venture
- Limited liability
- Similar to a corporation
- Bond representation according to % ownership
- Profit and loss sharing according to % of ownership interest
- Profit repatriation free of Chinese withholding tax

Equity Joint Venture   2

Foreign Investor or Special Purpose Vehicle

Chinese Partner

X

Y

Cooperative Joint Venture

X+Y = 100%
- Often used for infrastructure, and hiring projects
- Limited liability
- Similar to a partnership
- Board representation subject to negotiation
- Profit and loss distribution subject to negotiation
- Profit repatriation net subject to Chinese withholding tax

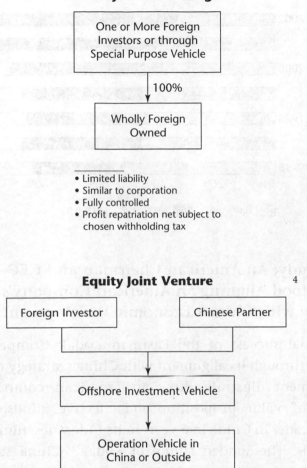

Wholly-Owned Foreign 3

One or More Foreign Investors or through Special Purpose Vehicle

100%

Wholly Foreign Owned

- Limited liability
- Similar to corporation
- Fully controlled
- Profit repatriation net subject to chosen withholding tax

Equity Joint Venture 4

Foreign Investor

Chinese Partner

Offshore Investment Vehicle

Operation Vehicle in China or Outside

A Bermuda holding company vehicle with a WOFE subsidiary or a joint venture subsidiary in China are useful structures for genuine global joint ventures between American and Chinese companies.

The graph below shows the mix over time of the deployment of FDI in Equity Joint Ventures, WOFEs, and Cooperative Joint Ventures:

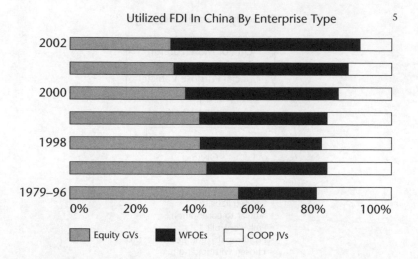

Utilized FDI In China By Enterprise Type ⁵

Case Study: An American Chairman and CEO who Understood Aligning an American Company's China Strategy with China's Economic Development Strategy

The initial success of the Eastman Kodak Company's China strategy through its alignment with China's strategy of economic development illustrates how an American company with a "win-win" value proposition and effective mindset became a market leader in China in 6 years in its industries: film, paper, and chemicals. The sudden failure of Kodak's China strategy after 2005 illustrates how quickly strategic mistakes can damage a company globally.

George Fisher became Chairman and CEO of Kodak in 1993 having been the Chairman and CEO of Motorola, Inc. He led both Motorola's 1987 and Kodak's 1993 pioneering expansions in China and is credited, in 2000, with making both investments unusually successful. He served as the Chairman of the U.S.-China Business Council (1997–1999) and Chairman of the Council on Competitiveness (1991–1993).

Upon assuming leadership at Kodak in 1993, Fisher defined three strategic objectives. Kodak would focus and define itself as the "World Leader In Imaging", would embrace the digital imaging technology which threatened Kodak's then dominant technology, and would become China's leading imaging company.

In 1994, he established within Kodak the Greater China Region (GCR), alongside the U.S. and Europe in Kodak's organizational chart. Fisher knew Kodak's China Strategy would take all-stars and staffed GCR with Kodak's very best people from around the world. Fisher knew that in a country changing as fast as China and so alien to non-Chinese habits and tastes, Kodak's GCR people needed to be very smart, flexible, and adaptable to surprise, stress, and culture shock. Equally important, Kodak hired excellent people from China, and worked with skilled professionals in China. Fisher made the China Strategy, which would be expensive, immune from otherwise across-the board budget cuts. Kodak's top management was committed to its China strategy and making it work in and aligning it with China's strategy. Fisher said:

> But, there was more to it than the team and the timing. We felt welcomed by the Chinese. We were confident that we could open up a new frontier in photography in a way that would benefit not only Kodak but also the Chinese people.

Fisher had learned at Motorola that Kodak had to have a win-win strategy. "If conspicuous benefits to China were not evident from our first proposals, we could spin our wheels for years." He knew the Chinese were superb negotiators and smart, no-nonsense, experienced managers who know what they need, what they want above that, and the value of extracting even more above that.

He also knew that there is no one-stop negotiating in China. Kodak had to negotiate with seven state-owned companies, six provincial governments, ten city governments and five ministries and commissions, several banks and trust companies, and local tax authorities everywhere. Fortunately, senior government officials stepped in and formed a Central Coordinating Committee that served as a single point of contact for all negotiations that nonetheless took four years, and were particularly difficult as no other company had done what Kodak was proposing and there was no regulatory road map to guide Kodak and the Chinese. China's investment laws and regulations had to be re-written because of the project.

Fisher knew there could be no deal unless the Chinese got three essential "wins". First, Kodak had to help address the overcapacity and underemployment in the SOEs whose plants were old and decrepit and product quality was second rate and inconsistent. Secondly, the SOEs had enormous debts, which China's government could no longer afford to continue to support. Thirdly, China needed new technology to make world-class products.

Kodak had its "musts" too. It needed a return on its huge investment, and a period when its huge commitment would not be threatened by other foreign investment. It could not keep supporting nonproductive assets, and it had to be compensated for its new technology and needed to keep complete management control, yet work hand in hand with local partners.

The complex deal defined in the negotiations left both Kodak and the Chinese with their essential requirements. Its main points were: Kodak would commit U.S. $1.2 billion to overhauling much of China's imaging industry and revitalize key factories, two obsolete plants would be closed and there would be a four-year moratorium on additional foreign investment, and two companies would be formed under Chinese law with Kodak keeping flexible management controls.

Kodak built a world-class plant in China, using its eleven decades of manufacturing experience, and modernized others. It hired and trained great workers, built a network of retail stores across China, worked hard to understand what Chinese consumers wanted from their pictures. It honored the environment, put safety first, and focused on employees' heath and working conditions. Sales climbed and then soared.

But getting profits out of China meant dealing with Chinese currency not being fully convertible. So, payments for goods and services purchased offshore, royalties paid for the use of technology, inter-company loans, and dividends for profits were used, but had to be very carefully negotiated.

Fisher also knew that Kodak could not assume that it would automatically be able to sell products made in China in China. Kodak's negotiations dealt with this. The best "win" for the Chinese would have been an agreement in which their factories supplied the Chinese market while Kodak in China would be only producing products for export. Kodak was able to develop a way around the laws preventing foreigners from entering the Chinese retail sector, not by flouting the law, but by using an ingenious interpretation of it and the excellent relationship between Fisher and China's Premier Zhu Rongji.[6]

Kodak employees in China rose from 30 to 5,000, and Kodak introduced the first Six-Sigma program, the highest standard for quality camera production and had an unprecedented safety record. It paid more taxes in the first six months in 1998 than the previous SOE company had in the previous 14 years. China's central government published a report on the Kodak project in the *People's Daily* crowning Kodak as a model corporate citizen and the project as a successful model of foreign investment and SOE reform. Kodak then leveraged this success in Xiamen to produce digital cameras in Shanghai, where it operates a software development center, and One-Time cameras in Xiamen. The number of Kodak Express Stores grew from fewer than 100 in 1993 to more than 5,000 in 2000 and the world class-rolled film made in China was exported to Japan.

Fisher indicated:

One of the keys to our success was that both sides knew we were embarking on something special. We all sensed that this was a pioneering venture suffused with risks for both sides. If only one side won, both would eventually lose. Everyone in the room had to tolerate a lot of ambiguity and surprise. Without genuine good faith, collateral goodwill, and a keen desire to succeed, talks could have, more than once, broken down. And it is equally important to connect with the Chinese on a human level. Despite cultures, background and perspectives, everyone has the same basic wants and needs. We understood this. We listened intensely to our Chinese hosts as they expressed their difficulties, and in turn, they listened to ours. Together we worked hard — there were many sleepless nights —to resolve the outstanding issues, and part of that good faith is making sure that no one loses face. This is very important in China, perhaps more so than in any other culture. In one or two instances, we actually made a small concession to prevent any possible embarrassment across the table. ... Anyone who signs up to do business in China must understand that full commitment means full commitment. But from that can come astonishing achievement.[7]

By 2000, Kodak in China had the number one market share in all categories: film, paper and chemicals; and China's roll film market moved in four years from seventeenth to second largest in the world. By 2004, Kodak and Fuji films had 90 percent of the Chinese market.[8]

Kodak announced in 2005, however, that its expectation that emerging markets, such as China, would buy its traditional film products because they were cheaper than digital substitutes had not worked because those markets were abandoning its traditional film products faster than expected.[9] Because of a failure by Kodak to correctly anticipate demand in China for digital photographic products, and perhaps an assumption that Chinese consumers would be driven by price considerations, Kodak's implementation of its China strategy stumbled. The

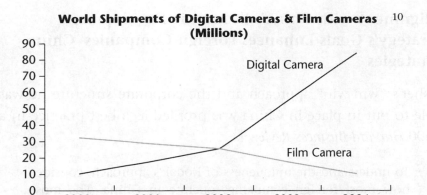

World Shipments of Digital Cameras & Film Cameras [10]
(Millions)

Source: Camera and Imaging Products Association

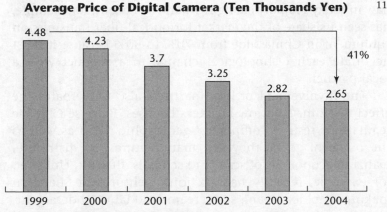

Average Price of Digital Camera (Ten Thousands Yen) [11]

Source: Japanese Cameras Industry Association

graphs above show the growth of demand for digital cameras and the reduction in their cost.

This miscalculation by Kodak manifests a failure to understand the Chinese market or a reluctance to abandon legacy business models in a global market changing faster than expected. Kodak has subsequently had larger fundamental problems in managing its business model as film has been displaced by digital technology.[12]

Alignment with China's Economic Development Strategy's Goals Enhances Foreign Companies' China Strategies

Fisher's "win-win" approach and the corporate structure he was able to put in place in China was profiled as a best practice in a 2000 *Harvard Business Review*:[13]

> To understand the uniqueness of Kodak's approach, consider how most foreign companies operate in China. The most common corporate structure is the joint venture, in which companies share day-to-day operational control with a local partner. But doing so can paralyze decision-making, a fatal flaw in today's rapidly changing markets. Lucent, for example, has seen its share of the market for optical-fiber transmission equipment in China slide from 70% to 30% because it must negotiate each technological change in a product with a local partner.
>
> The involvement of local partners also exacerbates the effect of China's narrow business licenses. Because Chinese regulations restrict companies' geographic reach as well as the range of goods they can manufacture and distribute, realizing economies of scale and scope is difficult. Unilever, for example, recently had six joint ventures in Shanghai making soap, ice cream, skin cream, and laundry detergent. Theoretically, a foreign company could consolidate the distribution of its various joint-venture products, but it would have to get consent from all its Chinese partners. That seldom happens because the partners fear that the products from their individual joint ventures would end up at a disadvantage.
>
> To avoid such complicated management issues, some companies have established wholly-owned foreign enterprises (WOFE), but they, too, have limitations. WOFEs have difficulty winning contracts and forging local alliances. China's local governments have routinely favored state-owned enterprises over foreign ventures, especially since 1999, when the industrial ministries in Beijing were abolished.

There is a better way for companies to compete in China. Since 1994, businesses have been able to register as joint-stock companies—a familiar corporate structure in the West. All of China's state-owned enterprises listed on the Shanghai and Shenxzhen stock exchanges have adopted this structure. But so far, only one foreign multinational has taken this route: Eastman Kodak.

Kodak's joint-stock companies, which I call foreign investor shareholding corporations (FISC), have allowed the company to achieve a high degree of operational control. The FISCs eliminate the trade-off between management control and market access by granting local partners minority stakes in return for their business assets, such as factories and trucks. Because local partners lose direct ownership of those assets, they can be excluded from the day-to-day management of them. But as part owners, they remain interested in helping the FISCs perform, which motivates them to help the venture secure access to the markets. The FISC structure also mitigates the economic impact of narrow business licenses. For example, Kodak doesn't have to get its local partners' consent to consolidate distribution of products from its different operations.

... Kodak has created two FISCs: Kodak (China), in which it holds an 80% share, and Kodak (Wuxi), in which it holds a 70% share. Kodak (China) purchase the assets of two domestic photo film manufacturers, Xiamen Fuda and Shantou Era, in return for 10% stakes and the right to appoint one board member each. Kodak named the remaining eight directors. ... For its part, Kodak put up $380 million in cash.

It is clear why the shareholding structure works for Kodak. But it is important to realize that it works for China as well. It gives Chinese authorities a face-saving way to allow industrial reform through the back door.

In the past, the photo industry had been almost entirely closed off to foreign corporations because the government wanted to develop a domestic photo film industry. Foreign companies like Kodak were restricted to licensing agreements or direct imports, which attracted heavy duties. But domestic manufacturers could not keep up with the industries' rapid technology innovations, and all but one was technically bankrupt by the mid-1990s. Kodak's proposal to create FICSs was therefore considered a good solution by Beijing authorities.... The photo industry is hardly unique. The Chinese economy is plagued by inefficiency and overcapacity, much of it due to China's highly protected domestic businesses.

... FISCs are well placed to obtain quick listings on the Shenzhen and Shanghai stock exchanges, making it easier for them to raise new capital.

For all these reasons many companies will probably follow Kodak's lead."[14]

Case Study: Motorola

Ted Fishman provides the following analysis of Motorola's China strategy:

Every month, 5 million new subscribers sign up for mobile-phone service in China. The country's 300 million mobile phone users make China by far the largest such market in the world. Hence, the world's makers of handsets need to be in China. ... Motorola invented the mobile-phone market in China. ... Robert Galvin, the company's ... long time chief executive, China, at a dreary state ceremony during a tour of the country ... turned to the minister of railroads and asked him whether he wanted to do a good job as minister and be done with it, or whether he wanted to create a world-class society. In doing so, Galvin tapped a thick vein of economic patriotism. ... Galvin and his team knew that eventually the transfer of technology to China would sow formidable Chinese competitors. Nevertheless, Motorola decided its best strategy was to get into China early. Before long, Motorola's reports to China's political leaders—infused with the same missionary vocabulary on industrial quality that had made the company a model for American manufacturers—were soon parroted by China's leadership. Galvin also brought Motorola's best technology to China. The proof today is in the size and efficacy of the country's mobile communications network: calls get through to phones in high-rises, subway cars and distant hamlets—connections that would stymie mobile phones in the Unites States.[15]

Motorola introduced Six Sigma in China. Fishman notes:

One of the biggest challenges facing Motorola and other global manufacturers is that Chinese suppliers are getting too good. Their quality, low-priced parts have helped create new, homegrown, and extremely aggressive competitors. More than 40 percent of the Chinese domestic handset market now belongs to local companies such as Ningbo Bird, Nanjing Panda Electronics, Haier, and TCL Mobile. Ningbo Bird will produce 20 million handsets in 2004, and is likely soon to nudge its way into the ranks of the top ten mobile-phone makers in the world. The domestic makers have become so strong that when Siemens found its mobile handset business in China wanting, it joined Ningbo Bird to gain both low-cost manufacturing and a developed distribution channel. Jim Gradoville, Motorola's vice president of Asia Pacific Government Relations said that the Chinese companies that emerged from the crucible of their market would be the leanest and most aggressive in the world, and a company like his would have no idea what hit it. So Motorola stays. Already the largest foreign investor in China's electronics industry plant, it tripled its stake there to more than US $10 billion by 2006.[16]

Business Week has commented:

If a company stays the course, the results can be remarkable. China contributed 9% of Motorola Inc.'s $31 billion in sales last year, and thanks to smart products and marketing, the Schaumburg (Ill.) based company is battling Nokia Corp, for leadership in the world's biggest handset market. Low cost exports from China, and the brainwork done at 16 labs, have also helped revive Motorola's fortunes. For many products, "China will become a larger market than the U.S.," says Motorola Asia Pacific Senior Vice President, Simon Leuing. "And it helps our global operation from the perspective of costs, quality and time to market."[17]

Motorola has had strong sales of its trendy cell phones, notably the ultra thin RAZR which improved its sales by 17 percent in the first half of 2005. The improved performance gives Motorola, the world's No. 2 handset maker by market share, some breathing room from its closest challengers, especially Samsung. Nokia, a global company based in Finland, dominates the industry with roughly a 33% market share globally. Motorola's performance contrasts with some other top handset makers, such as Samsung, which in the first half of 2005 reported a 46% decline in profit, due to increased completion and slackening demand for its cell phones.[18]

Motorola's dilemma, of how to cope with emerging Chinese companies' competitive advantages and the importance of the Chinese mobile phone market in the future of competitors in the global market, is a classic example of where a Genuine Global Joint Venture between Motorola and one or more of the formidable Chinese companies may be the only "win-win" strategy for Motorola.

Siemens' strategy of teaming up with Ningbo Bird, could be taken a step beyond just a business combination addressing Siemens' needs for a successful China strategy. The step further is a genuine global business joint venture. Motorola, an American company, might benefit from such a genuine global joint venture strategy. The theoretic synergies between an America and Chinese company doing so are enormous. Motorola and other American companies may benefit quickly and long term by such a new template of genuine global joint ventures, possibly using the Chinese Money Inside And American Money Outside Model.

Case Study: Huawei Technologies Co.

Such genuine global joint ventures could greatly assist Chinese companies. For example, Huawei Technologies Co., which, the

Wall Street Journal reported, in July 2005:

> ... has tried to use its cut-rate prices to take customers from Cisco Systems Inc and Lucent Technologies in America. However, Huawei has yet to land any big deals with big U.S. phone companies, such as SBC Communications Inc or BellSouth Corp, winning only some contracts with smaller firms. "It has taken longer than we thought" says Bai Yi, Huawei's business development director for North America and one of the first Huawei's executives in the U.S. "We still have a long way to go to learn about this market." With little experience in marketing, Huawei has struggled to build brand recognition in the U.S. It confused customers by using a new name for its U.S. business. With the headquarters in Shenzhen, China, hesitant to delegate, local executives have trouble adapting to the local culture. The company has been dogged by suspicions of cutting corners on intellectual property rights, and alienated some job applicants by pumping them for detailed technical information. Huawei's successful formula winning business in other countries with low prices hasn't worked as well in the U.S. market marked by long-term ties between phone companies and their equipment suppliers.
>
> The company's setbacks in the U.S. contrast with its recent progress elsewhere outside China. From the Middle East to Latin America and, more recently, Europe, Huawei has taken business from global giants such as Germany's Siemens AG and France's Alcatel SA. Of the 19 licenses issued around the world last year for high-end wireless networks known as "third generation", Huawei was involved in building 14 of them ... BT Group PLC, the large British telecom company, recently gave Huawei an important stamp of approval, awarding the Chinese vendor part of a $19 billion project.

Huawei has come a long way from its beginnings in 1988, when founder Ren Zhegfei, a former officer in China's People's Liberation Army [PLA], used a contact in the Chinese government to obtain some rudimentary telecom gear. Mr. Ren's background helped the company win military contracts during the early, lean years, according to former Huawei executives. Today the PLA accounts for less than 1% of Huawei's business, the company says. With $3.8 billion of revenue in 2004, Huawei still ranks far behind leaders like Alcatel, which had $15 billion of revenue last year. But Huawei is growing by nearly 50% a year, while established vendors are only just beginning to grow again after the telecom bust wiped out much of their business several years ago.

With eight regional headquarters and 55 offices around the world, the company expects this year's revenue from outside China will at least equal that from China for the first time. Of its global work force of 24,000, many are housed at Huawei's sprawling, modern headquarters in Shenzhen, in brightly painted dorms, surrounded by neatly manicured lawns, basketball courts, and swimming pools. The streets are named after famous scientists, such as Marie Curie and Deng Jianxian, a key developer of China's first atomic bomb.

Like the global push of CNOOC and other large Chinese companies, Huawei's expansion is fueled in part by cheap loans from the Chinese government. Last year, the company, which is owned by its employees, received a $10 billion line of credit from the China Development Bank, and an additional $600 million from the official Export-Import Bank of China for its international expansion.

But Huawei's push into the U.S. differs from its compatriots in one key way. While other expansion-minded Chinese firms are trying to buy their way into the American market, Huawei is trying to grow by lining up its own new customers.[19]

American companies will find, if America pursues a "containment" strategy, that Chinese companies like Huawei grow in other markets, at the expense of American companies globally. The window of opportunity exists now for American companies to choose, design, and deploy the Genuine Global Joint Venture Model with Chinese companies. As the need by Chinese companies for such genuine global joint ventures decreases, American companies will find themselves in an increasingly invidious position.

Business Week reported in July 2006:

Western telecom equipment makers have long looked down on China's Huawei Technologies Co. as a mere copier of their designs. But, last year, Huawei snared $8 billion in new orders, including contracts from British Telecommunications PLC for its $19 billion program to transform Britain's telecommunication network. The deal sent a chill through the rest of the telecom manufacturers. ...

Whether one chooses to confront or collaborate, the new multinationals are set to change the rules in industry after industry.[20]

Using the strategy of foreign and Chinese companies collaborating to meet new challengers, Nortel Networks and 3Com have formed telephone equipment and design ventures with Huawei.[21] Cisco is using the strategy of attacking Huawei's market share in China by forming a "tie-up" with Huawei's Chinese rival ZTE Corp.[22] A genuine global joint venture between Chinese champion companies such as Huawei and leading foreign companies may provide the greatest and most sustainable benefits for both the Chinese and the foreign partners.

6

Traditional Structures and Strategies and the Global Joint Venture Model's Advantages

Overview

This chapter compares traditional structures and strategies and the Genuine Global Joint Venture Model for foreign and Chinese companies for aligning their interests, combining their strengths, ameliorating their weaknesses, and collaborating. We present case studies that illustrate that foreign companies that understand the different mindset, assumptions, needs, and goals of the Chinese government and Chinese companies can use their own foreign styles in negotiating and working with Chinese companies, executives, staff, and government officials, providing they understand the Chinese way of thinking and "doing things." Chinese understanding of foreign business assumptions, practices, needs, and goals is growing. The Chinese government and Chinese companies have been dealing with foreign companies *in China* since 1978, so their practice in dealing with them has increased. But, since most Chinese companies have only been encouraged to "go global" since 2002, their familiarity, understanding, and integration into the world outside China is still nascent.

Joint Ventures, WOFEs, and the Genuine Global Joint Ventures

The following case studies, sometimes explicitly, sometimes subtly, illustrate the pragmatic business efficacy of "win-win" value propositions and strategies. They illustrate that having the "right spirit," and being committed to long-term relationships that are beneficial to China which train, assist, and reward Chinese partners are simple, humane, and profoundly attractive ways to earn the trust and relationships needed for American companies to succeed in China.

The case studies illustrate some of the generic challenges in doing business in China and useful approaches to doing so. In some cases, a Genuine Global Joint Venture would have increased the value proposition the companies offered the Chinese government and their Chinese trading partners. In selecting these case studies, we had in mind the management culture and structural challenges that the Genuine Global Joint Venture Model and US Money Outside And Chinese Money Inside China Model seek to ameliorate with their enhanced value propositions, corporate structures, and rewards for successful collaboration. As well as "going global," Chinese companies face fierce competition with foreign and other Chinese companies in China's domestic market.

The case studies do not directly illustrate the application of the Genuine Global Joint Venture Model and Chinese Money Inside And US Money Outside China Model, because these are new strategies.

Case Study: ASIMCO: American-Style Capitalism Doing Business in China

Jack Perkowski, an American investment banker, established ASIMCO in the 1990s to acquire, consolidate, and operate business in China. ASIMCO had over US$400 million, raised by Dean Witter and later GE's Pension Fund; and entered into operations which included 15 automotive component joint ventures, two wholly-owned component companies, and two joint ventures in the brewing industry, including one of China's brand leaders. ASIMCO's story is thought to be the subject matter of *Mr. China* by Tim Clessold, published in 2005, which is a primer of problems encountered by foreign companies doing business and investing in China in the 1990s. Jack Perkowski was quoted in John Stuttard's *The New Silk Road*[1]:

> To me, it all boiled down to one issue: the lack of capable management to deal with the challenges.... I start by looking at the universe of executives in the United States. After World War II ... companies in the United States had to learn to be competitive as they sought to become global players competing with their European and Japanese counterparts. In many cases, domestic and foreign competitors had inherent competitive advantages, so the U.S. companies had to become better at managing their businesses and, therefore, began to focus on improving management skills. "Management" became a science in the developed countries of the world. Business schools were established, and universities began offering MBA programs. Management development courses were prepared and conducted in many companies. These were designed to take raw managerial talent and provide enough structure to run a big company, while at the same time enabling managers to retain entrepreneurial instincts necessary to drive the business forward.... If you were to plot the management universe in the United States, what you would get is a bell-shaped curve, where the vertical axis is the 'number of people' and the horizontal axis shows managerial behavior, which is categorized as 'bureaucratic' at one end and 'entrepreneurial' at the other. If you have a problem with management in the United States, you call up headhunters, tell them what you want, and within a relatively short period of time you can have a team of people who are able to accomplish your objectives.[2]

In China from 1949 to 1978, China was a centralized, planned economy closed to foreigners. Managers of Chinese enterprises were allotted capital and labor and told to make specific products. They did not have to learn how to optimize capital or labor, how to use marketing research and advertising to determine what products to make and how to sell them, or manage distribution networks or customers.

As a result prior to 1978, virtually all managers in China would have been at the far left of the scale, very bureaucratic. On the other hand, in 1978, when Deng Xiaoping opened up the economy, the handcuffs were taken off. We all know that the Chinese are the most entrepreneurial people in the world. Beginning in 1978, a new class of managers was created, this time at the far right of the scale, very entrepreneurial. You saw it initially in the southern part of China, in Guangdong Province, next to Hong Kong. Now you see it all over China. Look at any city in China, and you have evidence of an entrepreneurial spirit driving China forward.

The problem for a company like ASIMCO, or for that matter any other multinational company is that you cannot afford to be at either end of the management spectrum. If the management you have in China is too bureaucratic, you can't get anything done. On the other hand, if it is at the other end of the spectrum, you can't sleep at night because these cowboy entrepreneurs practice a brand of management that no multinational company would feel comfortable with. You might be in the components business today and find that you are in the hotel business tomorrow.[3]

Someone over 40 has probably spent from 5 to 10 years during the cultural Revolution in the fields, without formal education. This generation has grown up with the "iron rice bowl" mentality. If Chinese managers come from a state enterprise, there is tremendous loyalty to the old ways of doing things, to the work unit. There is a need to divorce ownership from managerial control. This can be quite complicated to achieve. But I have great optimism, based on seeing the young talent joining our organization. They are the ones with the bright futures. For this group of people, our challenge is retention. As long as they see that they have opportunities for upward mobility, they won't change jobs for more compensation.

By training and keeping these youngsters, this is how we eventually make up for China's present management shortage.[4]

If you take a good company in China and try to make it into a good global company, it has to change—it can't stay the same. And, like most people, the Chinese don't welcome change. The argument that the Chinese use, at the level of general manager or deputy general manager, runs along these lines: yes, those techniques and practices may work in Europe and the United States. But this is China. China is different. They may actually believe that...But, we don't subscribe to the notion that because it works elsewhere it won't work in China. We think that, when you boil everything down, China actually operates the same way as other places. The laws of economics apply here as they do in every part of the world. However, the fact that Chinese managers are able to argue in this way gives them an immediate excuse for not changing.

In view of all this, we find that an expatriate must be quite outstanding. He has to have enough experience to overcome the credibility issue. He has to have had a substantial career prior to China...he has to be an extremely patient person, yet very persistent—someone who does not take no for an answer. He had to be willing to roll up his sleeves. You have to find someone at a high level in an organization, with the relevant experience, who is the right kind of person and willing to come to China and do things he or she probably hasn't done for 10 or 15 years. We have great difficulty in finding those individuals.[5]

ASIMCO's strategy was to choose the number one or two firm in the auto components and beer businesses in China with the idea that since these companies had reached that rank in China, they might be capable of becoming successful globally. ASIMCO's initial strategy was to use indigenous managers in the businesses it acquired. But, it found that 20% of managers in China were able to make the leap to the next level in "for profit" businesses. The second strategy was to supplement local management with experienced executives from Western countries. This was costly, and it was difficult to integrate them culturally into the Chinese operations successfully.

The Genuine Global Joint Venture Model's Advantages

The Genuine Global Joint Venture Model addresses these challenges by recruiting, as the Chinese company, one that is already a Chinese "champion" that is very competitive and wants to go global. The reciprocal rewards of the global joint venture must be attractive. The American and Chinese companies carry out the joint venture company's global strategy together combining their respective strengths and compensating for their respective weaknesses. A Bermuda holding company should be used for the joint venture. The Chinese company, with the American company's help in going global, carries out the joint venture's "China strategy."

As in the IBM + Legend = Lenovo deal, the commitment of both the American and Chinese company to the joint venture is highly public and vital to short-, medium-, and, therefore, long-term, success. The American company assisting the Chinese company to successfully learn how to go global makes the relationship far more useful and potentially sustainable than a joint venture between the same companies only inside China.

Case Study: Integration of American and Chinese Approaches: Artesyn's Strategy in China

Haley, Haley & Tan cite Artysen, an American multinational with headquarters in Florida, as having highly successful Chinese operations:

> Artesyn...has succeeded through playing the part of a chameleon. In managing its Chinese operations, Artesyn has metaMORPHED into an Overseas Chinese company using largely Western controls and taking a largely Western strategic perspective. Indeed, the four-step investment guidelines that its managers described to us mirror those of the Overseas

Chinese. Artesyn's investment guidelines for information-scarce China include:

1. Investing small amounts initially—Artesyn launches small subsidiaries until it gains confidence in its decision and in its knowledge of the new products and markets.
2. Investing in known environments—Artesyn invests where it either already knows the local authorities or where it can determine through research that the local authorities have a pro-FDI track record and display honesty in their dealings with investors.
3. Investing with history on their side—Artysen invests where the local economy has a vibrant private sector and does not tailor its business practices to those of SOEs.
4. Investing in locals—Artesyn works hard to find and train good, entrepreneurial local managers. The company however prefers competent foreign managers to locals who fail to show initiative.

Artysen has two goals with its Chinese investments. First, it does not measure success by the profitability of individual investments, but by the contributions made by those investments to overall corporate profitability; and second, it ascertains how the investments optimize and rationalize overall corporate cost structures.

Thus, Artesyn has undertaken managerial convergence in China by adapting Western planning models to fit local, uncontrollable, situations. For its Chinese strategy, Artesyn's managers follow the same planning procedures as at its US headquarters. However, they use personal judgment, subjective data, and information from reliable sources, to fill in the gaps in their objective data.[6]

Genuine Global Joint Venture Model's Advantages

If a company wishes to offer the Chinese partner a better and more sustainably attractive value proposition, the Genuine

Global Joint Venture Model entails that the joint venture will not merely be restricted to the Chinese market; where in time the management of the Chinese joint venture may feel they can move on and compete with the local joint venture owned by the foreign company.

Case Study: Identification and Training of Effective Managers[7]

Xi'an, the capital of Shaanxi Province, in northern China, was the site of one of China's ancient capital cities, but is now one of China's vast, less developed regions. It is a center for medical research and the manufacture and sale of traditional Chinese medicines. It is the location of one of China's most successful foreign joint ventures, Xian-Janssen, due to Johnson & Johnson's foresight and timing and the energy and imagination of Jerry Norskog, the Chairman of Johnson & Johnson China Investment Limited, and his management team.

In Norskog's view, what separates the winners from the losers in China is a foreign company's approach to choosing and developing people. Johnson & Johnson's approach is aggressive and makes profound sense because it focuses on finding and training the right people to be the employees carrying out its China strategy.

Johnson & Johnson searches for the best minds at China's best universities and colleges, and holds "career days," which it initiated in 1992. Johnson & Johnson focuses on solving the manager selection and development problems that are common in China as it makes its abrupt change from an SOE and socialist economy. Norskog states:

> ...the Chinese have great pride in their abilities, as they should. On the other hand, they completely underestimate how much ground they lost during the years between 1949

and 1979, when contact with the West was limited. There is an expectations gap. The young, intelligent, hardworking people don't really understand what they missed and don't understand how complex managing a modern business really is. Consequently, they tend to underestimate how long it takes to reach so-called international standards and how much work is involved.[8]

To effectively address these challenges and identify and train managers who could carry out Johnson & Johnson's China strategy, Norskog created a "management camp" modeled on Outward Bound and the program used by the U.S. Marines. Norskog and Chong Siong Hin, a former drill sergeant in the Singapore Special Forces, led the management camps. This worked well culturally as much of China's schooling embodies a military approach.

To take the foreignness out of the training, instead of referring to American management ideas, Chinese historical examples of leadership were referred to such as *Sun Tzu* or Mao Zedong's *Little Red Book*. The Emperor Qin Shihuang's exploits were used to show how Johnson & Johnson was going to build a national network in China and operate a chain of command. Norskog said: "This was not only fun, but more importantly it created a great deal of pride in our Chinese staff. We never tried to create an American company. We wanted to build a global company with Chinese characteristics."[9] Norskog said:

> Chong and I created an environment that was very competitive, very aggressive, just a bit over the top, just a bit crazy— an environment that expected just a bit more than it was reasonable to expect. These camps would provide us with an opportunity to really observe behavior and traits of character, which, in a one-on-one interview or in a resume, don't jump out at you. In these annual camps, we identified our potential leaders. They are held in the mountains. At a typical camp, everyone is in formation at 6.00 A.M. I lead—the President leads—the warm-up exercises. We jog three kilometers, come back, and have 15 minutes to change clothes, half an hour to

eat breakfast, and then we are in the classroom. We have a few short breaks during the day.

We developed a very interactive, competitive training program, which rewarded the kinds of behavior we wanted to see. For example, we rewarded people who stood up and shouted out their views. We rewarded people for taking initiative and for taking risks. We stimulated the kinds of behavior we value as a company, in stark contrast to "face" and other Confucian values.

Just imagine a week where you are exercising at 6.00 A.M. and seldom finish before 11 at night. In a 10-day camp, on perhaps three nights at least, we would go to two or three in the morning—as I said, a bit over the top, expecting more than is realistic—to determine who is ready for the types of challenges our company offers.

And then change—constant, constant change. For example, we would say, "Okay, break into teams. We want a 20-page letter to the Chairman of the Board on this subject and it's due the day after tomorrow." The next morning, we would say, "The Chairman doesn't speak Chinese, the letter has to be in English, and 20 pages are too much—he says he will only read 10—and it is due tonight instead of tomorrow." Then, at around lunchtime, we would say that the chairman has decided to visit camp; he is arriving by air this afternoon; but he can't stay long, so he only wants three slides in English. Change, change, and change—it drives them nuts.

Perhaps the most telling test came about halfway through the second week at three in the morning. We would arrange for someone to knock on the dormitory doors and shout that everyone had to come downstairs for a conference, in full business dress, as soon as possible, because a special meeting had been called. At that point, you really start to see the cream separate from the milk. Most people found that request totally unreasonable and would give logical reasons why they could not come downstairs. But we recorded the names of those who did come down. They were the winners.

> For all of the recruits, this was an incredible, exhausting, exhilarating learning experience, a "change your life" experience, and many of them loved it. Like the U.S. Marines, Chong and I challenged them early, and we also cut our losses early. Many said this is not for me, not my cup of tea. So, up front, we were able to identify people who were interested in our culture. This saved a great deal of time.[10]

Johnson & Johnson earned a reputation for effective training and Xian-Janssen earned a reputation as one of China's most successful joint ventures. Norskog said: "I would be surprised to hear of a single big pharmaceutical company in China that doesn't have at least one ex-Xian-Janssen executive on its management board, and we're very proud of that".[11]

This brilliant training program effectively addressed a key shared problem for foreign companies' China strategy and China's strategy: the training of profit- and customer-oriented managers in China's emerging Socialist Market Economy Capitalism. It also brilliantly sifted and developed the Chinese management talent the foreign company's China strategy needed to be successful in China.

Genuine Global Joint Venture Model's Advantages

The Johnson & Johnson case study illustrates how a foreign company can apply its own corporate culture in selecting and training Mainland Chinese executives and staff. These insights are useful in carrying out the Genuine Global Joint Venture Model, which may provide a broader scope and more interesting recruiting incentives and career paths for attracting Mainland Chinese talent and assist in motivating, retaining, and rewarding them for adding value globally rather than thinking locally and leaving to start or run competing businesses in the Chinese market, as Legend did after being a distributor of HP.

Case Study: Looking at Problems with Chinese Eyes with the Right Spirit

United Technologies Corporation has been in China since the first decade in the 20th century and reestablished business there involving its elevator company in 1984; and then invested US$ 300 million in the late 1980s and 1990s in rapid investments by its air conditioning, aircraft, and automobile parts companies through 23 joint ventures and one wholly-owned foreign enterprise (WOFE).

In 2000, Dr. Richard Latham was President of United Technologies International-China. He had been involved with China for over 30 years, was fluent in Mandarin, and had greater knowledge and experience of Chinese society, culture and business practices than many foreigners who headed multinational companies in China. A former missionary, he studied Chinese, obtained a Ph.D., and led the U.S. Air force Total Quality Management initiative in Washington D.C. He joined United Technologies with the objective of working in China. He has written a number of works on China, and was Chairman of the American Chamber of Commerce China. Dr. Latham says:

> To begin to understand how to operate in China, it helps to understand the differences between Chinese society and its people and the society and people you know back home. There is a Chinese way of looking at things and a Chinese way of doing things. However, this does not mean that the way you do business in China has to be entirely different from elsewhere. Every country is different, yet there are similarities. Unfortunately, too few executives who come to China have worked in many countries. They fail to realize that there are bureaucracies everywhere, that there are pollution and traffic jams, that the political and economic issues are remarkably the same, that there are trade barriers and complex social issues. So one has to understand where China is the same and where it differs and what impact these differences have, if any, on how one does business.

Dr. Latham's thesis is that foreigners must think from a Chinese perspective. He emphasizes three key differences between Western and Chinese perspectives.

> First there is the question of relationships. *Guanxi* (or relationships) is one of the first words a person learns when he or she comes to China. Anyone who has been around will tell you that networking and building relationships are important everywhere in the world. But newcomers here think that they have stumbled across something so entirely unique that only the Chinese are concerned with it. What is different about China is the intensity of preoccupation with relationship building, which goes on the whole time; it is an almost consuming aspect of Chinese life. Foreign managers fail to realize how pervasive it is, and that at every meeting, social or business, the Chinese participants are working on some aspect of the relationship.
>
> Another issue is the language, which is very different and can be difficult to learn. I don't want to overplay the importance of being able to speak and to read Chinese, although clearly it can be a useful tool. You can get by using English, but you may be missing 60 percent of what's going on. And that can't help but have an impact on productivity and the bottom line.
>
> I had a case in one joint venture where the financial and operating reports sent in English to the foreign manager showed different numbers than the Chinese-language reports issued to the Chinese manager. The foreign manager couldn't read the headings and the columns, so the Chinese partner had a better understanding of what was going on in the factory than the foreign factory manager.[12]
>
> The third important difference is that there is an absence of intermediary organizations in Chinese society. Although alumni groups and cultural associations have slowly appeared in China, there is no business or social organizations like those of the Masonic Lodges and Rotary Clubs. As a result, there are no mediating mechanisms between the state and the individual, and the latter, as always, would turn to his work unit in times of need. This is because the work unit has always

acted as a surrogate parent—in the provision of housing, education, healthcare, even arranged marriages; hence the nickname of "the iron rice bowl."

Dr. Latham states:

In a Chinese entity, the manager will take time to visit people who are in the hospital. He will visit older employees who have retired. There's a very personal touch to it. And we, the foreigners, are by and large unable to do that. So, employees continue to turn to the Chinese manager for many things because they receive that emotional comfort. I'm not saying that foreign-invested enterprises have to go completely Chinese in this respect. But we need to understand what the social dynamics are in the minds of Chinese employees. And we cannot easily change the expectations of the employees about their relationships with their Chinese managers.[13]

Advantages of the Genuine Global Joint Venture Model

The Genuine Global Joint Venture Model offers the competitive advantage of allowing the American company to offer the Chinese government real assistance in finding ways to enable Chinese companies to "go global." The traditional joint venture in China and WOFE models do not directly do so. In the Genuine Global Joint Venture Model, the Chinese learn to collaborate, rather than compete, with the American company. The American company can develop competitive advantages over foreign companies that are not collaborating with Chinese companies going global.

Case Study: Alignment of Respect for Foreign and Chinese Cultures and Needs[14]

Dr. Michael Portoff, the Chairman of Bayer (China) Limited, worked on Bayer's China strategy at Bayer's German headquarters in the early 1990s, and in 1993 was asked to implement the strategy. This combination of roles, rather than separation of the designing and deployment of a China strategy are an advantage.

Bayer's involvement with doing business in China dates back to the 1880s, but was interrupted by World War II and the Chinese Revolution. After the "Opening Up," Bayer's first joint venture was established in Shanghai in 1986. Bayer learned a lot from this experience and from operating two small representative offices in other cities. In the early 1990s, with Bayer's board of management and its business groups expressing increased interest in China, a major review of Bayer's goals and strategy in China was done. Part of the strategy that came into focus was the need to protect local sales in the longer term by planning for local production in China and to be close to its Chinese customers and participate in the economic life of China. Bayer's China strategy was clear, concise, and agreed upon internally. A delegation from Bayer visited China and presented the strategy to the Ministry of Chemical Industries. In 1993, Dr. Portoff negotiated a cooperation agreement with the Ministry of Chemical Industries, which was signed in the Great Hall of the People in Beijing. Bayer ensured that government authorities were kept informed of developments at both the central and local government levels. Dr. Portoff stated:

> You have to establish good relations with the central author-
> ities. In our case, this was the Ministry of Chemical Industry,
> SINOPEC, MOFTEC, the State Planning Commission, and the
> Ministry of Health. However, if you deal only with the cen-
> tral government, you will not succeed, because the provinces
> have their own powers, proceedings, and wishes. It has been
> Bayer's policy to balance the two and to approach and inform
> both levels of government.[15]

Twelve joint ventures and the establishment of one of the PRC's first holding companies followed. This was done step by step, and Bayer's China executives learned many lessons that were used in subsequent negotiations. Dr. Portoff comments:

> We cut short discussions with potential partners where the financial feasibility studies showed no realism or there was no meeting of the minds. However, in total, only four negotiations were terminated. We had to find the balance between the interests of Bayer and the relative strengths (and weaknesses) of our potential partners. Up till now, we have only signed up green field sites and haven't accepted to move into old premises that needed revamping. In addition, we have wanted large majority interests. We balanced the interest of the Chinese partner with the interest of Bayer, always in an open and frank manner. Potential problems were discussed at the outset, during the joint venture negotiations, rather than left to cause trouble after the joint venture was founded.[16]
>
> When it comes to choosing a joint venture partner, we have wanted to identify one for the longer term. As in a marriage, we wanted to choose the right partner and minimize the likelihood of eventual divorce. This takes time, and it is not just the courtship that can be lengthy. The average time taken by Bayer to establish a joint venture from the day the letter of intent is signed to the day the business license is issued has been approximately 18 months.... Relationships are also important in the West, but they are still more important in China and one of the principles of success in all walks of life. The problem is that individuals come and go, and therefore you have to develop something I call "institutional *guanxi*." ... Regardless of our ownership percentage, we have tried to treat our joint venture partners as equals. We have discussed problems face to face, sometimes for many hours. We have never put anything to the vote.... To survive in China, Chinese have learned to be flexible. Governments change. Laws and regulations change. Officials change. We cannot move as fast as we want or as fast as our head offices sometimes wish. In China, you must be patient. Things do not happen overnight.[17]

China remains, however, a complex country in which to do business. It has a different history and a different approach to doing business. These differences will not wash away. They will remain. When you form and operate a joint venture, the emphasis has to be on the word "joint." You have to understand that there are different points of view. But this doesn't mean you have to give in. To succeed you have to get the balance right.[18]

Bayer's approach of defining clear absolute necessities in its China strategy, presenting its value propositions on a continuous basis to all levels of government, and taking great care in selecting and respecting joint venture partners sidesteps pitfalls that some foreign companies' China strategies falter in.

Dr. Portoff understood that it is necessary to respect China's cultures and traditions without losing your own identity. "We have shown respect to our Chinese partners. But, it is also important not to try to change yourself. You cannot be Chinese. You were not born a Chinese and you cannot behave as a Chinese."[19]

The Bayer case is an interesting example also because the German and Chinese style of thinking and communicating have been contrasted as explicit vs. implicit, i.e., verbal communications

High and Low Context Communication

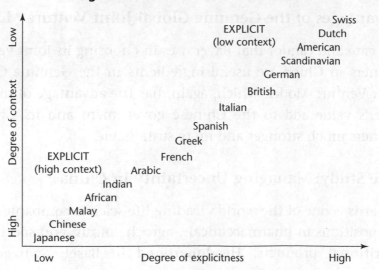

Source: Hall and Hall, Understanding Cultural Differences

being explicit and precise rather, as the Chinese do, relying on relationships and what is unsaid but understood more than the verbal or written contract.[20] The table above offers a spectrum of national stereotypes of implicit and explicit thinking and verbal traits.

Perhaps one of the important lessons in the Bayer case study is that providing there is respect and sensitivity to Chinese values and ways of doing things, the explicit communication of the foreign company's needs in a well-defined and thought-out China strategy that has strong and continuously communicated value propositions for the Chinese stakeholders can be judged to work by the German participant.

Perhaps also attention to detail is a common feature of the German and Chinese styles of thinking and communicating, which may be more pronounced in some cases than the American style of thinking and communicating.

Many observers have commented on the importance of having reliable intermediaries who can help foreigners and Mainland Chinese understand and reconcile differences.

Advantages of the Genuine Global Joint Venture Model

The care and candor that Bayer uses in choosing its joint venture partners in China are useful ingredients in the Genuine Global Joint Venture Model, which, again, has the advantage of making Bayer's value add to the Chinese government and its Chinese partners much stronger and more sustainable.

Case Study: Managing Uncertainty in China[21]

Novartis is one of the world's leading life science companies with top positions in pharmaceuticals, agrochemicals, and specialized nutritional products. Headquartered in Basel, Switzerland,

Novartis has a small home market and has to grow and prosper in markets in other countries. China's huge market and low production costs presents a competitive opportunity that companies like Novartis cannot ignore. Since China constitutes 22% of the world's population, which is a key market for health care, agricultural, and nutritional products, Novartis must succeed in China.

Novartis is subject to many uncertainties in developing its healthcare and agriculture products, which are highly subject to changes in government policy and regulations, market development and shifts, and the challenge of creating a profitable business in China as it transforms itself by embracing Socialist Market Economy Capitalism.

Novartis' value propositions in China's strategy is that foreign pharmaceutical companies bring products to China that were unavailable to handle diseases that traditional Chinese medicines were of limited effectiveness in treating, such as cancer, heart disease, and certain other ailments. China faces high costs in providing medical care. Western agrochemical products also offer important value propositions to China's need to feed its huge population and the Chinese government's desire for self-sufficiency in food production.

Novartis recognized that developing a good and close relationship with China's government required that its President regularly visit China's head of state and key ministers. To be a friend of China, and to work with China's government and spot policy changes, Novartis also worked in China on pharmaceutical and agricultural research projects important to the Chinese government and China's strategy. Novartis' doing so helps it manage the uncertainties in doing business in China.

Novartis is looking at China as a place for research and to investment in research as a way to develop a long-term relationship with China and hopefully to be considered an insider. "Like the

Chinese, we want a complete relationship, not just bricks and mortar."[22] Since research and investment in research is a priority in China's strategy and for the Chinese government, that is a superior strategy to withholding research and investments in research out of fear that China's weak intellectual property protection will destroy Novartis' value proposition and sustainable profitability in China. This is the only potentially winning solution for Novartis, which must succeed in China.

Novartis' China head, Terrence Barnett notes that: "We all welcome China as a member of the World Trade Organization. But there is probably overconfidence about the impact of WTO on our ability to do business in China in a freer manner, because WTO membership does not automatically confer that freedom. It will take time. There will be phase-in periods in different markets, and these could be relatively long. You only have to look at what the Europeans did with Japanese cars to realize that phase-in periods even in a region like Europe can be long. Cars were governed by a 15-year agreement."[23] Since Novartis works in industries classified as "restricted," Novartis must deal with the uncertainties encountered with joint venture partners:

> "We get a lot of support from our joint venture partners," says Barnett. "We get their interest. But regrettably, their objectives are sometimes different from ours. In most cases, the Chinese partners have minority stakes, and they are usually looking for an early return on their investment. By contrast, the foreign partner is usually looking much longer-term, particularly when a large plant has been constructed. In pharmaceuticals, as well as agro-chemicals, economies of scale are important and it takes some time before volumes are large enough to reduce unit costs sufficiently to make the operations economically sound. Further, foreign companies in China sometimes find that feasibility studies, often carried out five years earlier on the basis of limited experience of the country,

predicted positive financial performance that has taken longer in practice to materialize. When the Chinese partner discovers this, mutual trust can break down because it is typically the foreigner who prepares the business plan in the first instance. The problem gets worse still when the Chinese party, often part of a state-owned enterprise, has been given a financial forecast of significant returns from a Sino-foreign joint venture, which is in reality taking some time to achieve profitability.

"Then there is the issue of who manages the joint venture. The foreigner typically wants total control, just as he does in other countries. He considers that, having invested large sums, he is entitled to ensure that the business is managed to an international standard. On the other hand, the Chinese want significant involvement, even if they are a minority shareholder. There is the issue of 'face,' but also pride, in being part of a joint venture with a large foreign enterprise. Relationships can sometimes be emotional rather than objective."[24]

Novartis recognizes that when a joint venture has no chance whatever of meeting its objective, it is necessary to sever the relationship. But, in some cases, time and effort must be invested with joint venture partners to find new solutions such as new structures, which enable each to achieve their objectives. It is necessary to invest in people and in training.

Another uncertainty is that the future shape of China's market is very unclear. Novartis' response is to try to get closer to and understand both the urban and rural markets, and to understand customers' mentality and the way it is changing and how its products should be marketed.[25]

Genuine Global Joint Venture Model's Advantages

The good additional way to understand and benefit from uncertainty about the future shape of China's market is for American companies to partner with Chinese companies on a global rather than a merely Chinese basis. The value of the collaboration adds incentives for the Chinese government, which has enormous influence on the future shape of the Chinese market to ensure that genuine global joint ventures between leading Chinese and American companies prosper both in China and globally. Making the decision-maker your supporter and advisor is a competitive advantage in a rapidly evolving "Permission Society."

Case Study: Coping with Chinese Competitors in the Chinese market[26]

In 2000 Shell was the leading foreign oil company in China, with 20 wholly-owned or joint ventures; its annual turnover was US$400 million. Brian Anderson, Chairman and CEO, Shell Companies in North East Asia, stated:

> The biggest problem I have is getting a handle on the marketplace. All the rest is relatively straightforward for a company like Shell that operates in most countries around the world.... Matching our investment in China to the growth of the market is a tricky game.... In an old fashion world, the process of new investment would take longer. Today's world does not allow that. You just have to go faster. Of the US$1billion we have invested in China in the last 15 years, US$600million has been spent in exploration and production. We are the largest foreign equity oil producer in China. That sounds grandiose. In fact, at only 40,000 barrels a day, it's very small. We have an equity share of only about 1 percent of China's oil production. This shows you that the PRC Government hasn't really opened up the oil industry. We have been very cautious about investing in this sector because there have been a lot of burnt fingers as a result of oil companies' going into marginal areas and struggling to make them viable. We are profitable, and one of the few that can say that.

In oil products and chemicals, we have just finished our first cycle of investment of around US$300 million. It's been a patchy start. Some projects have worked better than others. None is profitable at the moment. But they are all very recent, built within the last two years. We expect them to come to profitability within the next two years. Oil products are a restrictive game in China. The PRC government *withdrew* the right from us to go into the retail market for fuels like petrol and diesel, which provide a shop front for oil companies. You will nevertheless see some Shell petrol stations. They stem from a grandfather clause in the legislation, which *allows us to use the arrangements that existed before the rules were changed.* So, by the end of 1998, we had about 30 filling stations.[27] (*Emphasis added*)

China is not going to allow foreigners to control its economy. In a Permission Society China's government can deliver on that shared goal with the Chinese people who remember the "century of humiliation." Nonetheless, Shell is in the game, and expects to be profitable. To not be in the game with 22% of the human race is to lose by default in the 21st century.

Anderson states:

Normally, in a new market, we would import our products and test the market out first. If the circumstances and financial projections looked right, we would then invest and build capacity. Here in China, that is not possible. You have to invest up front, and that is the killer. There is a further problem: over capacity being built in China at present because of over investment.... Additionally, Chinese competition is strong, and the rules of the game are unclear. It's a battle, but I'm optimistic because the country is led by some very smart people, and the market will eventually sort itself out.[28]

This manifestation of the "right spirit" holds out so much promise for the foreign-Chinese win-win relationship.

The Genuine Global Joint Venture Model's Advantages

The politically aborted CNOOC bid for Unocal has harmed American companies seeking to succeed in participating in China's economic development. American oil companies, whether Chevron or others, all other things being equal for the purpose of comparison, would likely benefit from quickly designing, entering into, and operating genuine global joint ventures with partially Chinese government owned oil companies "going global." It is hard to imagine any other means of American oil companies advancing their interests given the rise of the importance in the global oil markets of Chinese and Indian state-owned and financed competitors.

PART 3

Aligning American and Chinese Strategies and Needs

7

China's Permission Society Enters the World Trade Organization

Overview

This chapter examines China's World Trade Organization ("WTO") membership commitments and the realistic and unrealistic expectations of non-Chinese observers on what China's membership entails. China's financial markets and banking sector are examined from the perspectives of foreign observers' attitudes that are unaligned and aligned with the essential economic development and sovereignty goals of the Chinese government.

China's WTO Commitments

The Chinese government, in order to drive internal reforms and obtain competitive advantages, joined the World Trade Organization, committing China's domestic economy to major changes. The Chinese government used WTO membership to implement Socialist Market Economy Capitalism reforms within China and to add to the competitive advantages of "champion" Chinese companies going global.

China's Main Commitment in Services Under the WTO   1

Sector	Upon Accession	2003	2006
Banking	foreign currency business to all Chinese clients	Local currency business to Chinese Companies with geographic restrictions	no restrictions
Distribution retail	joint-ventures in Special Economic Zones and six cities incl. Beijing and Shanghai	foreign majority control of joint-ventures; all provincial capitals	restrictions of products only for foreign-controlled chain stores
Insurance life	50% foreign-ownership in joint-ventures		
Insurance non-life	branch or 51% foreign-ownership in joint-venture; 50% for large scale commercial risks and reinsurance	wholly-owned subsidiaries; 51% for large scale commercial risks and reinsurance (2004)	wholly-owned subsidiaries for large scale commercial risk and reinsurance
Telecom mobile	max. 25% foreign-ownership in joint ventures; limited to Shanghai, Guangzhou, Beijing	max. 35% (2002); relaxed geographic restrictions; max. 49% (2004)	no geographic restrictions

*different time schedules apply for other services

Source: WTO

Financial Services in China Under the WTO Protocol

The protocol for the accession of China to the WTO came into force on December 11, 2001. Although the WTO agreements include approximately sixty agreements and annexes, three agreements are fundamental: the General Agreement on Tariffs and Trade, covering goods; the General Agreement on Trade in Services, covering services; and the Agreement on Trade-Related Aspects of Intellectual Property Rights, covering intellectual property. Financial services are controlled by the services agreement (the GATS). The GATS Agreement imposes a most favored nations treatment obligation on all trade in services within China with several exceptions. The GATS Agreement requires that over time the Chinese government treat non-PRC service firms in the same manner it treats Chinese service firms. This includes allowing access to relevant markets.

For its admission into the WTO, China has made a significant and unprecedented market opening commitment as a developing economy. In addition to the drastic reduction of its tariffs on imported industrial and agricultural goods, it will liberalize foreign participation in its internal distribution systems and key industrial sectors such as telecommunications and construction.

Among the most far reaching market opening commitments is to open up China's financial services market. China agreed to gradually allow more branches of foreign banks to operate in more regions and to allow foreign banks to conduct Yuan business. China agreed to allow more access to foreign insurers, to make it easier for foreign insurers to invest in domestic insurers and set up joint venture insurance companies and to open up more geographical and services areas for foreign insurers. China also agreed to allow foreign participation in its rapidly expanding investment banking and fund management industries by initially allowing significant foreign minority stakes.

A Realistic View of China's "Permission Society" WTO Compliance

Lester Thurow summarizes some realities about China's compliance with its WTO obligations:

> China's entry into the World Trade Organization has been widely discussed inside and outside of China. An important psychological event, it signaled to everyone inside and outside of China that the leaders in Beijing want to play the global capitalist game. But by itself, joining the WTO was not an important economic event. China's entrance to the WTO should be seen as an instrument the leaders in Beijing could

use to persuade middle and lower levels of the bureaucracy to continue reforming China's economic institutions. Reforms could be defended as necessary to fulfill WTO requirements (blame the foreigners) when, in fact, the leaders in Beijing see them as necessary to keep economic progress going. If the Chinese leadership did not believe that these reforms were necessary for their own future success, they would not have joined the WTO. China was doing very nicely outside of the WTO.

In the future, if China's leaders don't believe that WTO requirements are in their long-run self-interest, they just won't conform to these requirements—*just as Europe does not conform to the requirements on hormones in meat; and the United States does not follow the rules when it comes to offshore tax advantages for its companies. The Chinese know they will not be kicked out of the WTO.* Fines are small, just a few billion dollars, for not following the rules, and one can always find clever ways around the rules without violating the rules. Korea gave tax audits to those buying Ford Taurus cars when Korea thought too many imported Fords were being sold. Nothing in the WTO rules says anything about who can be given a tax audit.[2] (*Emphasis added*)

China will not be the first or only WTO member to shape its WTO compliance around its own national needs. America is among the leading examples of a country that does just that. In that respect, China will be like America. In any event, America has little moral authority, as an exemplar of WTO compliance, to castigate China. Nonetheless, WTO members spend lots of energy castigating each other. The WTO creates a context for such recriminations, adjustments and adjudication of national interests.

As we have seen, foreign companies' "China strategies" face domestic Chinese companies, which blend private and public ownership and others that are privately-owned. In China's "Socialist Market Economy Capitalism," partly-privately and wholly-state-owned competitors enjoy the Chinese government's support without the previously more limiting "Communist Market" interference. Some Chinese companies are showing themselves to be capable of grabbing market share inside and outside China from major foreign companies.[3] Soon there will be complaints that China is supporting "unfair" competition. How internationally persuasive are such complaints? Even if they are very persuasive to Americans, America does not have an historical record of supporting "fair" competition.

The Fallacy That China Is More Protectionist Than America

After the American government's blocking of CNOOC's acquisition bid for Unocal, American political and business leaders have a lot less moral authority than they did previously to trumpet America's openness to Chinese companies or demand that China be wide open to American companies. The first major publicly traded Chinese company that sought to purchase a publicly traded American company was prevented from doing so, allowing an American company to successfully make the acquisition with a bid US$2 billion less than the Chinese company offered. China has a far better and longer record of openness to American investment and participation in its domestic market, than America has of permitting Chinese investment and participation in America's domestic market.

The Reality That the Central Chinese Government Is using WTO Membership in Reforming China's Domestic Economy So Chinese Companies Can Compete Globally

The Chinese central government in negotiating the WTO agreement reportedly consulted very little with the industrial ministries, provinces, and cities where foreign competition could threaten local business. Few localities are reportedly prepared to implement WTO obligations, preferring to stimulate local economic growth and reduce foreign competition. Provincial, municipal, and village governments derive much of their revenue from SOEs. Local and national officials can use constantly changing national, provincial, and local regulations and relationships. China's central government must manage or deal with competing demands among China's banking system reform needs, health and other public services, environmental needs, and cash-strapped local governments.[4] Foreign companies seeking competitive advantages should highlight the compatibility of their China strategy with China's strategy of economic development at all levels of government.[5]

The Aligned Perspective on Opening Up China's Financial Services Industries to Unrestricted Foreign Competition

Joint ventures, formerly the only way to operate in China, present problems for foreign venturers. Government officials often promote weak SOEs as joint venture partners with foreign companies. Chinese firms want to dominate their local markets and typically want to take profits out of joint ventures rather than reinvesting them. They often ignore the corporate governance rules American companies are accustomed to. Instead of using a joint venture, foreign companies frequently now use a wholly foreign-owned enterprise, which the Chinese government now permits.[6] American companies wishing to participate aggressively in China's financial services, and other sectors, are bound to feel the fallout of the American government's aggressive refusal to allow CNOOC to pay more than Chevron for Unocal. The blocking of the CNOOC acquisition by the American government was a turning point in

China's openness to accepting American companies. This should be expected, as the Chinese government cannot reward CNOOC jingoism.

Pragmatic American companies, in this "do as I say, not as I do" damaged political environment, that wish to participate aggressively in China's financial services and other sectors should present Genuine Global Joint Venture proposals to major Chinese companies. Such initiatives will signal their understanding that win-win value propositions and strategies must be offered to the Chinese government and Chinese companies. In sectors such as banking, where the China's central government predominates, American companies, sensitive to the needs of the Chinese government, will have competitive advantages. The competitive position of such American companies also will be enhanced if America and China's political leaders agree to implement a partnership and if American political and business leaders take an aligned and collaborative approach to Chinese companies going global.

Hank Greenberg, the former Chairman of AIG, who has over 25 years of experience in dealing with China, understands the prudence of an American company using an aligned approach. In explaining why China has taken so long to open the financial services industry, he stated in 2000:

> China did not have the experience, the institutions, the regulations, or the knowledge base to deal with external financial institutions. They had to take it step by step, and they have had their fits and starts. But they are eager to learn, and they had countless delegations here and there trying to gain an understanding of how to deal with today's financial institutions and the speed of global capital movement. If China had a convertible currency when the Asia crisis began, it would have been a disaster. They were pursued by many and urged to inaugurate a convertible currency, but all those voices were very still when Asia had

its problems. The best thing to happen was that China did not then have a convertible currency. In due course that will come, when China has the means and regulations to sustain a convertible currency. The same is true of financial institutions. My guess is that if China and the United States agree on WTO accession, there will be continued progress in opening the market to financial services, but it will be on a phased basis, as well it should be. They have learned a great deal in the last few years and they continue to learn. Hopefully, we will learn more about China and how to do business there.[7]

It took Hank Greenberg seventeen years of patient effort to obtain a license for AIG to sell insurance domestically in Shanghai, Guangzhou, Shenzhen, and Foshan, even though AIG signed a claims and reinsurance agreement with the People's Insurance Company of China even before the 1978 Opening Up. Greenberg chaired the first international business advisory council for Zhu Rongji when he was Mayor of Shanghai, and who later became China's Premier and a key force in the overhaul of China's SOE and banking sector.[8] AIG is reported to have made a US$500 million profit in China in 2004.

The Unaligned Perspective on Opening Up China's Financial Services Industries to Unrestricted Foreign Competition

In contrast, the unaligned approach urges the Chinese government to adopt financial service reforms that benefit foreign companies, and assumes that China's regulatory framework *can be and must be* like America's. The unaligned approach champions the interest of foreign companies in capturing control of China's huge and rapidly growing markets, and ignores China's need to protect its economic sovereignty. The Chinese government is unlikely to grant the unaligned approach's aggressive goals. Hank Paulson, America's current Treasury Secretary, while Chairman and CEO of Goldman Sachs, exemplified the unaligned approach. In 2003 he wrote:

> As China moves into the next stage of economic reform ... the country's new generation of leadership must respond with utmost urgency to a critical challenge—that is the restructuring of its ailing banking system. With 190% of [China's annual] GDP in total assets, the banking sector plays a dominant role in China's financial system, However, government-directed credit allocation (policy lending), lax supervision, and mismanagement of the central planning era have left China's banking sector burdened with massive bad loans, with the non-performing loan (NPL) ratio likely to be as high as 40%. As we have learned from financial crises around the world, including the 1997/1998 Asian Crisis and Japan's decade old economic malaise, problems in the banking sector have grave macroeconomic consequences. Monetary policy is likely to lose effectiveness when the banking sector is in distress; and an ensuing credit crunch could severely depress private consumption, corporate investment, and foreign trade, thus choking off economic growth and exacerbating deflationary pressures. If the banking system ceases to function properly, fiscal policy will have to assume the full burden of stimulating demand and growth, leading the widening budgetary deficits and higher long-term interest rates. Moreover, the required NPL resolution and recapitalization will entail massive fiscal costs, imposing a severe burden on the government budget and public sector balance sheet.
>
> While China has made substantial progress in economic restructuring and has recorded impressive GDP growth rates in recent years, its vast economic potential will not be fully realized unless it rapidly tackles its banking sector woes.[9]

Mr. Paulson characterized China's banking sector as:

> ... one of the worst banking systems in Asia, or even the world.... The good news, though, is that China has taken

some encouraging initial steps in the right direction. Instead of denial and delay, the government has embarked on a program of banking reform since 1998. Partial recapitalization, NPL carve-outs, asset sales, debt restructuring, and write-offs, combined with the early efforts to strengthen credit appraisal and risk management systems, have succeeded in fending off a full-blown banking crisis and in maintaining public and investor confidence.... As a key component of China's banking reform strategy, the government has been actively pursuing privatization of its largest state-owned banks.... In the coming two to five years, the Chinese government will likely accelerate privatization of its large financial institutions.[10]

Peter Sullivan, the Chairman of Goldman Sachs International, writing in 2001, stated:

While much remains to be done to complete China's push towards efficient capital markets, the political leadership has taken significant steps to lay the foundations of the necessary reform process. As I have pointed out, measures such as SOE restructuring and privatization are key to the further capital inflow into the country. At the same time, this capital flow will *demand* reform in corporate governance. Free markets and openness to foreign trade are *vital* for high economic growth *so is* good transparent corporate governance. *China will not be able to maintain this high rate of economic growth.* I believe China's economic success will *enable* it to join the United States, Europe, and Japan as global economic leaders, contributing to poverty alleviation and economic development in sub-Saharan, Africa, South Africa, and other less developed parts of the world, not least through the example that it will provide. As one of the major economic powers China must play an important role in safeguarding world peace and prosperity and its on-going economic transformation will be *judged* as one of *mankind's* greatest triumphs.[11] (*Emphasis added*)

Fred Hu, the Chairman and CEO of the Goldman Sachs Group and the Managing Director of Goldman Sachs, Hong Kong, writing in 2003 stated:

... public confidence in part stemming from state ownership
of the banks, strong liquidity, substantial foreign exchange
reserves, and significant fresh opportunities for quality loan
growth—should help the Chinese banking section escape the
worst of the possible outcomes. Barring an unexpected, sharp
macroeconomic downturn, China appears likely to be able to
avert a full-blown banking crisis within a five-year horizon.
That does not mean, however, that China can afford to relax
and just shrug off its banking sector problems.[12]

This unaligned perspective asserts an assumption that
China, to be successful, must be like America, Europe, and
Japan. But the reality is that China is not like those countries
and is very successful. It also asserts that capital inflow will
demand reform in corporate governance. But the deficiencies
that unaligned observers focus on have not stopped US$650 billion
in capital inflow into China from 1979 to 2006. Free markets and
openness to foreign trade have not been vital for China's high
economic growth from 1979 to date. The unaligned perspective
asserts that China will not be able to maintain its high rate of
economic growth. It recognizes the potential China has to be a
major economic power, but apparently does not recognize or
accept that China is likely to be the dominant economic power
in the 21st century. The unaligned perspective asserts that
China will be judged in comparison to and by the other major
economic powers in the world. But China may be less concerned, albeit not indifferent, to the views of foreigners than
the unaligned perspective assumes. The reality is that China
constitutes 22% of the human race, and may impose new rules
and set new precedents from a growing position of influence.

Even assuming the unaligned perspective turns out
historically to be correct, which we doubt because of China's
overwhelming competitive advantages, American business
leaders and companies that choose aligned strategies are likely
to have competitive advantages over those which choose

unaligned strategies. Even if American business leaders and companies choose the unaligned approach, other foreign companies seeking short-, medium-, and long-term competitive advantages over American companies will follow the aligned approach.

China will not allow foreign banks to control the Chinese banking sector due to the Chinese government and people's economic sovereignty concerns, which are not the driving concerns of Mr. Paulson in his role as Treasury Secretary or his former role as head of Goldman Sachs. In his senate confirmation hearings, Mr. Paulson indicated the problem of "global economic imbalances" and banking reform, a flexible or "market based currency" and exchange rate, and open markets in China would be among his priorities.[13]

Mr. Paulson will have to deal with the predictable consequences in China of "CNOOC jingoism" in America. What goes around, comes around. In the finance sector, deals involving Citigroup, Merrill Lynch, UBS, and JP Morgan have suffered delays amid a "backlash against foreign involvement in the economy" of China.[14] A Citigroup joint venture failed to reach agreement on buying a stake in China's Shandong Chenming Paper Holdings Ltd.[15] *The Economist* reported: "Chenming appears confident of finding alternative funding, saying in its weekend announcement it had applied for an RMB 6B ($735 M) long-term loan from a group of domestic banks."[16] The Carlyle Group, a U.S. private equity firm, has also been unable to close a proposed purchase of a Chinese machinery maker, although the machinery sector is officially open to foreign investment. These challenges facing American investment in China can only be exacerbated by "CNOOC jingoism." America now lacks the moral authority to resist such a backlash, and China is not a developing country that America or American companies can dictate terms to.[17]

The Chinese government permitted the first major cross-sector domestic investments by a Chinese insurance company in 2006. Ping An Insurance (Group) Co. was allowed to invest in a bank with 44 branches in its home city of Schenzhen, 52% owned by the Schenzhen city government. Ping An Insurance is 19% owned by HSBC Holdings Ltd. The insurance company was also permitted for the first time to invest in express way construction, with initial investments in three expressways being built in Northwestern China.[18]

The Fallacy That China's Banks Will Collapse in Insolvency

The Chinese government abandoned plans to liberalize China's capital account following the Asian Financial Crisis in 1997. The Chinese government has many economic management tools that the American government does not have. Among the most powerful is that the Chinese government uses compulsory saving schemes among China's huge population to generate huge pools of capital. China has a higher savings rate than America, Switzerland and Japan; although China's (purchasing power adjusted) per capita income of less than US$5,000 is 80% less than in those countries. The Chinese government's system of state-directed banks, insurance companies, and asset management companies enabled the Chinese government to use Chinese thriftiness to achieve greater control of China's economic development processes. Foreign banks, insurance companies, and asset management companies hope to be able to gain access to China's national savings pools. The Chinese government instead may follow Singapore's model of government-linked entities controlling investment allocation decisions, which results in government-linked companies having access to cheap and patient funding capital.[19]

The Reality Is That Chinese Government Is Upgrading China's Banking System's Management and Capital Base Without Losing China's Economic Sovereignty

Instead of China's banks collapsing under "the bad loans they were saddled with" as many observers predicted, the Chinese government used some of China's ingenuity, vast savings, and foreign currency resources. In other words, the Chinese government is using China's way of doing things and success to recapitalize banks, turn them into joint-stock companies,[20] sell stakes to leading major global banks,[21] and then have IPOs, which to date have been highly successful.[22]

The Chinese government is seeking and obtaining financial and intellectual capital investments by leading global banks as a key part of banking sector reform so that Chinese banks will be better equipped to compete with foreign banks in China. But foreigners can currently own only 25% of a Chinese bank. American and other foreign banks' proposed deals often seek to push beyond that 25% limit. Beyond that threshold, the Chinese banks currently lose many of the advantages in doing business in China that make it attractive to foreigners. Even if foreign banks succeed in getting beyond that 25% cap on foreign ownership, the Chinese government still controls the rules of the game. There have been a large number of investments by foreign banks in Chinese banks in 2005.[23] The Chinese government is strengthening the capital bases and management of what increasingly will be partially-state-owned banks in preparation for IPOs[24] and other international capital market transactions. It would be surprising however if the Chinese government would allow foreign control of Chinese banks. It is generally felt that a foreign bank, under WTO provisions seeking to operate in China without Chinese bank partners, would face a very difficult process.[25]

The Reality That Both China and America Are Permission Societies

China remains a Permission Society. At anytime that it is necessary to protect China's economic sovereignty and achieve its economic and other goals, the Chinese government *can, will, and must* change the laws, policies, or regulations governing foreign firms participating in business in China. American companies seeking to thrive in China should pragmatically factor that reality into their business plans.

How would the American government react if a Chinese bank sought to acquire more than 25% of a major, publicly traded American bank or financial services firm? After the American government's action in blocking the higher bid of CNOOC, a NYSE-traded company, for Unocal, the American government and American companies have little moral authority to criticize China's "Permission Society" behavior and *rule by law* rather than rule of law system. *America is also a "Permission Society"* from the perspective of the Chinese government and CNOOC and other Chinese companies who noted the American government's CNOOC jingoism.

As of July 2007, no American financial services group or bank has publicly offered a major Chinese bank a Genuine Global Joint Venture. The foreign banks that pioneer *Genuine Global* Joint Ventures with major Chinese banks will have massive competitive advantages over their peers. That is the next brilliant new move in "The China Game" for an American financial services firm or bank. In 2002, there were approximately 478 foreign financial service firms competing with each other for very limited licenses to do business in China.

The Fallacy That China's Banking System Must Follow Foreign Financial Service Sector Models

Observers who insist on projecting the classic 18th, 19th, and 20th century model of capitalism, and characteristics of American capitalism they are familiar with on China, do not see or do not accept that the new model of 21st century Socialist Market Economy Capitalism that China is deploying is different. It is a powerful new model of capitalism or an additional and different model of capitalism, that combines state ownership, China's multi-faceted competitive advantages, massive developing domestic market, cost advantages, and massive economic and intellectual wealth in the 21st century with the Chinese government's ability to make and revise the laws that "The China Game" is played by. An economically successful Permission Society like China, with its *rule by law* rather than *rule of law* system, has key features that many observers do not see or accept. The economic success of a rule by law Permission Society is a new phenomenon, and a paradigm shift, in 21st century capitalism and economic theory. It is a paradigm shift in the way the global economy works in the 21st century, which was not a factor in the 20th century.

Such observers do not see or accept that, for all but the past 200 years of its 5,000-year history, China has been the largest, most populated, richest, innovative, and civilized nation in the world. Instead, The World Economic forum, for example, sees China as a developing country that they ranked in 2002 as 33rd in growth competitiveness and 38th in macroeconomic growth among 80 nations. Such perspectives assume in effect, that when China grows up, it must be like America and other much younger societies. That is unrealistic.

Throughout 4,970 years of its 5,000-year history, China has been one of the most energetic, pragmatic, and entrepreneurial societies in the world. After a 30-year failed economic experiment with a communist ideology and planned economy that ignored the global economy, China has now, in less than 30 years, transformed itself again into the most entrepreneurial and competitive economy in the world. That achievement has endowed the Chinese government and people with even greater confidence, energy, and resources in the 21st century than were realities in the 20th century.

Nonetheless, even as non-Chinese observers grapple with the rapidly increasing competitive capabilities of the Chinese government and people today, they insist on assuming that China must either fail or become like America. They see or accept no other alternatives. The reality is that in the 21st century, it is China that is creating key parts of a new template for China's and the global economy. America may have to adjust to China, rather than China adjusting to America.

Many Foreign Observers Cannot Accept That the Chinese Government Is Pursuing a Different Economic Model of a Capitalist Economy

The cognitive dissonance of many observers, who assume their conclusion that China's capital markets must be like America's, rather than change their assumptions to fit the new realities of the success of Chinese capitalism, can be seen in the following October 13, 2005 *Wall Street Journal* article: "China's Economic Boom Masks Financing Limits of Big Firms." The article is unusually candid in stating that the projecting of Western financial assumptions on China's economic strategies furthers the hopes of American companies of generating business in China.

Strength in China's economy, including solid corporate-profit growth and surging foreign investment, is masking balance-sheet problems at the nation's largest companies, according to a report by Citigroup and Moody's Investors Services Inc.

The report compares 686 of China's largest listed companies with nearly 5,000 other publicly traded companies throughout the world, and it concludes the average big Chinese company is behind the global curve in developing a flexible financial structure. The report is to be presented at a meeting organized by Citigroup and Moody's today as they brief senior financial officers of about 100 of China's largest publicly traded companies.

The report, based on data reported for 2004 by the companies, ticks off a number of danger signs at big Chinese companies. They rely too much on simple bank lending. Half of their bank borrowing is for periods of a year or less. Nearly every dollar of profit earned by Chinese companies has been offset by new loans for investment. Only 13 Chinese companies have obtained an internationally recognized credit rating.

Capital markets provide few alternatives for longer-term funding. The report notes that the size of China's stock market, relative to gross domestic product, ranks behind that of every major economy, and the corporate-bond market is essentially non-existent.

It all adds up to rigid financial structures that don't allow Chinese companies much breathing room should economic fundamentals change. In contrast, companies elsewhere usually tailor their financing to be more adjustable to their individual needs and to changing conditions.

Carsten Stemdevad, Head of Citigroup's emerging markets financial strategy group in New York and the report's lead author, said one purpose of the report is to drive business to Citibank and Moody's by encouraging Chinese companies to turn to the U.S. companies for help in modernizing their capital structures. Still, he said, the report is based on data reported by the firms.

Many companies' *problems* are a reflection of China's heavily regulated financial system and *aren't necessarily indicative of poor corporate strategies. Chinese regulators have essentially frozen stock market fund raising for several months, while the continued poor performance of key stock indexes has discouraged many companies from participating in the market.*

Many companies are barred under government restrictions from issuing bonds. Controls on derivatives' activity limit their financing options.

Foreign banks have been quietly pressing for business with Chinese companies after Beijing gave the green light for the banks to handle commercial business nearly a year ago. *The foreign banks are also responding to signals that more-sophisticated hedging products are becoming acceptable to authorities.*[26] (*Emphasis added*)

What many observers miss or avoid is considering the reality that China and Chinese companies are succeeding, not only without an American-style domestic capital market, but also because of the role of the Chinese government in guiding Chinese economic institutions and policies and Chinese companies' development on a Chinese model rather than an American model. The graph below from the article reveals not just a Chinese economy in transition, but perhaps a fundamentally different economic model of one-party state-managed capitalism that is more advanced or more powerful perhaps in some ways than the American model of capitalism. The reality is that the Chinese government will tailor China's financial services sector to its evolving view of China's requirements rather than American companies' desires to penetrate and re-engineer China's economic development.

Western Assumptions About the Convergence of Non-Chinese and China's Capital Markets

Two articulations of Western assumptions regarding the necessary convergence of the Chinese capital markets with American style capital markets are set out below. In reading them, consider

Capital Comparison

Chinese companies rely far more heavily on bank lending than their counterparts in other countries; values as a percentage of gross domestic products

[27]

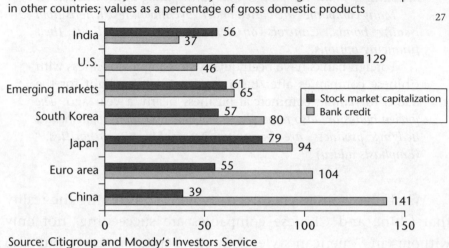

Source: Citigroup and Moody's Investors Service

whether the CNOOC-type bid for Unocal could be strengthened or weakened or both by the assumptions they make about how China's capital markets must operate, which are based on a simple comparison, without deeper analysis, of the model that China's capital markets will mimic America's.

While considering these articulations of Western assumptions, it is critical to recognize how adroitly the Chinese government has been in listening politely while proceeding to reform the Chinese banks with foreign capital and expertise, discussed in Chapter 9 and something no western country has. The Chinese government has access to the accumulated assets from China's 1.3 billion people's 40% of annual per capita national savings rate held in state-owned banks that pay little interest operating in a system where there have historically been few other places to put or invest money other than for citizens to keep it in cash. Many expert Western observers project their assumptions and experience of what a "sound financial services sector" is on China, and do not sufficiently factor in such profound differences between, for example, the American and Mainland Chinese ways of doing things.

The World Economic Forum's Report from Private Meetings during the 2005 China Business Summit was entitled *"Financial Services Community: Evolution of Capital Markets in China."* It included an Executive Summary and papers by Robert Morse, Managing Director and Chief Executive Officer, Asia Pacific Corporate and Investment Bank, Citigroup and Georges Ugeux, Chairman and Chief Executive Officer, Galileo Global Advisors, USA. Here are the examples of two articulations of Western assumptions regarding the necessary convergence of the Chinese and American styles of operating capital markets.

First we will consider the Executive Summary, which stated:

1. China's bond and equity markets remain "miserably small." Of total capital financing over the past six months, banks provided 98% with the fixed-income and equity markets accounting for a mere 1% each.
2. An efficient government bond market (as reflected by a true yield curve) is always a necessary condition for an effective corporate bond market. China's financial regulators are beginning to address some of the government bond market's deficiencies.
3. For an effective equity market, China needs to establish a "First Board" or "Super Board", not a "Second Board", and needs to keep the process fair and controlled and work with major stakeholders.

   Notwithstanding the problems on both the fixed-income and equity sides, several key reforms are underway in the capital markets:

1. Aiming to help turn the brokerage industry around, the government recently set up a fund to take care of individual

shareholders who have been victims of fraud. In the meantime, brokerage firms are being shut down, sold or merged, laying the foundation for healthier firms to emerge.

2. Signaling a major policy shift, this summer Beijing announced that listed companies would be required to convert all their shares to tradable status. (Previously, an estimated two-thirds of equity in local markets was tied up in non-tradable issues.)

3. In another hopeful sign, the different P/E multiple between Chinese companies listed on domestic exchanges and shares listed in Hong Kong or overseas has almost diminished to zero.

The reforms underway are likely to bear fruit, and by 2006–2007 you will again see a strongly-functioning, A-share (Shanghai and Shenzhen-listed) market, and the domestic market will begin to provide a viable source of fungible assets for corporations and opportunities for people making private investments in China today.[28]

Robert Morse's paper stated:

China's policy-makers recognize the need for a market-driven system for allocating capital efficiently. Now that impressive and aggressive measures are underway in reforming the commercial banking industry, establishing reliable capital markets is the next priority for China's financial system. Indeed, one can view reform of the capital markets as a logical and necessary extension of banking industry reform, a critical step in weaning China's economy from its historical over-dependence on bank lending as the primary source of credit.

For China's capital markets to be able to allocate capital efficiently, all three domestic markets need to function effectively—namely, the government bond market, the corporate bond market and the stock markets. Currently, the government bond market is the largest by far, but still lacks liquidity and does not properly set prices; the corporate bond market is nascent; and the stock market is in the throes of a long-awaited reform of the non-tradable shares overhang problem.

An efficient government bond market (as reflected by a true yield curve) is always a necessary condition for an effective corporate bond market. China's financial regulators are beginning to address some of the government bond market's deficiencies.

1. Fragmented markets (inter-bank, exchange traded, privately placed)
2. Unequal treatment of sovereign issuers (different tax effects)
3. Lack of benchmark issues
4. Uncertain issuance calendar
5. Lack of true market-making by dealers
6. Buy-and-hold behavior
7. Lack of hedging instruments

Once a dependable government bond yield curve develops, China's corporate bond market can evolve quickly. Private sector issuance has been minimal, and many of the bonds issued so far are fully backed by bank guarantees. The potential size of this market is enormous, but issuers and investors need to learn to properly price the varying risk of different issuers. Companies and their owners also need to understand the corporate finance theory that equity is more expensive capital than debt, and not the other way around.

China's domestic stock markets are larger and older than the corporate bond market, but stock prices have been declining for several years. Valuations of domestic A shares and international H shares have been converging, and this trend will continue. With the A share valuations approaching more reasonable levels and the expected removal of the non-tradable share overhang, these two key structural changes should pave the way for further growth and influence of institutional investors, and for a return of domestic investor confidence.

Georges Ungeux stated:

> Capital markets are an important asset for China. The "balanced development" defended by President Hu Jintao has in these markets a powerful engine for growth and a gradual mechanism to open the Chinese markets to domestic and foreign capital. However, this development requires a delicate balance between governance and control. Companies need to have access to capital to finance their growth: the past mechanism of state-owned enterprises financed beyond their credit worthiness led to the collapse of the companies as well as of the banking system. Sustainable growth needs the support of capital markets.
>
> Over the past few years, Chinese companies raised capital using mostly the domestic Chinese market, the offshore Hong Kong Market, and the United States capital markets. Most of the capital was raised in Hong Kong and, while the US markets were rather less significant, they have recovered their appetite for Chinese companies since 2004.
>
> By contrast, the share of the domestic stock exchanges (Shanghai and Shenzhen) steadily decreased to a point where they stopped playing the role domestic equity markets are expected to play: being the primary source of equity for their domestic companies. While the authorities were "shelving" the domestic equity markets they, in fact, shrunk them and the price of the A shares did not follow the evolution of the H shares or the ADRs. The measures taken by the government to insulate the domestic markets were due to the so-called "Asian Crisis" when the Yuan was under threat. Unfortunately, when the situation changed and China started piling up foreign exchange reserves, the markets remained fragmented.
>
> The losers of this situation are obvious: Chinese investors did not benefit from the growing appetite of international investors for Chinese shares, and only those companies that were allowed to issue shares outside of China benefited from a price level that produced a competitive cost of equity. In short, the insulation of the Chinese markets did not "protect" but "punished" domestic investors and issuers.

The road to a fungible market is not easy: one step is the change of the regulatory structure that gives the Exchanges a level of autonomy that allows them to list and de-list companies on the basis of the quality of those companies. The Chinese government is in fact unable to play its regulatory role, since it also has to act in the best interest of the exchanges. This regulatory presence has stopped the de-listing of companies that should never have been listed in the first place.

Now is the time to develop a true capital market structure: it will boost domestic capital markets and, more importantly, be a partner of the Chinese government in the "balanced development" of China.[29]

Is the Chinese government going to take such foreign experts' advice? The World Economic Forum's Report from Private Meetings did not include a paper from Chinese government authorities although many attended the meetings. Yasheng Huang[30] might argue that the result Georges Ungeux cites above is consistent with Chinese government policy of restricting debt-based capital and access by Mainland Chinese entrepreneurs to equity financing.

Since the model of capitalism with Chinese characteristics is working for China, why should China use the model of capitalism with American characteristics? The reality is that in economic terms, the Chinese model of capitalism is working better for China than the American model of capitalism is for America.

We are not suggesting that America should adopt capitalism with Chinese characteristics or remain on the road to becoming a Permission Society in a jingoistic reaction to China's economic growth. However, that may be what is in the process of occurring with the interaction of Chinese and American capitalism.

We are stating that in order for American and Chinese capitalism to prosper peacefully together, their differences must be understood and respected. We are stating that China's model of capitalism is validated by the fact that it "works" even if it is different from

America's model of capitalism. Understanding why China "works" requires that observers understand that, whether they like it or not, China's way of doing things does "work" and is becoming more important in the global economy of the 21st century every day.

Is There a Sustainable Powerful Alternate Model of a Capitalist Economy Emerging in China That Can Be Integrated into the American Model of Capitalism?

As seen, China has a very successful alternate capitalist economy to America's. It is possible that a prescient view of what China's financial services sector and capital markets are becoming might be best found somewhere between the assumptions of observers, such as Treasury Secretary Paulson and others with views unaligned with the Chinese government's economic sovereignty needs and development goals, and the economic sovereignty needs and developmental goals that the Chinese government is guided by and is implementing.

In any event, American companies wishing to participate and profit from China's economic development will have competitive advantages if they accept the possibility that the Chinese government is developing a brilliant alternate model of capitalism with Chinese characteristics that is not going to disappear soon. They might also benefit from examining the possibility that such an alternate Chinese model of capitalism may be sustainable. The evolving Chinese model of capitalism will adopt as much of America's model (and other nation's models of capitalism, i.e., Singapore) of capitalism as is prudent, and acceptable or optimum for China's economic sovereignty and sustained growth. It is unrealistic and imprudent to assume that China *can or must* simply mimic the American model of capitalism.

Such an evolving hybrid Chinese model of capitalism may have significant competitive advantages over American capitalism, which are not fully recognized by some observers yet, but will be very significant to American companies and the American economy in the decades ahead. For example, the financing structure of the CNOOC bid for Unocal, which was possible with China's model of capitalism, *will not be and is not possible* under the American model of capitalism and the capital structures that American companies, such as Chevron, have.

Building the Financial Service Sector in China

In Chapters 8 to 13, we will examine the opportunities, challenges, and the means available for foreign players and investors to participate in China's banking, insurance and reinsurance, stock markets, and venture capital businesses. In each business, we will provide an overview of the general market condition and the status of foreign participation and the means available in that business's regulatory environment in China for foreign players and investors. But we will focus on how American companies can align their fortunes with China's economic and social goals in win-win strategies, rather than zero-sum-game strategies that will not work, in dealing with a Permission Society that has the fastest growing and most competitive economy and largest developing market in the world.

8

Aligning American Companies' China Strategies with China's Financial Services Development Strategies

Overview

This chapter examines China's evolving financial services sector from the perspective of American companies selecting alignment strategies with the Chinese government and Chinese companies' needs. The Genuine Global Joint Venture Model is also considered in the context of the win-win development and integration of China's banking system into the global economy.

China's Economic Success Was Not Sustainable as a Zero-Sum Game

The Chinese government is protecting economic growth by restructuring the SOEs. Chinese and foreign purchasers will be allowed to acquire assets and opportunities at deep discounts in order to rapidly reengineer China's inefficient SOE-based economy with foreign intellectual and financial capital. The speed that this is to be accomplished reflects the decisiveness of

229

China's non-majority-rule decision-making system. The Chinese government made a courageous decision in 1998 to move away from the SOE system because it was not working. Many SOEs are being auctioned off to foreign and Chinese private interests pursuant to the Communist Party's new "He Who Invests Owns Policy."[1] It is the biggest and fastest economic restructuring in history, and resulted from hard decisions with short-term turmoil for medium- and long-term gain. The mosaic of Chinese and foreign acquisitions and joint ventures will, at an accelerating rate in 2005–2030, restructure the global and China's economies.

Foreign Companies' Zero-Sum-Game Strategies with Flawed Value Propositions Waste Critical Time

The Chinese government's decision to offer more attractive value propositions to foreign companies, such as joining the WTO, the "He Who Invests Owns" policy, and the sale of control of tens of thousands of SOEs and other imminent reforms,[2] offer major new opportunities. An American company that responds with win-win value propositions and finds creative strategies in dealing with its Chinese trading partners may have a more competitive "China strategy" than if the same company uses zero-sum-game value propositions and strategies.

Foreign companies without win-win China strategies may find in the coming years when the Chinese government is due to open China's domestic market to direct competition from non-Chinese companies, that they are the losers in a game of musical chairs. The seats worth having will be taken.

Financial Services Regulation: Preserving China's Economic Sovereignty

The Chinese government must naturally fear that allowing foreigners to acquire control of many of the tens of thousands SOEs will sacrifice China's economic sovereignty. They are concerned that Chinese companies will not be able to compete with foreign companies in China or internationally. The per capita assets of the top 500 Chinese enterprises are only 1.57% of those of the world's top 500 enterprises.[3] Chinese enterprises will soon have to compete with foreign funded enterprises at home and abroad. China's government has chosen to address these problems by speeding up the development of the joint stock mixed-ownership economy. Control of most SOEs is being sold to foreign and Chinese private interests so that Chinese companies will grow in scale and competitiveness.[4] However, the Chinese government will use this process to get the productivity, standard of living and other increases, from permitting foreign competition in China's domestic market, but shield Chinese companies from the full force of competition.[5] The Chinese government will retain control of the rules of the game in a "Permission Society" even when China is subject to the fuller impact of foreign companies competing with Chinese companies.

Primary Sources of Demand for Non-Chinese Financial Services Firms

The current Chinese financial system contains three major sections: banking, insurance, and securities market, with three regulatory authorities: CSRC: China Securities Regulatory Commission created in 1992, CIRC: China Insurance Regulatory Commission created in 1998, and CBRC: China Banking Regulatory Commission created in 2003.

The management challenge the Chinese government accepted was to privatize inefficient SOEs while not jeopardizing the economy in the process. The Chinese government plans to privatize step-by-step over 300,000 SOEs' assets that comprised 57.8% of the economy in 1978 and 32.8% in 2001. In 2002 the SOEs' assets were 65% business and 35% of non-profit, i.e., hospitals, schools, etc. 52.2% were

The charts below show the regulatory frameworks of china's financial services sector:

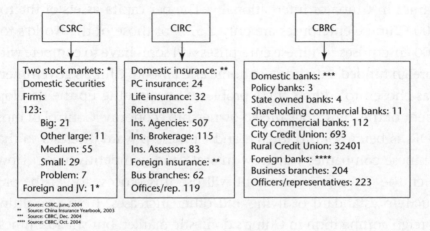

CSRC	CIRC	CBRC
Two stock markets: * Domestic Securities Firms 123: 　Big: 21 　Other large: 11 　Medium: 55 　Small: 29 　Problem: 7 Foreign and JV: 1*	Domestic insurance: ** PC insurance: 24 Life insurance: 32 Reinsurance: 5 Ins. Agencies: 507 Ins. Brokerage: 115 Ins. Assessor: 83 Foreign insurance: ** Bus branches: 62 Offices/rep. 119	Domestic banks: *** Policy banks: 3 State owned banks: 4 Shareholding commercial banks: 11 City commercial banks: 112 City Credit Union: 693 Rural Credit Union: 32401 Foreign banks: **** Business branches: 204 Officers/representatives: 223

*　Source: CSRC, June, 2004
**　Source: China Insurance Yearbook, 2003
***　Source: CBRC, Dec. 2004
****　Source: CBRC, Oct. 2004

owned by provincial and municipal governments and 57.8% by the National Government.[6] The Chinese government has not yet announced which of the 191 major SOEs that comprised 47.8% of the total SOE assets of US$1.36 trillion in 2001 that are owned by the Central government will be sold. Although unprofitable SOEs were one of the biggest problems in China's economic reform, the Chinese government has made tremendous change by restructuring, by public offerings of shares, and laying-off workers, without unmanageable social unrest. The total remaining SOE assets, especially their total profits, has increased despite Western observers' predictions. Some estimate that the private sector in China now constitutes 75% of the economic output and employment.[7]

Equity exchanges exist throughout China, and most have a membership structure and act as stock exchanges but are not regulated by CSRC, and trade on the basis of percentage of the total assets of an SOE rather than on the basis of the number of shares. For liquidity, some Equity Exchanges allow their members to trade as little as 0.5% of the total assets of the selling company. There are two types of exchanges, which since 2002 have tended to merge: Equity Exchanges from local governments used to sell SOEs and Technical Equity Exchange from local technology agencies used as an alternate mechanism for angel investors and venture capital firms to raise funds for high-tech start-ups or to exit from previous investments. In 2003, there were 97 Equity Exchanges with trading volume of over 650 billion RMB, of which eight had trading volumes above RMB 10 billion, and the Shanghai Exchange's trading volume of RMB 248 billion was 47.5% of the national total.

The Challenge of Aligning China's Strategy and an American Company's "China Strategy"

How can foreign companies profitably take advantage of the new phase of opportunities in China? We examine China's evolving financial system in this chapter, and then in the next four chapters, China's banking, insurance and reinsurance, stock exchanges, venture capital industries, and case studies of alignment opportunities between American companies' "China strategy" and "China's strategy."

Genuine Global Joint Ventures of Chinese and American Companies Can Help China's WTO Commitments Work Reciprocally for American and Chinese Companies

Nationalism and China's economic sovereignty requires the emergence of Chinese companies that can compete effectively in China's domestic market that WTO membership and other reforms help to create. In order for Chinese companies to be strong enough to compete in China's changing domestic market, Chinese companies must emerge that can compete successfully in the global market in many sectors.

We propose that American and Chinese companies consider the theoretically much more powerful Global Genuine Joint Venture

Model and the US Money Outside and Chinese Money Inside China Model. The value propositions of a global, rather than merely a domestic, China relationship between American and Chinese companies could bring a win-win paradigm shift in deal structures used. Unlike domestic joint venture and WFOE models typically used to date, these advanced models focus on successfully aligning China's strategy of economic development and global goals with foreign companies' China strategies. These advanced structures may, if successfully designed and deployed, present a sounder model, from both a foreign and Chinese perspective, than the usually used WFOE structure that does not include such critical alignment of interests, goals, and rewards of Chinese and American companies. The new models and advanced strategies and structures we present might provide a way for American companies with win-win mindsets to deal with some problems of doing business with a "Permission Society" bureaucracy and protectionism and in competing with wholly or partly state-owned Chinese companies.

In order for these advanced models and strategies to be more likely to work sustainably and profitably for all concerned, such genuine global joint ventures will have to be both genuine and global. The weakness of the domestic Joint Venture and WFOE models is that the foreign participants rapidly get past the apex of the curve of gratitude of the Chinese government. The advanced models and strategies we recommend will not work unless the Chinese government sees and sustains these models and strategies' merits and profitability in the real world. The business rationale in these models and strategies is that through their corporate structure of a global holding company outside China, in a politically and fiscally neutral jurisdiction, Chinese firms that are private or partly Chinese government-owned can participate in long-term global partnerships with foreign firms jointly owning a global holding company that receives profits from China's domestic market and the global market. That win-win approach can work if the Chinese government and American business leaders make it work.

The short, medium, and long-term success of such advanced models that seek to align and achieve both China's strategy and the China strategy of foreigners requires that all parties use a win-win approach. If any party uses a zero-sum-game approach, neither party will "win." In our view, if American and Chinese businesses cannot jointly prosper on a sustained and growing global basis as China's economic dominance develops, America and China will follow the path to trade war.

The success of such models enables the Chinese company chosen by its government to have the benefit of the foreign company's "know-how and know-who" so that it does not falter. It allows American business and political leaders to find and showcase a template of mutual success inside and outside China that zero-sum-game approaches by either are unlikely, if at all, going to provide.

The Genuine Global Joint Ventures with the US Money Outside and Chinese Money Inside China Model can and must be made to work profitably and sustainably by determined and resourceful American and Chinese partners. That can only occur with their full and genuine support on a daily basis by China's and America's business and political leaders. Chinese and American leaders can and must strive to prevent their failure for any number of a myriad of possible reasons. Chinese and American shareholders, management, staff, customers, suppliers, and service providers must be put in place that have and reward the abilities to make them work. Any individuals or participating companies must be replaced quickly and decisively if they do not successfully do so.

The Genuine Global Joint Venture Model, with or without the Foreign Money Outside and Local Money Inside Model, is a win-win approach to the search for strategies that fit emerging markets, is still a developing field in the business, and academic literature. The approach of many American companies to emerging markets often seeks to fine-tune zero-sum-game approaches to penetrating and dominating developing countries' economies.[8] A 2005 *Harvard Business Review* article stated:

> If Western companies don't develop strategies for engaging across their value chains with developing countries, they are unlikely to remain competitive for long. However, despite crumbling tariff barriers, the spread of the Internet and cable television, and the rapidly improving physical infrastructure in these countries, CEOs can't assume that they can do business in emerging markets the same way they do in developed nations. That's because the quality of the market infrastructure varies widely from country to country. In general, advanced economies have large pools of seasoned market intermediaries and effective contract-enforcing mechanisms, whereas less-developed economies have unskilled intermediaries and less-effective legal systems. Because the services provided by intermediaries either aren't available in emerging markets or aren't very sophisticated, corporations can't smoothly transfer the strategies they employ in their home countries to those emerging markets. During the past ten years, we've researched and consulted with multinational corporations all over the world. One of us led a comparative research project on China and India at Harvard Business School, and we have all been involved in McKinsey & Company's Global Champions research project. We have learned that successful companies work around institutional voids. They develop strategies for doing business in emerging markets that are different from those they use at home and often find novel ways of implementing them, too. They also customize their approaches to fit each nation's institutional context. As we will show, firms that take the trouble to understand the institutional differences between countries are likely to choose the best markets to enter, select optimal strategies, and make the most out of operating in emerging markets.[9]

The Genuine Global Joint Venture Model and US Money Outside And Chinese Money Inside China Models' successes, promotion, and proliferation are ways that a "Rights Society's" and a "Permission Society's" respective competitive advantages can be combined successfully in business in a "win-win" strategic game approach. Neither a "Rights Society," nor a "Permission Society," nor the needs and goals of American or Chinese companies, can reconcile locally and integrate globally on the zero-sum-game strategy approach. The very different "Rights Society" and "Permission Society" approaches, which work well respectively for America and China, cannot coexist prosperously and peacefully in the 21st century using zero-sum-game approaches. American and China's "ways of doing things" can integrate if win-win approaches are adopted and sustained in America and China's political and business leaderships' conduct. Since China's economy will become much larger than America's, a zero-sum-game approach is myopic.

China's Political and Business Leadership Must Help Genuine Global Joint Ventures Work

The Chinese government, as the regulator, a major shareholder, and a major customer of many of the leading Chinese companies, must help make Genuine Global Joint Ventures work and proliferate. It is in alignment with their strategy of using foreign financial capital, management skills, and technology to enrich Chinese companies and executives' business expertise, which is needed in the short and medium term to make China's economic success stable and to harness foreign "know-how" and "know-who" both inside and outside China.

9

Aligning American Companies with China's Banking Industry Goals

Overview

The Chinese government is strengthening China's banking industry by regulatory changes, recapitalizing it, and recruiting major foreign banking expertise through permitting investment in China's banks. But foreign ownership and participation will remain subject to the essential economic sovereignty and development goals and control of the Chinese government.

The Chinese Banking Industry

Foreign banks in China in 2005 owned a 1.9% market share according to a senior Chinese bank regulator. Over 160 foreign banks maintained branches or representative offices in China. Financial assets are concentrated in the banking system. Foreign banks have set up 225 branches and 240 representative offices with total assets of US$79.6 billion. They are trying to expand beyond their operations in the fast-growing coastal regions. In addition, 19 foreign institutions had bought stakes in 16 Chinese banks with an investment of nearly US$16.5 billion.[3] Chinese

Sources of Financing for Chinese Corporate/Government Projects 1

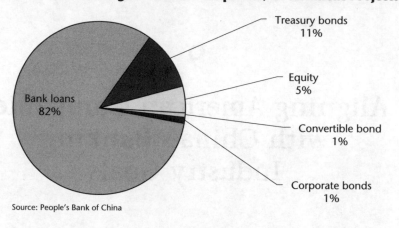

Treasury bonds
11%

Equity
5%

Convertible bond
1%

Bank loans
82%

Corporate bonds
1%

Source: People's Bank of China

2

In a League of its Own

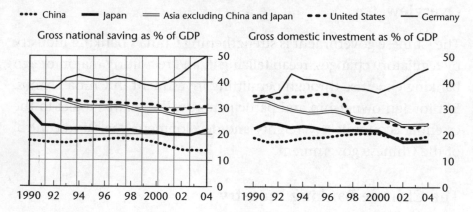

•••• China ▬ Japan ═ Asia excluding China and Japan ●●● United States ▬ Germany

Gross national saving as % of GDP   Gross domestic investment as % of GDP

banks have been enlisting strategic foreign investors to bring them cash and foreign expertise ahead of the opening of the banking industry expected in late 2006, when foreign lenders hope to access the vast Yuan business.

China has four large banks: The Industrial and Commercial Bank of China, the Bank of China (BOC), the People's Construction Bank of China, and The Agricultural Bank of China. China also has three "policy" banks: China Development Bank, The

Agricultural Development Bank, and The Export-Import Bank of China. In addition, over 90 city commercial banks representing approximately 4 to 5% of the domestic banking business, urban credit cooperative with approximately 5%, and rural credit cooperative and other small institutions with approximately 9%.

With China's accession to the World Trade Organization, Chinese banks are modernizing as fast as they can. The threat of increased foreign competition has forced the government, and some domestic banks, to pick up the pace of internal reform. First, the People's Bank of China (PBOC), the country's central bank, has been restructured to prevent SOEs from getting easy money. Previously, the PBOC was organized along the same lines as other central-government agencies, which meant that nearly every level of government across China had its own central-bank branch. This has created a unique dual-control problem in China. Not only must the PBOC branches follow the policies dictated by their head-quarters, they must also listen to the local government. This structural scheme makes the banks subordinated to the local government, and forces them to finance budget deficits and fund ailing SOEs. The central bank is shaped into nine regional branches. Because the rearrangement cuts across local party lines, the People's Bank will be able to better monitor the branches of the four state banks, which also faced pressure to supply credit to inefficient local state enterprises.

Reform of the SOEs themselves is seen to have a huge bearing on China's economic future. As much as 80% of the country's bank loans are to SOEs. Meanwhile, the truly private sector is getting less than 5% of bank lending. China's banks have billions of Yuan worth of bad loans to SOEs. The central government is seeking to balance their books by transferring bad debts to asset management corporations while making its banks function along commercial lines.

Another reform move by the Chinese government involves the creation of asset-management companies to take banks' bad debts and swap them for equity. The Chinese government has transferred hundreds of billions of dollars in bad debt out of the banking system and onto the balance sheets of government asset management companies. Outside China, when asset-management companies (AMCs) are created to take bad loans off overburdened banks, they take them at less than face value.

Some more enterprising Chinese banks, like the China Construction Bank and Industrial & Commercial Bank of China, are moving into fee-based businesses like insurance and fund management, seeking to sell financial products through their large branch networks. Meanwhile, state banks have started to lend more to the private sector and high-tech industries, areas they have traditionally ignored. In addition, Chinese banks are forming alliances with one another to sharpen competitiveness against foreign banks.

The central government is taking time to lift various restrictions on foreign banks that sharply curtail their ability to conduct business. While most foreign banks' competitiveness lies in their diversification, they, like the rest of domestic banks, have been restricted to core banking businesses in China such as lending, deposit taking, and transaction banking. Licenses were granted to foreign banks to have local currency business, all of which are in Shanghai and Shenzhen. An even smaller group is allowed to borrow from and lend to local banks.

Some Chinese banks with foreign investors are permitted to do local-currency business with Chinese clients. Foreign-currency business is limited to select cities. American financial institutions require approval, granted on a discretionary, case-by-case basis, for new representative offices and branches.

American financial institutions will gain controlled market access. China will allow internal branching and provide the same rights (national treatment) for all newly permitted activities. It will also expand the scope and geographic opportunities for foreign banks to conduct local currency business consistent with China's economic sovereignty.

Joint Venture Banking in China

On February 1, 2002, the "Regulations on Administration of Foreign-Invested Financial Institutions" were adopted by the State Council. The regulations govern the following financial institutions established and doing business in China, banks with foreign capital that have their head offices in China, finance companies with foreign capital that have their head offices in China, and finance companies operated in China as equity joint ventures by foreign financial institutions and Chinese companies or enterprises. The People's Bank of China is the responsible authority for the oversight of foreign-invested financial institutions.[4]

In spite of the increasing importance of the Chinese insurance industry and developing Chinese stock markets, the Chinese banking industry remains dominant. At the end of 2003, China's domestic banking system included three policy banks, four big state-owned banks, eleven shareholding commercial banks, 112 city commercial banks, 693 city credit unions, and 32,401 rural credit unions. Within the Chinese banking industry, the four major state-owned banks (Industrial and Commercial Bank of China, or ICBC; Agriculture Bank of China, or ABC; China Construction Bank, or CCB; and Bank of China, or BOC) are still the principal players. They controlled about 55% of the total Chinese bank assets. Even though their market share has been reduced from 62% at the end of 2001,[5] they collectively handle the direction of money flows inside China.

The Dominant Position of the Chinese Banking Industry in China's Economy

At the end of 2003, the total assets in the Chinese banking system was 27,639.45 billion RMB; the total assets of the Chinese insurance industry was 912.28 billion RMB; and total market capitalization in Chinese domestic securities market was 4,245.77 billion RMB, including the non-tradable and non-liquid state-owned shares and legal shares. The banking industry was still by far dominant, accounting for 84.3% of the Chinese financial industry. If we exclude legal shares and state shares, the total market size would be only 1,317.85 billion RMB. In that case, the insurance industry and the securities industry together only accounted for 7.5% and the banking industry was responsible for an amazing 92.5% of the total end-of-year financial assets. The dominant position of the banking industry inside the Chinese financial system is formidable in China's economy. The banking system, and therefore, the financial system, is not flexible and not efficient in the rapidly growing economy, where private sectors account for two-thirds of

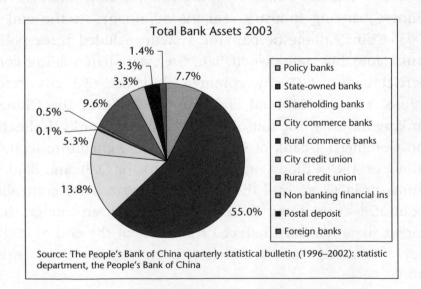

Total Bank Assets 2003

- 1.4%
- 3.3%
- 3.3%
- 7.7%
- 9.6%
- 0.5%
- 0.1%
- 5.3%
- 13.8%
- 55.0%

Legend:
- Policy banks
- State-owned banks
- Shareholding banks
- City commerce banks
- Rural commerce banks
- City credit union
- Rural credit union
- Non banking financial ins
- Postal deposit
- Foreign banks

Source: The People's Bank of China quarterly statistical bulletin (1996–2002): statistic department, the People's Bank of China

the total GDP, but only less than one-third of the total loans. The capital demand for the private sector is far more than its supply. Consequently, firms are actively seeking private sources of money, including venture capital.[6]

In July 2001, the Chinese government estimated that the total unofficial private placement finance reached 700 billion ¥uan.[7] In 2004, the total underground finance in urban areas represented an astonishing 28.7% of all legal and formal bank finance. The worst province was Heilongjiang with an estimated underground finance of more than half of the legal banking finance. The situation in the countryside was even worse. The curb-market rate in China was estimated at 11.6% in June of 2004.

Banking with Chinese Characteristics: Foreign Banks Vs. China's Control of China's Banking Industry

As seen, the mantra of western financial commentators are demands for the opening up of China's banking system and dire threats of China's banking system's internal collapse if China's government does not adopt a Western style-banking model.

That is not likely to be what happens. As mentioned, China is solving the non-performing loan problem by recapitalizing banks with money from its huge foreign currency reserves, brokering joint ventures or investments in leading Chinese banks by leading foreign banks, and restricting the access of foreign banks to China's market. Foreign banks are making inroads into China's domestic market, but the barriers to entry remain high. Foreign banks were only permitted to open one branch and two sub-branches every two years, must undergo qualification processes and demonstrate minimum number of years of profitability, and are limited in both the amounts of Yuan they may expatriate and in the range of products they can offer. Opening a branch or two a year, they will never be able to compete with The Bank of China, which has 11,000 branches nationwide.[8] The Chinese government's anxiety about an onslaught of major international financial institutions after China's WTO accession is reportedly easing. Foreign banking assets as a percentage of national totals dropped from 2.48% to 1.62% in 2004. Foreign banks have realized how hard it is to do business in China.[9]

Banking offers a classic example of the combination of preservation of China's economic sovereignty and competitive advantages China's government has in running a highly competitive "Socialist Market Economy." The Chinese government makes the rules in China and can change the rules in China. They could not do that if China becomes a "Rights Society" before Chinese business interests are able to compete inside and outside China with foreign companies. China will find its own form of market-oriented banking reforms. China will not simply adopt foreign banking models because countries that did suffered as a result in the 1997 Asian Financial Crisis.[10]

Premier Zhu Rongji's highly successful management of the reform of SOEs and the Asian Financial Crisis in 1997 was successful in spite of being very different from what the International Monetary Fund and other non-Chinese observers thought was required.[11]

China's Socialist Market Economy Capitalism will continue to have features and rules that are specially designed, used, and changed to protect China's sovereignty and economic development. Zhu Rongji used the tools of command and market economics to bring inflation down from 21.7% in 1994 to 1% by mid 2002, while maintaining an average 8% growth rate over the same period. Laurence Brahm has pointed out that Zhu Rongji:

> ... streamlined and rationalized China's banking and financial systems, taking on and closing down the investment and trust

companies, old bastions of an unregulated system in the early stages of transition. He steered China through the Asian financial crisis without devaluing the Yuan, strengthening the currency in the process. The reforms Zhu has overseen as Premier have involved reengineering the state-owned enterprises, cutting government bureaucracy by half, and replacing the 'iron rice-bowl' system with the framework of a modern social-security and insurance-based healthcare and pension system. Such reforms have involved more than structural changes and institutional capacity building. They have required the reengineering of Chinese society as a whole.

The execution of any International Monetary Fund or World Bank reform measures in Russia, Eastern Europe, Central Asia, Mongolia, Indonesia, South Korea, or any other transitional economy has received praise from Washington, D.C. and the predominantly pro-Western international media. However, one must ask honestly: how many of these reforms have been successful in carrying out economic structural capacity-building, raising lifestyles, invigorating these economies, and establishing social and political stability in these countries? It is hard to imagine the leader of any other country daring to take the political risks inherent in tackling economic and financial challenges on such a scale as China's. Yet, Zhu has done so and, arguably, succeeded. In doing so, he has ignored the formulas and sacrosanct IMF prescriptions for developing countries. Many of those who accepted the economic panacea proffered by Western academics have lived to regret it. Zhu, however, developed his own practical model suited to Chinese realities, his own theory for the 'managed marketization' of China's economy. And China's economy is all the stronger for it today.[12]

Since the American government politically blocked the CNOOC higher bid for Unocal because it did not want Chinese companies acquiring American publicly traded companies, America no longer has the moral authority to complain about China not opening up its financial service sector to American companies' domination.

10

Aligning American Companies with China's Insurance and Reinsurance Industry Goals

Overview

This chapter examines the advanced alignments of foreign companies' China strategies with China's economic development goals, which are being pioneered by Bermuda companies. American companies should emulate such alignment strategies. The developmental needs of China's nascent insurance and reinsurance industries and the challenges the Chinese government and Chinese companies face are examined. The competitive complexity and hurdles foreign companies face are examined so that the competitive advantages of win-win strategies aligned with the Chinese government's and Chinese companies' needs can be understood.

The Chinese Government's Needs in Rapidly Developing China's Insurance and Reinsurance Industries

In April 2004, a senior Chinese government policy maker told the regulators and executives of China's domestic insurance industry that the Chinese domestic insurance industry was comparable to England's in 1856 and that, with WTO entry, foreign insurance companies would be able to apply for national insurance licenses and compete with Chinese domestic insurers. Mr. We Dingfu of the Chinese Insurance Regulatory Commission then listed the problems Chinese insurance companies had, including that China's insurance companies had low investment returns, SOE- trained management, unautomated financial and claims data management, focused only on marketing and premium growth, unimaginative products, and widespread belief among Chinese that domestic Chinese insurance companies would not pay claims.

Under China's WTO responsibilities, foreign insurance companies can apply for full national licenses since 2006. How quickly the review and granting of such licenses takes may be a function of how well the Chinese government is assured that foreign companies will not take over China's domestic insurance market, perhaps putting China's weaker domestic insurance companies out of business, because of the foreign companies' greater experience, expertise, capital, product range, data processing and other advantages.

China's Insurance and Reinsurance Market Background

The People's Insurance Company of China (PICC) was created in 1949 after the nationalization of all insurance companies, and there was no domestic insurance until 1979. PICC had a monopoly until 1986, when a second license was issued to another SOE. In 1992, the first foreign insurer was licensed. The Chinese government did not use insurance products in China's planned economy social welfare system. But the reform of the SOEs, the social security system, health care, housing, etc. move social responsibility for related risks from the government to individuals and enterprises. In 1978, SOEs produced 80% of

China's industrial output, employment, and fixed investments. In 1998, those roles of SOEs had fallen to 40%, 45%, and 50% respectively.[1] This corresponded with the development of China's insurance industry.

It is still in its early stages and has attracted major foreign companies that see the combination of the opening up of China's insurance market, with a 1.3 billion population, with their national average of 40% of annual income savings rate, weak and inexperienced Chinese domestic insurance companies, as a profound opportunity for their growth. The issue is how soon that growth will occur and how much of China's insurance and reinsurance can foreign companies access and control. The gross premium volume in China has risen from US$1.6 billion[2] in 1986 to $48.6 billion in 2003, and was growing in 2004 at an annualized rate of 25% per year[3] and is rising. Foreign companies' share remains small at 2% and they are restricted from third-party automobile insurance, which constitute over 70% of non-life policies sold.[4]

The Chinese government is gradually removing itself from directly having the role of ultimate risk bearer. Under China's communist-planned economy, SOEs operated directly by government, provided lifetime welfare benefits including free housing, medical care, and pensions. As in other sectors of the economy, the Chinese government needs the expertise and capital of foreign insurance and reinsurance companies to help create China's 21st century insurance and reinsurance products and services. But the Chinese government does not want the foreign insurance and reinsurance companies to take over China's insurance and reinsurance industry which is vital to China's transitioning social security system so vital to China's stability, their leadership of the reform process, and China's economic sovereignty. The Chinese government's challenge is to create an effective insurance and reinsurance industry in China with foreign expertise and capital while maintaining control of that new industry.

Because China has been closed to foreign business and has 1.3 billion people, the Chinese government is able to attract the foreign expertise and capital to rapidly establish China's insurance and reinsurance industry as part of China's new social security system. As in other sectors of China's economy, it is unlikely that the Chinese government will voluntarily sacrifice China's economic sovereignty for economic development. The Chinese government's goals are to have China's insurance and reinsurance industry remain under the government's control and benefit Chinese enterprises, while effectively protecting China's people.

With such a large population, rapid-growing economy, and constant improvement of its people's living standard, the insurance industry in China thus enjoys tremendous market potential. Entering the 1990s, the Chinese insurance market initiated a limited opening up to the outside world with Shanghai and Guangzhou as the experimental basis. By the end of 1999, there were 26 insurance institutions in the whole insurance industry of China. Among them, 13 Chinese-solely-funded insurance companies, 9 foreign-funded insurance companies, and 4 joint ventures. By 1998 the insurance revenue of the Chinese insurance industry was 127.35 billion RMB Yuan, 16th in the world, with insurance coverage intensity 1.57 percent or the 77th in the world, and insurance coverage depth of 100 RMB Yuan 66th in the world. Thanks to the deepening reform and effort of the policy implementation of expanding the social security industry, the insurance industry of China enjoys fast growth. According to an estimate made by the China Insurance Supervisory Commission, the growth rate of the market size of China's insurance industry would reach an annual average of 12 percent in 5 years, and the insurance revenue reached 280 billion

RMB Yuan by the end of 2005, with insurance coverage density (insurance premium per capita) of 2.3 percent and insurance coverage depth of 230 Yuan.

On the date of China's accession to WTO, the Chinese government granted seven foreign insurance companies permission to form joint ventures or set up branches in China and issued them licenses to conduct various insurance businesses in this mass market. Seven insurance licenses were issued in one day. This sought to indicate the government's determination to realize the promises in the WTO agreement. A number of international insurance companies had been preparing for such an opportunity for many years. The number of foreign insurance companies operating in the China market has exceeded the domestic companies since 2004. China will become the biggest market for life and non-life insurance products and services. However, the situation in the China market is very complicated. The heavy government regulations and restraints, the big gaps between eastern and western China, and different customer and organizational behavior are some examples. Foreign and domestic insurance companies need to design and develop products and services to fulfill the special needs and suit the special environment in China.

China's Insurance Industry Growth

The Chinese insurance industry is one of the fastest growing sectors in the Chinese economy. Insurance premiums in China increased 32%, 44.8%, and 27% in 2001, 2002, and 2003. By the end of 2004, the total insurance premium in China reached 431.81 billion Yuan, and the total assets of the Chinese insurance industry reached 1.18 trillion Yuan. Given the tremendous growth in the market, the industry itself is still very young and far from developed. The insurance density was only US$35.3, compared with countries like Switzerland with US$5,660.3, and the United Kingdom with US$4,058.5. China has a long way to go. Even if we exclude the population factor, the Chinese insurance industry is still at a very low level. The insurance penetration ratio (the percentage of total insurance premium over GDP) was only 3.33 (%) compared with UK 13.37 and Switzerland 12.74. By 2003, there were 61 insurance companies in China, including 24 domestic companies and 37 foreign ones, and 5 reinsurance companies. Among the 46 biggest insurance companies in the Fortune 500 in 2003, 27 of them had already established subsidiary companies or branches inside mainland China. In addition to the insurance companies, there were 503 insurance agencies, 115 insurance brokerage firms, and 83 insurance assessor firms. On December 11, 2006, the WTO grace period for the Chinese insurance was over, and the industry had to completely open its door to the foreign competitors. The Chinese insurance market is going to be more and more attractive for the foreign investors.

China's insurance industry brought in $19.27 billion in premiums in 2000, an increase of 14.5 percent over 1999, according to the China Insurance Regulatory Commission (CIRC). Total income from premiums topped US$20 billion in 2001. By 2005, the total value was expected to constitute 2.3 percent of the total gross domestic product value. The average premium per person was $27.78. But despite its rapid growth, the insurance industry is still only a small part of the entire economy—less than 2 percent—compared with 11 percent in Japan and 8 percent in the United States. The total assets of China's insurance companies reached $40.75 billion, an increase of 14.5 percent over 1999. Of this, $7.23 billion, or 37.5 percent, of the total premium income came from property insurance. This marks a 14.8 percent increase over 1999. US$3.69 billion was paid out to insured property claims, or 51.1 percent of property insurance premiums. Life insurance income increased 14.4 percent to $12.05 billion, accounting for 62.5 percent of the total premium income, and $2.68 billion was paid out against life insurance claims.

By 2000, 17 foreign insurance companies had been granted permission to operate some form of insurance business in China, and 89 firms had set up representative offices waiting for permission to establish their own insurance operations in China. With China's WTO membership, however, this figure is expected to jump dramatically. On accession, the Chinese government indicated it will initially approve licenses for seven European companies, two Japanese companies, one South Korean company, and three United States companies. China's insurance market is characterized by its small size relative to its potential future size, a limited variety of insurance products, relatively high costs, lack of Chinese consumer education about the role of insurance, and a lack of a rule of law environment, particularly in the area of enforcement. Another factor in the growth of the insurance industry is that China's undeveloped financial markets limit investment vehicles for insurance premiums. A second factor is China's memories of its pre-1949 experience of foreign domination and control of its insurance industry. Analysts say foreign companies will need to do thorough due diligence before entering the market, then build up long-term relations with Chinese local governments and potential consumers. They also will need to develop business plans that prepare their companies to be long-term players.[5]

The China Insurance Regulatory Commission estimated that in the next five years, the annual growth rate of the Chinese insurance industry will be sustained at about 12 percent. The Beijing-based China Mainland Marketing Research Co. in 2001 surveyed residents of Beijing, Shanghai, and 20 other cities about insurance. The categories of insurance policies most commonly held by the urbanites surveyed were pension insurance, medical insurance, and life insurance, held by 17.4 percent, 15 percent, and 14 percent, respectively. The percentage of those with insured property was comparatively low. Only 3 percent of those surveyed held policies on personal property, and only 1.7 percent held auto insurance policies. The survey also shows a dramatic increase in the number of families in the low and average income brackets who hold insurance policies. Thirty-eight percent of families with monthly incomes lower than $120.77 and 40 percent of families with monthly incomes from $120.78 to $241.55 bought insurance in 2000. Forty-three percent of families with monthly incomes between $241.56 and $362.32 bought insurance, and the figure for families with monthly incomes greater than $362.32 was 44 percent.

The People's Congress is considering new rules that continue the prohibition of property insurers carrying on life insurance business, but with the permission of the relevant regulatory agencies, property insurers may engage in short-term medical insurance and casualty (accidental death) insurance.

The CIRC is increasingly allowing China's insurance funds to invest in securities investment funds. For example, Ping An Insurance Company of China, New China Life Insurance Company and the Manulife-Sinopec Life Insurance Co have been allowed to invest all their revenues from "premium unit-linked products" in securities funds. Unit-linked products are a category of life insurance product where premium income is invested and returns go to policy holders. Until recently, no more than thirty percent of these funds could be invested in the securities market. The bulk was invested in bank deposits, treasury bonds, corporate bonds, and inter-bank loans.

The Chinese insurance industry is not earning significant interest on these assets as Western insurance and reinsurance companies typically do as an essential part of their business models.

The Chinese government faces a major challenge in creating effective "for profit" executives in China's emerging insurance and reinsurance industry. In 2005, China's insurance industry earned only a 3.6% return on assets. But the Chinese government removed restrictions preventing insurance companies from investing in banks and also is encouraging infrastructure investments by insurance companies.[6]

Problems Facing China's Insurance and Reinsurance Industry

Like the banking industry, China's insurance industry will face adjustment challenges from joining the WTO. Most life insurance companies in the country have payout obligations that are significantly greater than their current return on investments. The industry is dominated by a few companies. Shortages of actuaries and professional insurance management staff have contributed to poor business practices. In quality of service and business skills, the country's insurance companies lag behind international ones. Domestic insurance companies will have to make serious efforts at adopting international business and prudent practices so that they can adjust to the international competition.

The Chinese government has several concerns. The industry might be subjected to unsound cutthroat domestic competition. Some domestic companies have sold large quantities of expensive fixed-interest-rate insurance policies at the peak of business operations. But since assuming these policies, the government has cut bank savings interest rates seven times. The resulting spread in margin losses threatens the viability of local companies, and some economists say the potential losses could trigger an insurance reimbursement crisis—posing the most severe challenge the industry has ever had to face. It has been estimated that the spread in margin losses alone could cost the insurance industry as much as US$6.04 billion, against total assets of US$40 billion.

Others fear that the biggest challenge posed by the increased presence of foreign companies to Chinese insurers isn't so much in gaining business as in winning consumer confidence. A survey conducted by Horizon Research showed that 51 percent of the respondents favored foreign insurance companies even though most of them had had little experience with foreign insurers. The reason appeared to be due to mistrust, specifically a fear that Chinese insurers might defraud them.

China's insurance industry has its own list of complaints. For example, the government limits the use of insurance funds to control risk, which has reduced the rate of insurance investment returns. In order to expand, the industry needs to standardize and rationally expand operations by offering new insurance products and by taking advantage of investment returns that are better than the world's average.

The market of financial services in China will be further opened up in the years to come. Given the wealth generation and the lack of well-developed service providers, the potentials are enormous. But the challenge is how to limit the risk and make the most of the potential benefits.

The inefficiency of Chinese domestic capital markets is one major factor seen by observers to be holding back China's economic development. But the international capital markets support of the global expansion of Chinese companies may exceed the direct foreign investments China raised from foreign sources in the past 25 years. Examples in 2003 are the US$3.5 IPO billion of China Life[7] and in 2004 the US$3 billion

Ping An Life's IPO.[8] Ping An Insurance Group announced a net income increase in the first half of 2005 of 49% of which 83% came from Ping An. London-based HSBC Holdings PLC owns a 19.9% stake in the company. Ping An said its investment returns had surged by 69% as the net rate of return on the investments increased. "Ping An has done very well in terms of trimming the losses on its equity investment and allocating more assets to higher-return bond investments," said one capital market analyst. China Life was part of a Chinese-government-owned insurance company that was reorganised into three parts before China Life's IPO. Ping An is the first privately-owned Chinese insurance company. These are the first of many IPO and subsequent equity and debt offerings by Chinese companies in and outside China that can raise the huge amounts of capital needed to redefine the global economy sooner than many anticipate.

Against this background, we will consider how two foreign reinsurance companies have sought to assist the Chinese government and insurance companies. In doing so these companies, relatively unknown in China, have quickly distinguished themselves among the plethora of foreign companies coveting major roles in China's evolving financial services sector.

Alignment Opportunity: China's Insurance and Reinsurance Industries' Needs

The Chinese government needs these problems remedied quickly so that foreign insurers do not completely take over the nascent Chinese domestic insurance industry. But how will the Chinese government take an SOE industry and turn it into a "for profit" industry? How can the Chinese government and insurance regulators quickly train SOE executives to be for-profit managers in increasingly publicly listed companies?

Case Study: The China Bermuda Society's 2004 Chinese Executive Education Initiative

The Chinese government, insurance regulators, and executives are struggling to rapidly upgrade Chinese insurance management techniques. In February 2004, the Co-chairs of the China Bermuda Society, John Milligan-Whyte and Dai Min, recognized the desire of foreign insurance and reinsurance companies to enter the China market and the management challenges facing the Chinese government in developing that market. They saw how a foreign reinsurance company's "China strategy" could be aligned with China's urgent need. They developed a plan for a very sophisticated insurance executive education program to teach Western insurance management techniques needed to achieve the development goals of China's insurance and reinsurance companies. They then convinced a Bermuda reinsurance company, XL Capital, to accept their proposal that it sponsor an executive education program designed to meet the needs of Chairmen, CEOs, and CFOs of China's property and casualty companies. XL Capital was incorporated in 1987 and had grown rapidly into one of the most innovative and successful reinsurance companies in the world.

The proposal John Milligan-Whyte and Dai Min made to XL Capital aligned the foreign company's "China strategy" with "China's strategy" in developing its insurance and reinsurance executives. Dai Min recruited Professor Liu of Remnin University and Professor Zhang, Chairman of the Insurance Department of Remnin University. Jerry de St Paer, XL Capital's CFO and Honorary Chairman of the China Bermuda Society, approached Jerry Rosenbloom and Neil Dohorty of Wharton's School of Insurance and Risk Management, America's most respected senior executive education insurance department, with the proposal that professors from Wharton and Remnin

University and executives from XL Capital teach the program. A dinner was held at the Great Hall Of China in April 2004 honoring XL Capital. The China Insurance Industry Executive Leadership Program was announced by XL Capital in March 2006. The program was developed in conjunction with the Aresty Institute of Executive Education at the Wharton School of the University of Pennsylvania and co-sponsored by the Guofa Capital Market Research Center, and is the first Sino-Foreign insurance leadership course endorsed by CIRC.[9]

Sponsoring the program "with the right spirit" provides a strategic opportunity for a reinsurance company that was not known in China. The foreign reinsurance company was able to immediately acquire strategically valuable recognition, respect, and gratitude from China's insurance regulators and also, through such an executive education program, from the top executives of the major Chinese insurance companies. From the perspective of a foreign company, how else could it quickly and effectively distinguish itself from other foreign competitors seeking footholds in China other than by earning respect and gratitude in China by exhibiting the "right spirit" and aligning the foreign company's enlightened "China strategy" with "China's strategy" of developing its insurance and reinsurance industries?

Case Study: ACE Education Program for China's Insurance Regulators

On its own initiative, a major Bermuda company, ACE, created an education program for Chinese insurance regulators in 2004. This is another example of a foreign company adding value to its China strategy by helping Chinese regulators with challenges the Chinese government has in building an advanced insurance and reinsurance regulatory system and industry.

The April 6, 2004 Dinner at the Great Hall Of The People in honor of XL Capital's support for the China Insurance Executive Leadership Program.

XL Capital recruited the Aresty Institute of Executive Education at Wharton School of the University of Pennsylvania to help develop the China Insurance Industry Leadership Program.

Case Study: Ace-Huatai Joint Venture in China

ACE Limited (NYSE: ACE) was incorporated in Bermuda in 1987 and grew rapidly into one of the most successful, innovative, and largest reinsurance companies in the world. In 2002, ACE entered into a strategic partnership with Huatai Insurance Company of China, seeking to perform a leadership role in China's growing property/casualty insurance market. Huatai was formed in 1996 by 63 sponsoring shareholders representing China's premier companies. Huatai provides a diversified product line including commercial and personal property, automobile, liability, oil and gas, marine hull and cargo, and aviation. In 2002, Huatai had branches in Beijing, Tianjin, Shanghai, Nanjing, Shenzhen, Oingdao, Dalian, and Guangzhou; and had been approved by the China Insurance Regulatory Commission to open another 18 branches and 22 sub-branches. By December 31, 2002, Huatai had total assets of approximately US$600 million and total premium of US$77 million, a 34% increase over the previous year. ACE acquired 22% of Huatai's outstanding shares for total consideration of approximately US$150 million. ACE and Huatai can leverage ACE's extensive product range, access to global investment capability, and sophisticated underwriting and Huatai's extensive, high-quality customer base and seasoned local management expertise to create a strong platform for growth. This alignment of ACE's and Huatai's China strategy and need for foreign management and investment expertise fell short of a Genuine Global Joint Venture, but was an advanced and intelligent structure that enables ACE nationwide access to China and the fastest growing and largest market in the world.[10]

The Competitive Advantages of a Win-Win Strategy Aligned with China's Needs

The competitive and regulatory challenges examined below that face a foreign company without a win-win China strategy aligned with the Chinese government and Chinese companies' needs are greater than the competitive and regulatory challenges facing the same company if it had a win-win China strategy aligned with the Chinese government and Chinese companies' needs.

Competitive Overview of Foreign Insurance and Reinsurance Companies in China

Being a "good corporate citizen" is especially important in China. American companies with "the right spirit" that assist the Chinese government in meeting its goals for China's insurance industry can distinguish themselves among a plethora of competitors. America licenses and regulates insurance companies on a state basis. China carries that licensing limitation even further. For example, Prudential PLC recently received a new city license in Jinan in Eastern China. Prudential PLC says its life insurance joint venture in China, CITIC Prudential Life, has been awarded a life insurance license for the capital city in Shandong Province. The license is Prudential's first in Shandong, which will complement its successful operations in nearby Beijing, Jiangsu and Shanghai. It took AIG, with Hank Greenberg's intense and relentless albeit patient effort, decades to get its first insurance license in China. In addition to such regulatory hurdles, the competition for the right to sell insurance in China is fierce.

A 2005 Swiss Study[11] included the following analysis of competition among foreign insurance and reinsurance companies in China:

The insurance industry in China: a highly concentrated market–until now

For a long time, the Chinese insurance market was not an issue for foreign companies. It was only in 1992 that AIG managed to gain a foothold in China and obtain a license to establish an insurance company. The life insurance provider AIA that AIG then set up remains the only player in China that is fully controlled by a foreign parent. It has been able to gain a market share of approx. 2%. Other foreign groups have bought into domestic players, though their stakes have not been allowed to exceed 24.9%.

Domestic Companies	Number of Branches	Strategic Foreign Investors
China Life Insurance	35	
Ping An	35	Dai-Ichi Life
		Goldman Sachs*
		HSBC*
		Morgan Stanley*
China Pacific	32	none
New China Life	29	Meiji Life
		Zurich Financial
Services		
Minssheng Life	4	none
Sino Life	4	Millea Group
Taikang Life	23	Winterthur
Taiping Life	15	Fortis

Source: Milliman Global Insurance, July 2004, Swiss Re sigma 51200, PWC Insurance Digest
*HSBC plans to acquire stakes in Ping An currently held by Goldman Sachs and Morgan Stanley, raising its holding to 19.9%

China's WTO entry will change this limit, however. Since 11 December 2004, all geographic restrictions are lifted, and foreign companies can apply for national licenses.

Foreign Insurers

Company	Market Share* Operation in:
AIU	0.35% Shanghai, Guangzhou, Shenzen
Ming An	0.21% Shenzen, Haikou
Tokio Marine & Fire	0.09% Shanghai
Winterthur	0.04% Shanghai
Samsung	0.03% Shanghai

Foreign Insurers (*Continued*)

Company	Market Share* Operation in:
Royal & Sun Alliance Plc	0.03% Shanghai

Mitsui Sumitomo	0.03% Shanghai
BoC	0.02% Shanghai
Chubb Insurance	0.01% Shanghai
Liberty Mutual	n.a. n.a.
Allianz	n.a. n.a.
Sompo-Japan Insurance Inc.	n.a. n.a.
Federal Insurance	n.a. n.a.

Source: Milliman Global insurance, July 2004, Swiss Re sigma 5/2004; *market share in 2002

Many foreign companies have opted to enter the Chinese market by way of joint ventures:

Foreign (joint venture)	Number of Branches	Foreign Partners
AIA	8	AIG (100%)
Aegon - CNOOC	1	Aegon (50%)
Allianz Dazhong	1(3 planned)	Allianz (51%)
Aviva - COFCO	1(3 planned)	Aviva (50%)
Axa - Minmetals	2	Axa (51%)
China Life CMG	1	CMG (49%)
Cigna & CMC	1	Cigna (50%)
CITIC Prudential	2	Prudential UK (50%)
Citi (Travelers)	1	Citigroup
CNP	0	CNP
Generali China	2	Generali (50%)
Haier New York Life	1	New York Life (50%)
Heng An Standard	1	Standard Life (50%)
ING Capital	1	ING (50%)
John Hancock Tianan	1	John Hancock (50%)
Manulife Sinochem	3	Manulife (51%)
Nissay SVA	1	
Pacific - Aetna (ING)	2	Aetna (ING) (50%)
Sino-US MetLife	1	MetLife
Skandia-BSAM	1	Skandia (50%)
Sun Life Everbright	2	Sun Life (50%)

Source: Milliman Global Insurance, July 2004; Swiss Re Sigma 5/2004, PWC Insurance Digest

China's life insurance market continues to be dominated by major national players: China Life, Ping An and China Pacific retain a share of over 90% in the market. Yet the reason why so many companies are nevertheless pushing into China is obvious: The expected market growth is so attractive that international companies active in rather saturated markets do not want to miss this business opportunity.

An international comparison also makes apparent the deficit in life-insurance products, even if the upside potential in terms of penetration (insurance premiums as a percentage of GDP) does not look all too attractive. This impression can be countered, however, by the argument that GDP is expected to continue to grow strongly. Moreover, there simply is no federal pension system in China at the moment, which leaves tremendous room for private pension funds)

Comparison Life Business 2003

Country/Region	Penetration	Density*
China	2.30%	25.1
Japan	8.38%	2'927.9
U.S.	4.38%	1'661.4
U.K.	8.97%	2'724.9
Switzerland	7.43%	3'290.6
Europe	4.65%	729.3
Asia	5.67%	138.4
*USD premium per capita		

Source: Swiss Re Sigma 5/2004, 3/2004; Penetration = Premiums/GDP

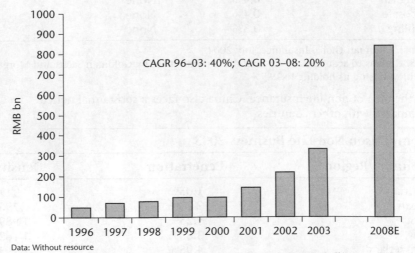

China's life insurance: Gross premiums written

CAGR 96–03: 40%; CAGR 03–08: 20%

Data: Without resource
Source: Boston Consulting Group: Building Professionalism - The next step for insurance in China

At the moment, it is hard to predict which distribution channels will ultimately dominate. Yet bancassurance activities have already gained influence. According to the China Insurance Development Report 2004, bancassurance revenues rose from near zero to almost USD12 billion. This is also the likely reason why HSBC recently announced plans to increase its holding in Ping An, China's second-largest life insurer, to 19.9% by acquiring stakes from Goldman Sachs and Morgan Stanley.

The picture is largely the same in non-life insurance. Local players continue to dominate the market as well, with the three biggest providers controlling over 90% of the market. The clear leader, PICC, is losing market share but continues to dominate about 70% of the market.

Company	Market Share	Strategic Foreign Investors
PICC	70.5%	AIG (9.9%)
CPIC Property	13.1%	none
Ping An Property	10.6%	HSBC (10%)*
		Morgan Stanley (6.8%)*
		Goldman Sachs (6.8%)*
		Dai-ichi(1%)
Huatai	1.0%	Ace (22.1%)
Tianan	0.9%	None
Sinosure	0.7%	None
China United	0.7%	None
Da Zhong	0.7%	None
Yong An	0.4%	None
Sinosafe	0.4%	None
TaiPing	0.3%	None

Source: Milliman Global Insurance, July 2004
*HSBC plans to acquire stakes in Ping An currently held by Goldman Sachs and Morgan Stanley, raising its holding to 19.9%

In the area of non-life insurance, China also faces a substantial deficit compared with other countries.

Comparison Non-Life Business 2003

Country/Region	Penetration	Density*
China	1.03%	11.2
Japan	2.28%	795.2
U.S.	5.25%	1'989.7
U.K.	3.83%	1'162.4
Switzerland	4.95%	2'193.3
Europe	3.20%	500.9
Asia	1.82%	44.5
*USD premium per capita		

Source: Swiss Re sigma 5/2004, 3/2004; Penetration = Premiums/GDP

The following factors play a decisive role in creating demand for non-life insurance:
• A positive GDP development
• Risk awareness (general liability can only be conducted to limited degree so far)
• Compulsory insurance (e.g. motor liability insurance only became compulsory on a national level as of 1 May 2004)
• Exposure to natural catastrophes (Swiss Re estimates that China suffered some 25% of the global economic losses that resulted from natural catastrophes between 1994 and 2003). Yet of these 25%, the insurance industry helped cover less than 1%)

The distribution of premiums therefore comes as somewhat of a surprise compared with more developed insurance markets.

CHINA: NON-LIFE PREMIUM SPLIT 2002   12

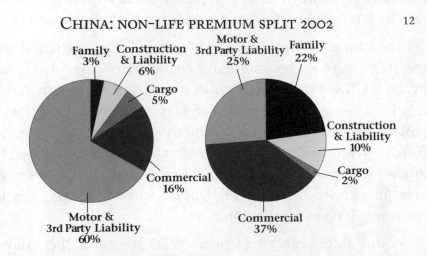

Family 3%
Construction & Liability 6%
Cargo 5%
Commercial 16%
Motor & 3rd Party Liability 60%

Motor & 3rd Party Liability 25%
Family 22%
Construction & Liability 10%
Cargo 2%
Commercial 37%

The results of the non-life insurance industry, the combined ratios (combination of non-life claims ratio and expense ratio), appear to be favorable in an historical comparison. A Swiss Re study showed that the combined ratios consistently were below 100% between 1999 and 2002, with the lowest level, 93%, reached in 2002. It is doubtful whether this favorable development will be upheld in the future.

For one, even China's business mix should see a shift toward segments that traditionally have a higher combined ratio (e.g. general liability). What's more, insuring natural catastrophes is bound to become increasingly important also in China, which will make results more volatile, From this point of view, it will be key for the national Chinese competitors to have adequate capital resources at their disposal. It remains to be seen when exactly the national watchdog CIRC will indeed step up pressure on these companies. International actuary Milliman believes that timing one's market entry will be more essential for financial success than being first to market. (Milliman, Global Insurance, July 2004).

Against this competitive background, an American company facing Chinese insurance regulatory framework without a win-win China strategy aligned with China's developmental needs is at a competitive disadvantage.

China's Insurance Regulatory Discretion

There is a lot of room for discretion affecting foreign companies' participation in China's economic development in China's insurance regulatory framework. A high-quality value proposition for China offered by a foreign company is a competitive advantage.

The China Insurance Regulatory Commission is charged with the oversight of foreign-invested insurance companies. As required by the GATS Service Schedule on accession to WTO, foreign life and non-life insurers, and insurance brokers, were to be permitted to provide services in Shanghai, Guangzhou, Dalian, Shenzhen, and Foshan. Within two years of accession, foreign life and non-life insurers and insurance brokers will be permitted to provide services in Beijing, Chengdu, Chongqing, Fuzhou, Suzhou, Xiamen, Ningbo, Shenyang, Wuhan, and Tianjin.

Within three years after China's WTO accession, there should be no geographic restrictions. Foreign non-life insurers should be permitted to establish as a branch or as a joint venture with 51% foreign ownership. Within two years after China's accession, foreign non-life insurers should be permitted to establish as a wholly-owned subsidiary, i.e., with no form of establishment restrictions. Upon accession, foreign life insurers should be permitted 50% foreign ownership in a joint venture. According to the GATS Service Schedule, internal branching for an insurance firm will be permitted as geographic restrictions phase out. The minimum registered capital for an insurance equity joint venture and a wholly foreign-owned insurance company is RMB 200 million, or the equivalent in a freely convertible currency. The minimum registered capital must be actually paid in. The capital contributions of the foreign insurance company must also be made using a freely convertible currency. Branches of foreign insurance companies must have operating funds of an amount equivalent to RMB 200 million in a freely convertible currency allocated by the head office without requiring compensation from the branch. The CIRC may increase the above minimum amounts based on the foreign-invested insurance company's business scope and scale of operations.

The "Regulations of the People's Republic of China on Administration of Foreign-Invested Insurance Companies" came into force on February 1, 2002. These regulations replace the older regulations and operate in combination with other regulations. Where these regulations are silent regarding administration of foreign-invested insurance companies, the Law of the People's Republic of China on Insurance, as well as other relevant laws and administrative regulations and other relevant state regulations apply. These regulations apply to insurance companies operated in China by foreign insurance companies, together with Chinese companies or enterprises on a joint equity basis; foreign-capital insurance companies in China invested in, and operated by, foreign insurance companies ("wholly foreign-owned insurance companies"); and branches in China of foreign insurance companies ("branches of foreign insurance companies").

A foreign insurance company, wholly foreign-owned insurance company, or branch of foreign insurance company, that applies to establish a foreign-invested insurance company must have at least thirty years of experience in carrying on insurance business; a representative office in China that has been established for at least two years; at a minimum, assets for the year preceding the application, of US$5 billion; must be subject to effective regulation by the competent authorities of the applicant's home country; must meet the solvency standards of the

applicant's home country; the applicant's home country authorities must agree to the application; and the applicant must
meet other regulations that can and will be introduced by the
CIRC in China's Permission Society context.

11

China's Stock Markets

Overview

China's domestic stock markets, introduced in the early 1990s as a cautious, controlled experiment, have quickly grown to an impressive size. With a combined market capitalization of approximately \$600 billion,[1] China's equity markets are now the Asia-Pacific's second largest after Japan and dwarf all other emerging markets in Asia, Latin America, and Eastern Europe. Despite their infancy, the markets have played a unique role in China's economic transformation. They have served as catalysts for corporate restructuring, turning many chronically inefficient state-owned enterprises into modern, profit-driven corporations. More than 1,200 companies are listed on the domestic exchanges in Shanghai and Shenzhen (and another 120 or so are listed in Hong Kong and New York).[2] However, American companies should recognize that Chinese government control of the access to debt and equity capital is likely to remain a key focus of public policy in China as the various components of China's financial services and capital markets are designed and deployed.

China's Capital Markets

Companies of global significance such as China Mobile, Unicom, and PetroChina have fundamentally altered China's corporate and investment landscape. Corporate governance, a concept totally alien to the Chinese public just a few years ago, has now become the buzzword in Chinese boardrooms, the media, and in the hallways of regulatory authorities. Long indulged in the "soft-budget constraint" of central planning, many of China's listed firms are for the first time under pressure to achieve a better return on equity. China has $200 billion of assets to monetize, which could mean about $10 billion a year in equity deals during the next 10 years[3] or much more.

Although the second board for emerging companies was delayed due to the crash of NASDAQ, there are a reported 450 companies waiting for listing on the Hong Kong Stock Exchange as an alternative. Hundreds more are waiting to be listed on the Shanghai and Shenzhen markets.

Capital Raised in China's Stock Market

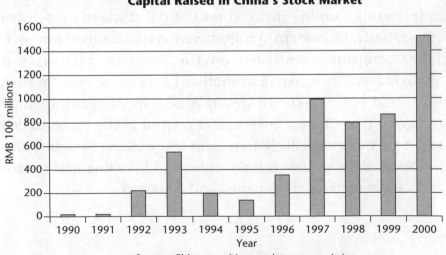

Source: China securities regulatory commission

Structural Problems and Constraints in China's Current Capital Markets

However, the markets created by the central government as an alternative funding conduit from centralized banking lending have constraints and structural defects. Many such problems have been identified and are either corrected or are in the process of being identified and rectified. It remains worthwhile to point them out as they represent both risks and opportunities for foreign companies.

First, the initial quota listing system and related corruption in obtaining such quota flouted a free and efficient market place directing resources to the most efficient use. Many companies got listed, not on the strength of their earning power, but on political connections and their ability to get approval. Therefore, initially, many companies that should not have been financed were the first batch to benefit from public investment as the investment opportunities were limited, in view of the quota

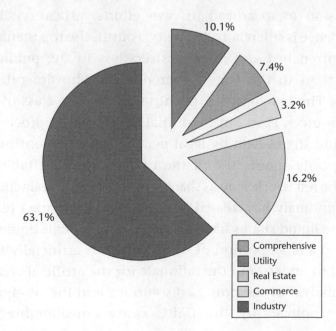

system, causing a waste of social resources. This in turn has given rise to accounting irregularities those under-performing companies use to overstate their earnings and manipulate their stocks. The China Securities Regulatory Commission (CSRC) has abandoned the quota system. However, it will be a few years before the skewed market restores its inherent integrity. There is a very urgent need to completely set the listing process free so that the market can operate, as it should, channeling limited social resources to the most efficient and deserving users. Second, the pool of listed companies does not represent the real market and is overly concentrated in a few sectors. The companies listed are largely dominated by state-owned enterprises and in the manufacturing sector. This in turn gives rise to problems for asset managers in terms of risk diversification and investment choices. Third, investors' rights are not adequately protected in terms of regulatory enforcement and private legal actions. Although the situation is improving with the hiring by the CSRC of the head of the enforcement division of the Hong Kong Stock and Futures Commission to spearhead its own efforts, private civil action jurisprudence is still relatively scanty. Fourth, the top management is too entrenched and often answers less to the public shareholders than to the largest shareholders who are often state agencies. The management talent, as a separate class of mobile social resources, is still in the initial development process. Fifth, the illiquid shares held by legal persons and state entities; are a problem only about 30% of the total market capitalization is liquid. The rest is locked up as shares not eligible for public circulation.

This anomaly has created a very dangerous market feature in which the liquid shares have an unreasonably high liquidity premium and a large portion of social wealth is artificially trapped. It is hard to understand the rationale for the artificial creation of this anomaly. But the proposed solutions and the on-again and off-again policies by the CSRC cause considerable market instability. The Chinese government has realized that all these trapped shares need to be freed up or they will limit the viability of the capital market. There exists enormous potential for foreign companies in solving these problems.

Investment Banking Legal Framework

The investment banking market was largely closed to foreign investors and banks. Prior to the commitment made under WTO membership, there was only one foreign investment bank which had only a limited operation in China. Morgan Stanley entered into a joint venture as a minority partner with China Construction Bank under the name of China International Capital Corporation (CICC) mainly engaged in deal origination for offshore securities offerings. CICC had been issued the license to engage in domestic investment banking activities. Under the WTO agreement, China has agreed to further open up the investment banking and brokerage businesses to foreign investors, allowing 33% of equity ownership to be gradually increased to 49% over three years. Many Chinese broker-dealers are looking for foreign partners to stay competitive and to learn the advanced investment banking technologies from international players, both in underwriting and other fields. Given the need for mergers and acquisitions and reorganizations in China and the limited experience the Chinese investment banks have in this field, this should be a field for growth.

In keeping with China's WTO commitments, the "Rules for the Establishment of Securities Companies with Foreign Equity Participation" came into force on July 1, 2002.[4] The rules over companies are transformed when foreign shareholders are assigned or subscribe to share rights in domestic securities companies, and for securities companies where foreign shareholders and domestic shareholders have contributed the capital and established the company jointly.

Securities companies with foreign equity participation may engage in the following types of business: distribution of shares (including ordinary Renminbi shares and foreign-investment shares) and bonds (including government bonds and corporate bonds); brokerage of foreign-investment shares; brokerage of, and dealing on one's own behalf in bonds (including government bonds and corporate bonds); and other business approved by the CSRC. Foreign-investment shares include those listed in China (B shares) and abroad.

Securities companies with foreign equity participation must meet the following requirements: (i) the registered capital must comply with the provisions in the Securities Law on the registered capital of general securities companies; (ii) the shareholders must meet the qualification requirements specified in the Rules; (iii) capital contribution ratios and the forms of capital contributions must comply with the provisions of the Rules; (iv) the company must have at least 50 persons who have obtained the qualification to engage in securities business in accordance with CSRC regulations; it must also have necessary accounting, legal and computer professionals; (v) the company must have sound internal management and risk control systems; it must also have appropriate internal control technology systems for the administration systems areas such as organizational structure, personnel, information, and business implementation in distribution, brokerage, dealing on one's own behalf and other such business; and (vi) the company must have a place of business that meets requirements and qualified trading facilities.

A foreign shareholder of a securities company with foreign equity participation must meet the following requirements: (i) the country where the shareholder is located must have sound securities laws and regulatory systems; (ii) The country's securities regulatory authorities and the CSRC must have concluded a memorandum of understanding on securities regulatory cooperation and must be maintaining an effective relationship of regulatory cooperation; (iii) the shareholder must have lawful securities business qualifications in the country where it is located; (iv) it must have been engaged in financial business for at least ten years and must not have been subject to major penalties from securities regulatory authorities or judicial authorities in the preceding three years; (v) each risk control and monitor indicator must have met the requirements of the regulatory authorities and the provisions in the laws of the country where the shareholder is located for the preceding three years; (vi) the shareholder must have sound internal control systems; and (vii) the shareholder must have a good reputation and business record in the international securities market; foreign shareholders who buy into, or acquire equity in, wholly Chinese-owned securities companies also must meet the above requirements.

Domestic shareholders of securities companies with foreign equity participation must meet the qualification conditions for securities company shareholders stipulated by the CSRC. At least one of the domestic shareholders of a securities company with foreign equity participation must be a wholly Chinese-owned securities company. The ratio of the foreign shareholders' shareholdings or the ratio of equity they hold in a securities company with foreign equity participation may not exceed one-third altogether (including direct holdings and indirect holdings). At least one wholly Chinese-owned securities company among the domestic shareholders must have a shareholding ratio or must hold an equity ratio in the securities company with foreign equity participation of not less than one-third. When a wholly Chinese-owned securities company is converted into a securities company with foreign equity participation, the shareholding ratio of at least one of the wholly Chinese-owned shareholders must be not less than one-third.

If securities companies with foreign equity participation merge or a foreign securities company with foreign equity participation merges with a wholly Chinese-owned securities company, the newly established, or continuing, securities company must fulfill the conditions for securities companies with foreign equity participation stipulated in the Rules. The company's business scope and the share rights or equity ratio held by the foreign shareholder must comply with the provisions of the Rules.

If there is a foreign shareholder among the shareholders of a securities company established after a securities company with foreign participation has been split, then the company's business scope and the share rights or equity ratio held by the foreign shareholder must comply with the provisions of the Rules.

In June 2006, the Swiss bank UBS moved closer to setting up the first foreign-managed Chinese brokerage firm. UBS and two Chinese partners are reportedly planning to take over an indebted Chinese Securities firm, Beijing Securities, in a venture to be named UBS Securities and may be allowed to underwrite domestic stock and bond issues and trade domestic securities. Although UBS may only hold a 20% stake, it may be allowed to have management control.[5]

China's Asset Management Industry

In Beijing, Shanghai, and Shenzhen, more than 3,600 companies are engaged in the private funds business. Estimates are that these companies control US$84.6 billion of capital. Most of the funds are invested in the stock markets where the value of all circulating shares is approximately US$193.3 billion.[6] In this section, we will identify the primary sources of the burgeoning demand for fund management services in China;

outline fundamental regulations governing international fund managers in China describe the operations of some of the international players in the fund management business in China today, and list the most intractable obstacles to fund management profits in China today and in the near future. Under WTO, foreign investment banks and asset managers would be allowed to be 33% investors in domestic stock brokerage firms and fund-management companies. The threshold was scheduled to increase to 49% by December 2004.

Demand for equity mutual funds in China fell after mid-2004 due to disappointing stock market returns. Credit Suisse's expansion into China's US$63 billion mutual fund market saw the joint venture fund, of which it owns 25%, lose 51% of its assets under management in the first three months, despite the fund's strong performance and a rebound of the Chinese stock markets. Analysts attribute the outflow of assets to Credit Suisse's joint venture partner, Industrial and Commercial Bank of China, which is believed to have pushed to attract money from its 370,000 employees and clients to invest in the fund. Schroeder's also lost nearly half of its assets in its Chinese maiden fund in 2005.[7]

The Chinese Securities Industry

In 2004, the Chinese securities industry had two stock exchanges: the Shanghai Exchange and the Shenzhen Exchange, with an SME board adjunct to the Shenzhen Exchange. The securities system also consists of a total 123 domestic securities firms (working as investment bankers). Among them, there were 21 big and relatively strong ones, and 11 large yet financially less sound firms. These two groups accounted for 26% of the total securities firms in China, but about 65% of total net assets.

At the time the stock market was established, China was in the planned centralized economy era. There was a debate among

Chinese scholars as well as government officials as to whether or not a typical capitalist mechanism such as a stock market was justified under a socialist economy. To maintain the government ownership and to rationalize the operation under a "socialist economy," the shares issued by the listed companies contained three types: the legal shares belong to the company as a legal person; the state shares belong to the government (who are representative of all people in China), and the market shares, the only portion allowed to be sold on the stock market.

The market shares were about one-third of the total market value, and they were the only shares liquid and tradable. The three-portion share system remains valid until today. It brought huge problems in the stock market and was a fundamental barrier to the further development of the Chinese securities market.

Pension Funds in China

Government officials in China have repeatedly announced the Chinese government's desire to upgrade the management of China's pensions funds, which manage the pensions of 150 million people nationally.[8] The funds run deficits year after year.

The Regulatory Framework for Fund Management Companies

The "Rules for the Establishment of Fund Management Companies with Foreign Equity Participation" came into force on July 1, 2002.[9] The rules control joint-venture investment funds. In order to operate in China, a foreign shareholder of a fund management company with foreign equity participation must meet the following conditions: it must be a financial institution that is established and in good standing under the laws of its home country and it must not have been subject to major penalties from any regulatory authorities within three years prior to applying for a license to operate in China; the securities laws and regulatory systems of its home country must be sound; the home country's securities regulatory authorities and the CSRC must have concluded a memorandum of understanding regarding securities regulatory cooperation and must maintain an effective relationship of regulatory cooperation; and the actual paid-in capital of the fund must not be less than the equivalent of RMB 300 million (US$36 million) in a freely convertible currency.

The ratio of the foreign investment shareholdings or the ratio of equity held in a fund management company with foreign equity participation cannot exceed 33% altogether (including direct and indirect holdings). Within three years following China's entry into the WTO, the cap was to be raised to 49%. The capital contributions of foreign shareholders must be made using freely convertible currencies. The chairman of the board of directors, the general manager and the deputy general manager must meet the qualification requirements stipulated by the CSRC for holding senior management positions in fund management companies.

Joint venture fund management companies must submit applications materials to the CSRC. After preparation for the fund management company is completed, the domestic and foreign applicants must submit commencement of business application materials to the CSRC.

Within 30 working days after accepting the application for commencement of business, the CSRC shall decide whether to approve, defer approval of, or refuse approval for commencement of business. If the CSRC intends to defer or to refuse approval, it must give written notice to the applicants and explain the reasons.

Within 30 working days after obtaining the approval document from the CSRC, the shareholders of a fund management company with foreign equity participation must carry out company registration or change the company registration with the industry and commerce authorities. Where the Rules are silent regarding establishment, changes, termination, business activities, supervision, or administration for fund management companies with foreign equity participation, other relevant regulations of the CSRC apply.

The Present Foreign Fund Management Companies

With all these powerful attractions for foreign-fund managers, it is not surprising that many have quickly moved into joint ventures. JP Morgan Fleming Asset Management has surpassed its peers, having worked closely with Shanghai-based Huaan Fund Management Co. Two major Chinese banks, the Bank of Communications and the China Construction Bank, have established strategic partnerships focusing on open-ended funds with Chase Manhattan Bank of the United States. The Bank of Montreal recently signed a contract for cooperation in mutual fund management with the Shanghai-based Fullgoal Fund Management Co. The Canadian bank has thus become the eighth foreign financial institution to find a local partner in preparing to tap China's much-coveted mutual fund management industry.[10] US-based Prudential Insurance announced that it intends to establish a joint venture fund management company in China. Prumerica Financial, the brand name under which the Prudential Insurance Company will conduct its business in China, signed a letter of intent to establish a fund management firm with Shanghai-based Everbright Securities, one of the top 10 securities companies in the country.[11] UBS Asset Management has signed an agreement with China's Guotai Fund Management Co. on business cooperation including the establishment of open-end mutual funds. UBS will provide technical assistance including product development while Guotai will help UBS develop its branch name and business in China.[12] China Southern Fund Management Company Limited and HSBC Asset Management

(Hong Kong) Limited signed agreements over full-range cooperation in fund management in Shenzhen in Guangdong Province.
China Southern Fund Management Company Limited and HSBC
Asset Management (Hong Kong) Limited signed agreements over
full-range cooperation in fund management in Shenzhen of
Guangdong Province. The cooperation will be carried out in fields
such as product designing, marketing promotion, client service,
business operational procedures, and investment management.

The joint venture agreements typically provide for the foreign
bank to provide the Chinese bank with services and consulting on
items such as open-ended fund schemes, technological support,
and personnel training. The Chinese banks, in turn, provide consulting and services for the foreign partner and strategic assistance
and market placement as the joint venture expands its fund
business in China. Experts said the agreements would help bring
the operation of China's open-ended fund business in line with
international practice.

As the major players are jockeying for market position, there are
many concerns about China's emerging regulations. Foreign
parties are concerned that they cannot obtain control over their
investments.[13]

12

Aligning American Companies with Chinese Companies in China's Venture Capital Business

Overview

The Chinese government's 1979 to 2006 stage of economic reforms attracted more than US$650 billion of foreign capital some of which was invested in SOEs and other government-favored companies. At the same time, Chinese government-owned banks provided capital on easy terms or without repayment to such favored companies. Various restrictions limited the access of privately-owned Chinese firms to both foreign and domestic sources of equity or debt capital. This was a key factor in the Chinese government's retaining the ability to govern the political and economic reform process. Some American companies, such as IBM, have developed win-win criteria and value propositions in China. As China is a critical economic driver now, American private equity and venture capital firms are increasingly required by their investors to have credible China strategies. This is changing the American private equity and venture capital system and contributing to the evolution of China's private equity and venture capital businesses. The Chinese government's strategy of making China the innovative economy of the world creates the conflict of achieving that goal and retaining the ability to govern the political and economic reform process.

China's Private Equity and Venture Capital Businesses: Conflicting but Evolving Goals

Before the 1980s, there was not a term in Mandarin for "venture capital" because the concept was foreign to China. Chinese-government-owned or favored businesses were financed by state funding and bank loans. Privately-owned businesses were funded by personal savings, operating profits, and later by financing by overseas Chinese, and then American venture capital firms in the 1990s.[1]

Yesheng Huang's *Selling China*[2] documents how the Chinese-government-managed or directed economic reforms increased the size of China's economy, but did not address allocation inefficiencies in China's economy. He emphasizes the stifling effect the policies selected by the Chinese government have had on both privately-owned Chinese companies and China's private equity and venture capital businesses' ability to facilitate the growth on Mainland Chinese entrepreneurs or their businesses.

The Chinese government's priority was reengineering and refinancing selected major SOEs, allowing other SOEs to disappear or be acquired in the transition to a "Socialist Market Economy Capitalism." In order to retain the ability to manage the economic and political reform process, a key goal of the Chinese government, was to suppress the rise of a domestic entrepreneurial class that might challenge the government (as happened in the former Soviet Union).

The Chinese government's desire to move China from "the factory floor of the world" to the "innovative economy of the world" is affected to some degree by the economic reform programs used by the Chinese government previously.

The invitation by Jiang Zemin for Mainland Chinese capitalists to join the "Communist Party of China" reflects an acceptance by the Party's leadership of the necessary and acceptable political input of such persons, but within the context of the stability that the Party provides. The Party is currently, and for some time to come, essential to China's economic reforms and continued economic growth. Accordingly, the Party is changing incrementally and pragmatically, in order to retain the ability to lead the economic and political reform process in China.

The Private Equity and Venture Capital Business in China

Andrew Tan and John Grobowski of Baker McKenzie[3] indicate that in 2003–4:

> Currently China's private equity market is small and evolving compared to the mature market economies, with about 200 to 300 venture capital companies (also known as start-up investment companies) established in China as at 2003. It is estimated that these private equity companies are currently investing US$6 billion in China. At the same time, there is a strong interest in investment in China among offshore private equity companies and funds, some of which are targeting almost exclusively Chinese business opportunities.
>
> Chinese institutional investors, including pension funds, insurance companies, and banks are not permitted to invest in the private equity market under Chinese law. The key sources of private equity in China are:
>
> 1. Government- or quasi-government-owned private equity companies investing in domestic high tech companies favored by the government.
> 2. Private equity funds set up by large privately-owned or mixed-ownership corporations.
> 3. A limited number of private equity companies with foreign investment.

4. A limited, but steadily increasing, number of high-net-worth individuals.

Despite the absence of a well developed infrastructure for private equity investment, China is attracting more private investment in the technology, manufacturing and financial sectors, as well as in distressed assets.

A total of 58% of the venture capital funds raised in 2002 came from domestic sources, with 35% from government sources and 23% from domestic enterprises. In 2003, the proportion of funds from government sources dropped slightly, while the proportion of funds from domestic enterprises increased by 7%. Funds from foreign sources dropped by 6% in 2003.

Fundraising from 1994 to 1996 grew at the modest rate of 5% to 7.5% per year. From 1997 to 2000, fundraising accelerated at a rate exceeding 70% per year. After the dot. com crash in 2000, the annual rate of growth decreased to 21.9% in 2001 and 9.3% in 2002. In 2003, fundraising experienced a negative growth of 13.9%, partly due to the SARS outbreak.

There was a shift in investment focus from 2002 to 2003 from early stage investment (mainly in the high tech sector) to later stage investment in more traditional industries, such as manufacturing. This is largely due to the Chinese government's recent push to accelerate the privatization of SOEs in traditional industries.

In 2003, 33.33% of venture capital project exits were through domestic trade sales and 25% of exits were achieved through acquisitions by the founders (entrepreneur buyback). In contrast, a mere 5.36% of exits were achieved through an IPO…. This is largely due to the onerous restrictions in China on IPOs.[4]

The Chinese Venture Capital Business: History and Development

Venture capital is one of the fastest growing economic forces in China. Its role is developing in a very different economic and social environment than the American venture capital business.

The tremendous growth in the venture capital business in China is a mixed story. Venture capital firms' investments in China in 2004 increased 28% compared with the previous year, and total deals invested in grew 43%. But the Chinese domestic venture capital business did not do that well and the foreign venture capital firms overshadowed them. The total investment amount for foreign venture capital firms is over 250% higher than that of the domestic firms.

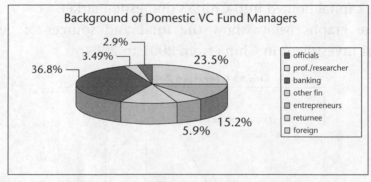

Source: Cheng(2004).

The graph above shows the background sources of Chinese domestic venture capital fund managers. The development of the Chinese venture capital business occurred in five stages:

1. Seed stage: from 1986 to 1991, the first Chinese domestic venture capital firm was established and the venture capital industry was small and scattered.

2. Initial development stage: from 1992 to 1996, when Deng Xiaoping's south China tour stirred another round of venture capital movement in which the domestic venture capital firms were all government initiated and government funded.

3. Rapid growth stage: from 1997 to October 2001, when CSRC officials declared that the secondary securities market was ready to launch and the Chinese venture capital

contained not only government entities, but also privately-owned Chinese venture capital firms and foreign venture capital and corporate venture capital companies.

4. Receding stage: from 2001 until the end of 2002, when the government stopped its efforts to open up a secondary securities market in Shenzhen and venture capital investment in China declined.

5. Re-booming stage: from 2003 to date, when several successful venture capital exits emerged and foreign venture capital poured into China's domestic market.

The graphs below show the total and sources of venture capital investment in China from 2001 to 2004:

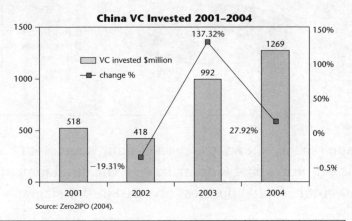

Source: Zero2IPO (2004).

13

	Total VC invt, SM	Foreign VCs, SM	Foreign %	Domestic VCs, SM	Domestic	Other**
2001	518	258.0	49.8%	260.0	50.2%	0.0
2002	418	208.6	49.9%	194.8	46.6%	3.6
2003	992*	823.0	83.0%	169.0	17.0%	
2004	1269	794.4	62.6%	319.8	25.2%	12.2

Source: Zero2IPO

*The 2003 numbers did not distinguish foreign VCs and Sino-foreign joint venture VCs.

The booming of venture capital in China after 2003 largely reflected the triumph of international venture capital firms. More and more foreign venture capital firms came into the Chinese market. Venture capital and foreign direct investment in Mainland China reached $51.4 billion in 2004. The reasons for the new wave of foreign capital flowing into China include, but are not limited to, the Chinese economy remaining strong, with enormous growth potential. In the summer of 2003, many businesses stopped operation, and restaurants and theaters closed their doors because of SARS. But the economy came back strongly in the fourth quarter with an astonishing 9.1% growth rate. The growth remained robust in 2004, and the Chinese government took measures in an effort to control potential overheating of the market. But overall, demand for venture capital investment has been increasing.

The anticipation of the appreciation of the Chinese Yuan also plays a role in the trend. Increasing pressure has been put on the Chinese government to let its currency appreciate. Many domestic scholars also argued the positive aspects of the currency appreciation, but the appreciation of RMB has been gradual. It will either stay where it is or go up. Consumer spending is increasing in China. Under this circumstance, foreign capital invested in China will certainly remain strong. Disposable income per capita for city residents, for instance, increased 12.1% the first quarter of 2004 compared with the same period previous year, and 13.2% for that of the rural dwellers.[5]

China is experiencing continuous economic growth and, at the same time, domestic labor costs remain low and inflation is under control. In the next 10 to 15 years, Chinese labor costs are not expected to grow very rapidly. The percentage population between ages 15 and 64 grew from 61.5% in 1982 to 70.4% in 2003.[6] Given the labor force structure, even though rapid economic growth has created many new jobs, the labor market will continue to be over-supplied.

Many successful exit cases caught the attention of venture capital firms worldwide. In 2004, the Chinese venture-backed companies achieved 21 IPOs overseas, and raised a total of $4.67-billion. At the end of 2003, Ctrip had its IPO on NASDAQ. That signaled the beginning of a wave of Chinese venture-backed companies going public overseas. Venture capital firms that participated in those investments became big winners. For example, the Carlyle Group invested US$8 million in Ctrip in 2000. Four years later, this investment grew to US$100 million when it exited in an IPO. In 2004, SMIC had its IPO on both the New York and Hong Kong stock exchanges. It raised $1.8 billion on NYEX, the third largest IPO of the year. More Chinese venture-backed companies had IPOs in 2003 and 2004 than in all previous years combined. Here are some success stories that happened in 2004. Linkstone was listed on NASDAQ and brought its venture capital investors, Acer, Index, Mitsubishi, and Temasek huge profits. Shanda, an Internet game company, created a similar result. Mengnu, a traditional dairy company, went public on the Hong Kong Stock Exchange. Another Chinese Internet company, Kongzhong, had its IPO on NASDAQ. On its first trading day on September 30, 2004, 51job.com closed at $21.15, a 51.07% increase from its opening price. Jinrongjie, or JRJ, also went public on NASDAQ.

In addition to such successful IPOs, many venture-capital-backed companies provided successful exits for their venture capital investors in mergers and acquisitions. For example, eBay bought the Chinese Eachnet for US$30 million in 2002. All Eachnet VC investors, Whitney & Co., AsiaTech Ventures Limited and Orchid Holdings, enjoyed substantial profits. Yahoo! (Hong Kong) purchased the Chinese Internet company 3721. Amazon.com purchased its Chinese counterpart, Joyo, where registered online users already had reached more than 5.2 million. Tom.com bought Leitingwuji. China's successful exit stories in 2004 stimulated the increasing venture capital flows into China.

Venture capital funds from the U.S., Europe, and Asia invested in the Chinese market in 2004 and 2005. The trend for the venture capital business in China was slightly different from its counterpart in the U.S. The U.S. venture capital investment results improved in 2004, but the improvement was far less impressive than that of the venture capital investments in China. The American venture capital business took a tremendous downturn starting from 2001 until 2004. China's venture capital investment hit its low in 2002, but had a comeback in 2003, when venture capital investment jumped more than 300% in a year. However, the enormous increase in Chinese venture capital investment in 2003 only indicated the massive capital inflow into China, and did not reflect the trend for the Chinese domestic venture capital business.

Examples of Alignment Opportunities for American Companies

American private equity sources and venture capital investors could harvest rich rewards in assisting in the commercialization of the intellectual capital resources that many Chinese inventors and start-up scientific, medical, or technology companies have. Since the private equity and venture businesses are nascent in China, Mainland Chinese individuals with such intellectual capital, which can be deployed anywhere in the world, should be very attractive investment opportunities for American corporate and private venture capital firms. Mainland Chinese leaving China to work or be inventors or entrepreneurs in America can develop Chinese intellectual capital through foreign companies investing in China. In due course, after successful foreign start-ups, the Chinese inventors often return to China with both the intellectual capital and Western start-up experience useful in assisting the development of China's private equity, venture capital business, and "innovative economy of the world." They are being indigenously deployed and are succeeding in developing "champion" companies in Mainland China.

American companies want the lower-cost talent and labor in China and access to Chinese domestic demand. Genuine Global Joint Ventures, structured through Bermuda holding companies owning WOFEs, would facilitate both if an American company partners with an excellent private Chinese firm going global that is well managed and profitable. As discussed in chapter 4, investments in such genuine global joint ventures through a Bermuda holding company is a potential competitive advantage. Such holding companies can be listed on the Bermuda stock exchange as part of an early private placement round, in preparation for a public financing and listing on NASDAQ or the Hong Kong or Singapore stock exchanges.

Domestic Venture Capital Firms Vs. International Venture Capital Firms in China

The venture capital business in China has "re-boomed" since 2003. Many major overseas venture capital firms have come to China, such as Accel Partners, Granite Global Ventures, Redpoint Ventures, and Venrock Associates. NEC, for instance, invested $150 million in venture capital plays in China in one year. Its investment in SMIC brought an enormous profit. In 2004, a Silicon Valley venture capital delegation came to China twice to explore the market. Among the prestigious venture capital firms in the delegations were SVB, DCM, Kleiner Perkins Caulfield & Byers, and Sequoia Capital.

However, the expansion of the venture capital business in China does not reflect the whole story. The "boom" is mainly from foreign venture capital firms in China. The domestic venture capital firms show a different trend. While foreign venture capital firms are increasing their investments in China, Chinese domestic venture capital firms were retreating. According to the Research and Development Center at the Ministry of

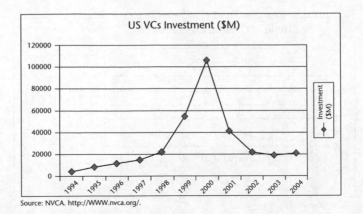

Source: NVCA. http://WWW.nvca.org/.

Science and Technology (MOST), the Chinese domestic business was in a relatively declining phase. The total number of venture capital firms reduced from 296 in 2002 to 233 in 2003. In addition, the total money raised by the domestic venture capital firms reduced from 58.2 billion Yuan in 2002 to 50.1 billion in 2003. The Chinese government was worried that the domestic venture capital business was shrinking. The graph below clearly shows this trend.

Before 2002, Chinese domestic venture capital investment was bigger than that from the foreign venture capital firms. In 2001, the total domestic venture capital investment in China was US$260 million, and the amount from its foreign participants was US$258 million. But the change took place in 2002, and the trend continued and accelerated. In 2002, of a total of US$418 million invested in China, the amount from the domestic venture capital firms accounted for only for $194.8 million, 46.5% of the total, and whereas foreign VCs contributed $208.6 million, or 49.8%. In addition, Sino-foreign syndicated investment accounted for 3.0%, and Sino-foreign joint venture invested 2.5 million, or 0.6% of the total. Even though the investment amounts of foreign and domestic venture capital firms were very close, the number of deals invested was much bigger for the Chinese domestic venture

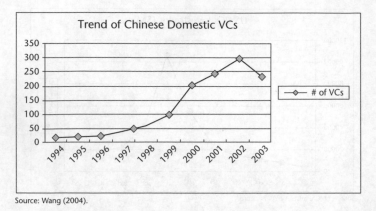

Source: Wang (2004).

capital companies. One hundred and sixty-eight deals accounted for 74.3% of all deals invested in that year. This phenomenon indicated that the average investment amount of the Chinese domestic venture capital firms was much smaller than that of the foreign companies: 1.2 million vs. 4.9 million.

As shown in the graphs above and below, the development of the Chinese domestic venture capital business took a downturn starting in 2002, when the investments from foreign venture capital firms surpassed that of the domestic firms. The difference was minimal, but it was the starting point of this trend. In 2003, the differences between investments from domestic and foreign venture capital firms grew into an astonishing $654 million, with the amounts invested by foreign venture capital firms being about

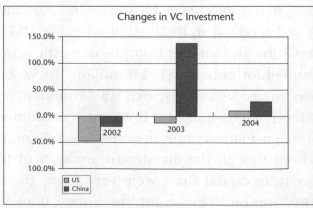

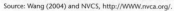

Source: Wang (2004) and NVCS, http://WWW.nvca.org/.

487% that of amounts invested by domestic firms. Even if we consider the $300 million lump sum invested in SMIC, the total investment from the foreign venture capital firms was still 309% higher. In 2004, foreign venture capital firms' investments continued that trend, and accounted for 62.6% of the total venture capital investment in China that year. Observing this trend, the Chinese government warned that measures would be considered to stimulate the domestic venture capital business. In order to explore what measures the Chinese government could take, we need to first understand the reasons behind the downturn.

Barriers to the Development of Chinese Domestic Venture Capital Firms

Several important factors are responsible for the declining trend of the Chinese domestic venture capital business. Two important aspects are the legislative and legal environment and the financial and economic framework. Both factors explain why the Chinese domestic venture capital firms have tremendous competitive disadvantages. Many researchers have explored the first set of factors, but only a few have examined the second feature.[7] We will examine both, with an emphasis on the second.

The legislative and legal environment within which the domestic venture capital business operates restricted its development. This environment includes aspects such as company formation, fundraising, post-investment management and monitoring, and exiting. For example, Chinese company law requires that the total amount of registered capital be in the company's account at the time of registration, yet only half of that amount is allowed to be legally invested. This requirement generated a tremendous waste of capital and created enormous operational inefficiency. Fundraising activities were sluggish because of the limited funding sources and the registration requirement.

Venture capital is a value-adding investment. Venture capitalists put a lot of time and energy post investment in management and monitoring.[8] However, for the Chinese domestic venture capital firms, post-investment monitoring is very difficult. One reason is that most of the domestic venture capital firms are very young. More than 85% of them were set up after 1998, and close to two-thirds of the firms were established after 2000. Many fund managers in the domestic venture capital companies lack relevant experience.

In addition, many domestic venture capital firms were created by government agencies, especially local subsidiaries of the MOST, because MOST has been the primary agent promoting the Chinese domestic venture capital business. Consequently, when the government initiated venture capital companies, the officials who were responsible for technology funding naturally became the managers of the companies. Transforming government officials into venture capitalists almost overnight is difficult and over 36 percent of the domestic venture capital fund managers were previously government officials. Another 23.5% were former professors and researchers with limited operational experience. The third-largest category was people with backgrounds in banking and non-banking financial institutions. The domestic venture capital managers usually have limited relevant venture capital experience, but their strength is the ability to learn, and their familiarity with the business environment in China and their skill at more established networks in China and "guanxi" or the art of relationships.

Exiting their investments is another of the major obstacles to the development of the Chinese domestic venture capital firms. Foreign venture capital firms have the advantage in channeling IPOs to foreign stock exchanges and companies. But for the domestic firms, the underdevelopment of the domestic stock markets, including the main board and the newly established SME board, is the major barrier to their exit.

The financial and economical framework in which the domestic venture capital firms operate is the other major factor impeding the development of China's domestic venture capital firms. As discussed, the financial system in China is still dominated by its huge but inefficient and inflexible banking system. On the one hand, the state-owned banks, known as the "Big Four," remain dominant in the Chinese banking system, and the banking system dominates China's entire financial sector. The Chinese banking system directs the flow of the supply of funds mainly to state-owned enterprises. For example, in April 2003, about 70% of all loans made by state-owned commercial banks went to SOEs, semi-SOEs (the enterprises whose controlling shareholder is government), or public enterprises (the majority of the publicly listed companies are SOEs). But the driving forces of China's economy, the private sector, and the SMEs are major sectors requiring funds, but receive little support from the Chinese banking system.

The private sector finds it very difficult to get debt or equity capital. The banking system is big, inefficient, and inflexible; and funds from non-banking sources are limited and very expensive. Two channels address the situation: underground finance and alternative finance such as venture capital. Even though underground finance has been illegal and prohibited, it grows at an amazing rate. At the same time, people increasingly see venture capital as an alternative finance channel to banking because it is a Chinese-government-approved, legitimate, flexible, and approachable finance channel. Venture capital provides one of the few sources in China of capital for developing private companies, which do not have access to debt or public listings.

With this financial structure, the Chinese venture capital business is given multiple tasks by the Chinese government. It is required to continue to serve as one of the important economic development strategies, providing long-term, non-speculative investment to the high-tech industry and to support the nation's innovation and technology transfer programs. It also has the mission to provide alternative financing wherever it is needed: whether it is high-tech or traditional company, whether it is a startup or a matured enterprise, whether it is a SME or a SOE. As long as it is in need of capital, a Chinese company looks at venture capitalists as alternative funding sources.

The current financial system has created this tremendous task, which is more than the Chinese venture capital business is able to fulfill. In addition, the Chinese venture capital firms currently must work with the Chinese government's inconsistent policies and non-collaborative attention. The inconsistency of the Chinese government's existing approach to the venture capital industry's development is obvious when we examine the national goals set up by the MOST and other government agencies.

Promoting the Chinese High-Tech and Technology Transfers

MOST is the leading government agency for the establishment and development of the Chinese venture capital business. MOST started the Chinese venture capital initiative and helped to set up the very first Chinese venture capital firm, China New Technology Venture Capital Company. The objective of this initiative was to promote China's high-tech industry and support innovation and technology transfer. The Chinese technology development programs initiated by the MOST include:

1. The 863 programs
2. The Torches Programs

3. The high-tech zones with 53 national high-tech zones and 81 provincial-level zones

4. The 973 programs—National Basic Research Programs of China

5. The National New Product Program

6. Innovation Fund for Small Technology-based Firms

The execution and expansion of these programs need funding. Either the government or private sources funded most of the programs. For example, the Torches program received a total funding of 5368.6 million Yuan in 2003, of which most was from enterprises themselves. Government funding was only 2.9%, bank loans accounted another 30.2%, and funding from foreign sources was 1.7%. Venture capital firms are encouraged to fund the companies nurtured by the Torch program. However, the efforts of MOST have not been without difficulties. One major obstacle is the limited sources of funds. China's high-tech zone is another. The national new high-tech zones were established by the MOST primarily for the promotion of new and high-technology innovation and development. The first of these zones was set up in Shenzhen in June 1985 in the Shenzhen Science and Technology Industrial Park, a municipal high-tech zone. In May 1988, the State Council approved the first of the national new high-technology zones: the Beijing New Technology Industrial Development Experimental Park. At the same time, the State council issued 18 favorable policies, laying the foundation for the further development of the Chinese new high-tech zones system.

In August 1988, the Chinese government established the Torches program, and stated that one of the major objectives of the Torches program is the establishment of the new high tech zones and the high-tech entrepreneur centers (technology incubators). The zones were encouraged to make breakthroughs in

the electronic information, software, bioengineering, photo-elec-
tro-mechanical integration, new materials, new energy sources,
and environmental protection industries. By the end of 2003,
there were 53 national new and high-tech zones, and over 200
local ones including 83 at the provincial level. The basic statistics show that a total of 136,321 enterprises registered inside the
53 zones, among them, 32,857 have their major operations
inside the zones and 79.4% of the firms are private high-tech companies. The total jobs created by the national zones reached 3.8
million.[9]

Some famous high-tech enterprises, such as Legend, Stone,
and Founder emerged from the zones. In addition, the high-tech
zones serve as a network to link research bases to the technology
enterprises, in an effort to further promote a knowledge-based
economy. For example, the Zhongguancun area in Beijing is
a highly concentrated cluster, with a total of 68 universities
and 232 research institutes scattered in the area of 75 square
kilometers.

The tremendous growth of the new and high-tech zones
increasingly needs funding. GDP growth and money supply (M2)

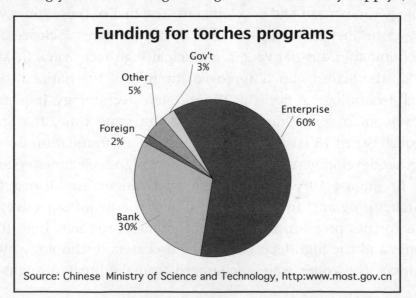

Funding for torches programs

- Gov't 3%
- Other 5%
- Foreign 2%
- Enterprise 60%
- Bank 30%

Source: Chinese Ministry of Science and Technology, http:www.most.gov.cn

growth have been in similar pattern, but not that of high-tech growth. The high-tech growth outpaced that of the national GDP and of the money supply. The high-tech growth curve only includes the growth rate of the mid-size and large Chinese high-tech firms' annual output. But, many small and private firms contribute a great deal to the Chinese high-tech development. By the end of 2003, the nation's non-state-owned technology firms numbered 124,937, up 14.2% from the previous year. Among the 124,937 firms, 76.9% were private enterprises including 27.6% technology proprietorships.[10]

During 2000 to 2001, the Chinese high-tech industry boomed with a moderate GDP growth and a tight money supply. At the same time, the Chinese venture capital business experienced a remarkable growth. The two events may not be completely unrelated. The growth of a strong high-tech industry in China needs a long-term, non-speculative, and patient financing mechanism, and venture capital proves to be on the top of the list of potential mechanisms.

While MOST is promoting high-tech industry by developing a venture capital system in the new high-technology zones, other Chinese government agencies may have a different agenda. As early as 1991, the Chinese government announced "relevant governmental agencies may encourage the establishment of venture capital funds inside the high tech zones, to support high-risk technology research and development. In some high tech zones, where conditions permit, venture capital companies should be established." In May of 1995, the CPCCC and the State Council emphasized again: Financial institutions will have to support technology development, build up technology venture capital, and establish venture capital organizations. All these policies were geared to the establishment and development of a Chinese venture capital business to support the nation's high-technology growth. At the same time, a different set of policies were set up where venture capital was seen as a financial tool to help small and medium-size enterprises.

In 2002, the Chinese People's Congress passed the SME Promotion Act, which stated that the central government will establish an SME development fund and enable a favorable tax policy to promote venture capital investing in SMEs. The SMEs in China are now driving forces for the economic development and largely responsible for the rapid growth. By the end of 2003, there were 29.3 million SMEs in China, accounting for about 99% of all mainland-China-registered companies. The SMEs contributed 51% of China's GDP, and over 60% of China's total export goods. In 2002, SMEs created more than 85% of all new jobs, especially in the retailing area where SMEs absorbed over 90% of employment in the industry. The growth of SMEs needs extra funding and extra capital sources.

By inducing venture capital as a convenient channel for financing the SMEs, several Chinese government agencies have to be involved, compromises have to be made, and necessary consensus has to be achieved. As a result, no single government agency is solely responsible for issues related to venture capital industry. No single government office is the leader in corresponding and collaborating among the ministries and agencies in the promotion, regulation, or legislation of venture-capital-related issues. Most important VC-related policies would require collaboration and cooperation among several ministries, usually seven of them, including the MOST, the MOF (Ministry of Finance), the NDRC (the National Development and Reform Commission), the PBC (People's Bank of China), CSRC (China Securities Regulatory Commission), the Taxation Bureau, and the MOC (Ministry of Commerce). As in any other situation, a case where many are responsible is comparable to a case where no one is responsible. The Chinese venture capital business is currently in this unfortunate position.

Countries vary in how much venture capital money is being invested in their high-tech industry. In Israel, for instance, 97% of all venture capital is poured into high-tech development. Switzerland is the second highest with 88%. The next is America, where 85% of all venture capital funding went into the high-tech sector. In China, a big difference exists between domestic and foreign venture capital firms in terms of high-tech investment. Foreign venture capital firms in China put most of their capital, 76%, into Chinese high-tech industry, whereas it accounted for less than half of the domestic venture capital investment. The variation can be largely explained by the analysis of the Chinese domestic economic and financial system and the legal and legislative structures, which are the major factors explaining the investment patterns of the Chinese venture capital firms.

The Goal of Being the "Innovative Economy of the World" Conflicts with Other Chinese Government Policies

The Chinese government's goals to promote the nation's innovation and technology transfer needs to be re-examined. In addition, the lack of skilled and experienced fund managers also plays a major inhibiting role because it takes a lot of experience and a strong technological background to be able to identify good technology and innovation at their early stages.

Venture capital investment in China experienced enormous success in 2003 and 2004, when venture capital investment increased 137.3% and 27.9% respectively. Yet that remarkable achievement was largely from the performance of the foreign venture capital firms. Compared with their foreign counterparts, the Chinese domestic venture capital firms were not as successful. The total amount invested by the Chinese domestic venture capital firms was down from US$260 million in 2001 to US$194.8 million in 2002, and decreased to US$169 million in 2003. In 2004, the

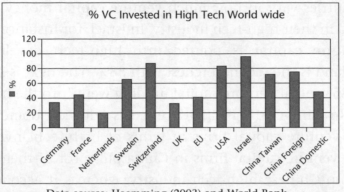

Data source: Haemming (2003) and World Bank,
http://www.worldbank.org.

Chinese domestic venture capital investment was up to US$319.8-million, but still was less than half of that from the foreign firms.

Because of the particular economic and financial arrangements in China, the Chinese venture capital firms have encountered tremendous difficulties. The difficulties came not only from the legal and legislative arena, but also from the Chinese current economic and financial structures. The Chinese domestic venture capital business provides more than venture capital in China; it serves also as an alternative financing mechanism, a good substitute for the inefficient and inflexible bank financing. To solve the Chinese venture capital business's problems, objectives, policies, and legislation set by the Chinese government should be reexamined.

China and America's Unique Potential as Innovative Economies of the World

Robert Thelen, Chairman of ChinaVest has stated:

> Until China's regulatory environment becomes more conducive for financial investors to sell their investment interests to others, venture funding for Chinese companies will not reach its full potential. However, I am confident that today's leaders in China understand this point, and will do

what needs to be done to ensure a vibrant and successful venture capital industry in the years ahead.[11]

It will be interesting to see how the Chinese government decides to allow the domestic Chinese venture capital business to develop or languish. The development of domestic Chinese venture capital firms may occur at some point in the deployment of the Chinese government's "Innovative Economy Of The World" strategy and strategy of regaining scientific and technological innovation leadership after 1800. Allowing Chinese domestic venture capital firms to compete successfully in China with foreign venture capital firms may occur as the governing party continues its absorption of entrepreneurs as members. China's economic and political reforms reduce poverty and create a vast middle class as well as a very wealthy class. A key factor in the evolution of China's domestic venture capital business's role will be the governing party and the Chinese government's ongoing assessments of how to achieve economic and political reform without unbalancing the harmony China requires. That is a key factor in all aspects of the Chinese government's management of the banking, insurance and reinsurance, stock markets, venture capital, and other financial service industries in China.

Countries all over the world wish to duplicate the innovative and financial success of the venture capital and technology companies based in "Silicon Valley" in America. But Robert Thelen believes that Silicon Valley's success is a result of the depth and efficiency of America's capital and consumer markets and the freedom with which commercial ideas can be shared and used while being protected in America. In his assessment, no other country, with the possible exception of China, can reproduce all those assets. He identifies eight key ingredients in being "the innovative economy of the world":

1. Capable entrepreneurs to lead, to take risk, yet willing to listen to outside advice and to put shareholder interests above all else;
2. Strong research-based universities, with an emphasis on basic research without regard to business applications or profits;
3. A ready supply of skilled and unskilled labor;
4. Middle management talent in areas such as finance, marketing, sales and business development, and strategic planning;
5. Liquid and efficient capital markets;
6. A strong and growing domestic consumer market;
7. A diverse economic base; and
8. Rule of law.[12]

The Chinese government is in the process of assembling and combining those skills and functions within its evolving system of "capitalism with Chinese characteristics."

Case Study: IBM Venture Capital Group[13]

IBM's Venture Capital Group's mission is to accelerate IBM's growth and increase the acceptance of IBM's vision, strategies, standards, and architectures in the venture capital community and their invested companies. IBM's Venture Capital Group proactively builds strategic relationships of *mutual value* with top-tier venture capital firms and mutually *beneficial* client, business development, and technology sourcing and partner relationships with venture-capital-funded companies early in their life cycle. The overarching objective is to establish a strong external innovation ecosystem and emerging partner and client base.

The "mindset" for partnering that IBM Venture Capital Group uses in China is to partner with companies with a unique technology solution or value proposition that have considered their overall business plan needs of their company. Suitable potential partners must have a willingness to adopt IBM technologies and must be able to bring a new customer to IBM. Then IBM does a deal and if it goes satisfactorily, then another deal, and then formalizes a relationship. Partnering often comes before an acquisition. In acquisition candidates, IBM also looks for strong strategic fit, good acquisition economics, and easy to integrate with IBM's existing arrangements.

Case Study: ChinaVest[14]

American venture capital companies bring new skills, insights, and credibility to promising Mainland Chinese companies. ChinaVest was one of the first American private equity funds to focus on Mainland China. It initially worked with Chinese operating outside of China. In 1987 ChinaVest invested in LuK Industrial Company, which built an assembly factory for television sets in Schenzhen and helped the company develop stronger financial controls and a domestic sales strategy, and helped it become one of the first companies with mainland manufacturing facilities to list on the Hong Kong Stock Exchange.

ChinaVest also invested in Santa Fe Transport, a start-up company operating from Hong Kong that planned to provide distribution services for the multinational oil industry operating in China and offshore. Recognizing that seeking a license for Santa Fe Transport from the Ministry of Communications, which had an association with Sinotrans, would involve a conflict of interest, ChinaVest developed "the oblique approach to Chinese bureaucracy," in which a license was obtained from the Ministry of Petroleum, which did not have a vested interest in Sinotrans, and Santa Fe Transport became the first foreign transportation company to form a joint venture permitted to operate in Mainland China. ChinaVest also helped Santa Fe Transportation expand its services and revenue, and financial and strategic planning, and helped engineer its sale to a larger European logistics company. This win-win relationship gave the company further marketing and financial capabilities and the foreign company obtained operations in China.

In 1997, ChinaVest invested in AsiaInfo, a start-up by Mainland-Chinese-born, American-educated entrepreneurs who had worked with multinational companies. Their business plan was to use their engineering talents and experience to help Chinese telecommunication companies construct information networks. With ChinaVest's help and validation, AsiaInfo was able to list on NASDAQ.

Domestic Venture Capital Firms Vs. Foreign Venture Capital Firms

The emergence of a domestic Chinese venture capital business is a significant social and economic aspect of China's economic and political reform. In 2004, the Chinese venture capital business's total venture capital investment in China made a breakthrough in reaching $1.27 billion, a 28% increase from the previous year and total deals invested in increased 43%.[15] Yet the booming of the business does not mean that the obstacles to the development of venture capital in China have been removed.

China's venture capital business must be seen in the context of the dynamics and transformation of the Chinese economic reform and particularly the Chinese financial system.[16] Compared with foreign venture capital firms, the domestic venture capital faces more difficulties and challenges. To promote indigenous firms and domestic venture capital business in China, different driving forces have to reconcile and the Chinese government has to prioritize its objectives. The Chinese domestic venture capital business's evolution serves multiple goals.

Economic reform and development certainly is an important goal shaping the venture capital business. The legal structure, the exit mechanisms, and the financial system are key factors in determining Chinese venture capital operations and performance Venture capital fundraising and exiting is more difficult in a bank-dominated economy such as China than in economies with active and vibrant stock markets.[17] An advantage in the U.S. venture capital business is the existence of a robust capital market compared to the relatively weaker venture activities in economies dominated by bank financing, such as Germany, Japan, and China.

Understanding the Chinese economic and cultural environment is critical to the success of the venture capital business in China.[18] Vaughn[19] linked the Chinese venture capital business to the Chinese financial framework, but did not further explore the relationship of the two. Apart from Vaughn's work, very little has been done in examining the Chinese venture capital under the framework of the context of the Chinese financial system, the process of its reforms, and its restructuring.

It is useful to look at the framework of the economic reform of the financial system in the context of China's domestic venture capital business's short yet dynamic history and its development and to compare the domestic and foreign venture capital firms investing in China. The current economic and financial structure of China makes it very difficult for the Chinese domestic venture capital business to compete with their foreign counterparts. It also makes it difficult for Mainland Chinese companies with foreign venture capital support to list on domestic Chinese stock exchanges.[20]

13

Alignment Opportunities for American Companies with China's Educational Challenges

Overview

This chapter examines opportunities for American companies to align their strategies in China with the Chinese government's educational, regional economic development, social welfare goals, and labor costs and conditions. It notes that one of the legacies of the Cultural Revolution is an unusual society-wide and interregional understanding of the needs of China's rural poor, which will assist the Chinese government in ameliorating regional disparities.

The Chinese Government's Regional Disparity and Education Goals

Reducing regional disparities is a focus of President Hu Jintao and Premier Wen Jiabao who want to alleviate poverty in the interior provinces by encouraging investment and infrastructure there.[1] *The Wall Street Journal* commented:

> China's leaders spent the New Year Holiday with locals in the impoverished countryside, where growing discontent has

315

spilled over into violent protests. The leaders pledged to do more to improve living standards. ...

China's communist leadership has made poverty in the countryside a key priority, as it acknowledges that three decades of economic and social reforms have left great swathes of the population behind.

Clashes between officials and villagers, angry over forced land seizures and inadequate compensation for farmland and layoffs, have been increasing. Last year, the government said there were 87,000 cases of public disorder, an increase of 6.6% on 2004.

Hu told Kang Haifa, a farmer, that the government's aim was to bring more wealth to the countryside, so they could eat as well every day as they do during the New Year Holiday ...

The Chinese premier used his two-day trip to east China's Shandong province to call for affordable health services for the rural population, most of whom struggle to get by on a few hundred dollars a year. Wen gave money to a farmer whose wife has been sick and told other villagers to take better care of the family. ...[2]

National leaders often curry favor by such tours and gestures. But there are important cultural and historic reasons why the connection between China's elite and poor, between the strong and the weak, may not be fully felt by some foreign observers. China's cultural tradition emphasizes citizens' obligations to others they know rather than to the rule of law. It is a society that values consensus. America has evolved farther from its agrarian roots than China.

One of the ironies of history is that Chairman Mao's economically and socially disastrous Cultural Revolution may bear valuable fruit 30 years later. China's universities were closed and China's urban privileged were sent to be "re-educated" in China's rural life. China's youth, including those who have become China's leaders today, experienced and, more importantly, felt and understand emotionally China's rural suffering and need. That gift of knowledge, obtained through hard experience, ironically, is the national "glue" that helps the Chinese government address regional disparities that otherwise could undermine China's continued economic, social, and political development and sovereignty.

Americans and American companies that can empathize with China's leaders and people will find their own innate feelings of compassion and altruism will have profound impact in China's Permission Society. China is not America, but people are people. An American with the "right spirit" and candor and whose word is their bond, will find a deep responsiveness in China's leaders and people. The "right spirit," candor, and integrity are the language of "moral authority" that Americans and Chinese feel emotionally and intellectually, even across the divides of language, culture, history, and self-interest.

Education in China: People as a National Treasure

One of the Chinese government's challenges is to change the educational system so that China can become a developed nation able to contribute effectively with America and other nations in science and technology. China produces many superb students. Increasing and enriching education in all parts of China is a way to reduce inequality, instill hope, and prevent the social instability that could reduce FDI and the governability of China which is a danger generated by regional disparities.

The Chinese government views the reform of China's schools as critical to China's economic growth strategy. Their goal is to have high school attendance rise from 40% in 2005 to 70% by 2010 and 85% by 2020. Their goal is to have university attendance rise from 13% in 2005 to 20% by 2010.[3]

At the end of the Cultural Revolution, 40% of Chinese were illiterate. In 2005, 85% are literate, with 95% literate between the ages of 12 and 40. China has 218 million children in 457,000 elementary schools and 66,000 junior high schools and 33,000 high schools taught by 10.6 million teachers; but spends US$56 billion or 3.2% of China's GDP on education.[4]

In 1986 the Chinese government established a law requiring all children to receive at least nine years of free education. However, government spending on education has not matched the pace of economic growth. China has not yet reached the target set in 1993 to be reached by 2000 of spending 4% of China's annual GDP on education. The goal now is to reach that level by 2010. In 2001, China's total spending on education, as a percentage of annual GDP, was slightly ahead of India's. Currently India is spending a higher percentage of GDP on education than China. There has been more than a 300% increase in tertiary students since 1999, which currently number 15 million students, and is expected to increase to 25 million students by 2010. Greater government funding of education is required. Students and their families are doing their best to pay for educational opportunity. This national problem is an opportunity for American corporations to address.[5]

Seventy-five percent of China's 500,000 elementary, junior, and high schools are far away from the coastal areas where 500 million Chinese are participating in China's surging economy.[6] How can American corporations help the Chinese government bring 21st century education to 800 million in rural China? What is a good 21st century education and how can 800 million inland Chinese participate in it?

The Chinese government is working to improve the education of rural children. It has capped the amount schools can charge families for textbooks and other fees. In 2003, it launched a $96 million-a-year program subsidizing the cost of textbooks in poor areas. Working with Hong Kong billionaire Li Ka-shing, the government has provided satellite dishes and personal computers to 70,000 rural schools at a cost of $1.2 billion and plans to double that by 2007.[7]

Case Study: Endowing Peking University

Peking University, also known as Beijing University, is one of China's most impressive universities, with an international reputation for the very high quality of its students and for its history of intellectual independence. Peking University, for historic reasons, lacks the huge endowments the top American universities have acquired over hundreds of years of capitalism. But Peking University's founding in 1898 was greatly assisted by the efforts and generosity of the donations from American "friends of China." Today, one-third of Peking University's budget comes from the Chinese government and two-thirds must come from private sources, which are predominantly Chinese students and their families or communities.

In response to this, the America-China Partnership Foundation, a forum for leaders of American and Chinese companies, is helping to fund Peking University's Endowment Foundation and to provide scholarships for American students to study in China and Chinese students to study in America. American and Chinese private donors and corporations interested in contribution to the Peking University Endowment Foundation and these scholarships can contact Dr. Deng Ya, Secretary-General of the Peking University Endowment Fund in Beijing and Dai Min, President of the America-China Partnership Foundation in New York.

The education of minds and characters of American and Chinese leaders of the future is an effective focus for collaboration. Americans one hundred years ago helped in founding, funding, and constructing three of China's greatest universities, which is profoundly remembered in China. The caliber of Quingua, Peking, and Tshinghua Universities is as high in the sciences as anywhere in the world. This is especially remarkable given how the Cultural Revolution decimated China's institutions of learning.[8] President Hu Jintao chose Yale University to deliver a speech on April 21, 2006:

On the preceding page – front row left to right:

Madam Jin Juanping, Vice President of Peking University Press; Madam Dai Min, President of the America-China Partnership Foundation; Dr. Deng Ya, Secretary-General of Peking University Education Foundation

Back row right to left:

Professor Li Shixin; Mr. John Milligan-Whyte, Chairman of the America-China Partnership Foundation; Dr. Xu Zhihong, President of Peking University; Dr. Chen Wenshen, Executive Vice President of Peking University; Mr. Hu Jun, Peking University Education Foundation.

Coming to the Yale campus with its distinctive academic flavor and looking at the eager young faces in the audience, I cannot but recall my great experience at Qinghua University in Beijing 40 years ago. Indeed, what happens during one's school years will influence his whole life. I still benefit greatly from the instruction of my teachers and my interaction with other students. Yale is renowned for its long history, unique way of teaching and excellence in academic pursuit. If time could go back several decades, I would really like to be a student of Yale just like you.[9]

Later in his speech, President Hu Jintao expressed his gratitude to Yale:

Exchanges in culture and education and young people serve as a bridge for increasing understanding between our two peoples. They are a major driving force for the healthy and stable growth of China-U.S. relations. Yale is a forerunner in conducting China-U.S. educational exchanges and providing an important platform for cultural exchanges between the two countries. One hundred and fifty-six yeas ago a Chinese young man named Rong Hong entered Yale. Four years later he graduated with distinction and received a Bachelor of Arts degree, making him the first ever Chinese graduate of an American university. Later a group of young Chinese followed in his footsteps and studied at Yale. Over the past twenty years Yale has accepted over four thousand Chinese students and undertaken more than eighty cooperation programs in culture, science and technology, and education in China. Last summer, Yale sent the first group of students to China for internships and some among them became the first foreign interns to work with China's Palace Museum. I wish to take this opportunity to express my appreciation to you, Mr. Levin [President of Yale University], and for Yale for the efforts you have made to promote exchanges between our two peoples.

    To enhance mutual understanding between young people and educators of the two countries, I announce with pleasure

here that we have decided to invite one hundred Yale faculty
members and students to visit China this summer. I am
sure you can look forward to an enjoyable experience in
China.[10]

How Can 800 Million Rural Chinese Participate in China's Success?

The director of curriculum development at China's Ministry of
Education says: "the lack of creativity is a fatal disadvantage of
Chinese education...Students can cram and recite...They remember but don't understand." The emphasis is being changed from
lecturing and tests to in-class experiments and discussions. But
how do you teach what has not been taught to teachers when
they were students?

Alignment Opportunities

Shantou University provides a blueprint for China's educational
reform. It is a public university, but gets much of its funds from
Hong Kong billionaire Li Ka-shing who recruited ethnic Chinese
academics, many of whom travel back and forth between their
home universities and Shantou University.

> This star-studded corps of American-trained educators wants
> to ditch tradition and remake Shantou in the image of a U.S.
> university. They're introducing new teaching methods,
> overhauling the curriculum, and giving Shantou's 8,000
> students more responsibility for their own education.
> Instead of a set of required courses, Shantou now has a credit
> system, the first of its kind in China...Above all, the
> reformers are focused on educational quality. The goal is to
> replace rote learning, a tradition that dates back to the Han
> Dynasty, which introduced exams for would-be mandarins,
> and instead emphasize creativity. In the past, students
> crammed only to spit back the information on tests... The

Shantou experience could serve as a model for other Chinese schools. Political leaders are setting their sights on higher education and aim to boost university enrolment sharply.[11]

Li Ka-shing, one of the wealthiest Chinese, is very active financially in Mainland China and recently invested in a major Chinese bank.

Case Study: The Right Spirit at Lucent

American corporations wishing to align their success in China with China's success can play major roles in addressing the Chinese government's regional disparity amelioration and education goals. Lucent is an excellent role model. In 2000, Randy Yeh was one of the few executives born in Mainland China who was leading the China operations of one of the world's largest multinational companies.

Lucent works with Chinese government ministries to understand China's telecommunications and to work in partnership to find solutions, and applies the same approach with its Chinese customers, China Telcom and Unicom, and its joint venture partners. Yeh stated:

> Following the signing of the Memorandum of Understanding with the former Ministry of Post and Telecommunications in December 1995, we have worked closely with China Telcom. China Telcom emphasizes technology leadership, and they are very good at building networks. So, we explored standards together. They visited Bell Labs. After that, we developed together a plan to build a DWDM (Dense Wavelength Division Multiplexing) transmission link between Wuhan and Xi'an. It has been a great success, generating 10 gigabits a second of transmission capability, which is the highest in China. After this experiment, China Telcom decided to adopt DWDM technology for its entire transport network. This is an example of a win-win partnership. It will enable China Telcom to embrace change and allow us to be part of these developments.[12]

Like all other multinational corporations in China, Lucent finds that making such win-win relationships work is a "challenge" and takes "hard work." Yeh said: "…I want to stress one thing: You have to look at it from the other person's point of view. You will always have differences, but if you act fairly, frankly, and honestly, you can make a joint venture succeed. When there is fairness on both sides, frank discussion can happen and a relationship can be built. Understanding can be established and trust will develop. Once you have trust, many things work in China. When you try to negotiate a contract, for instance, in a very formal fashion, there could be many difficulties. But if you get to know each other well, you can become friends and trust each other. You have a sound understanding and then many things can be put on the table, looked at from both parties' angles, and get resolved. The final solution may be different from what you initially conceived, but your partner in China is capable of thinking in very creative ways in China to meet your need. You can develop a win/win partnership."[13]

All six of Lucent's joint ventures in China were profitable from 1997, and four of them are among the joint ventures with the best return on investment in the telecommunications industry in China in 1997. Yeh emphasizes the importance of training local talent in order to deal more effectively with China's fiercely competitive telecommunications industry:

> My feeling is that we still need to spend more energy and time to develop the overall skills of our people. There is still a significant experience gap between our Chinese employees and their counterparts, for instance, in the United States. We have established training and career development plans for all employees to demonstrate to our people that we are serious and that we have their long-term interest at heart. We also have repeatedly communicated our corporate values, for example, integrity, focus on results, customer dedication and care about the communities we live in, in

order to build the right spirit and behavior in our people and in our business."[14]

Focusing on the "right spirit," Lucent has supported Project Hope, a charity that helps underprivileged Chinese children go to school in a village three hours from Beijing in Hebei Province where a new school was built and many children have been "adopted" and supported by Lucent employees and their families. Yeh proudly states:

> "Every two or three months we go together to see these kids, their families, and the teachers. Sometimes we take the children out to Beijing to see educational exhibits, such as the aquarium. Sometimes we help by donating libraries and organizing computer training for the teachers, or by planting trees. Over the years, this has become quite an event in the village. Now, every time we go, the whole village turns out to see us. This has been a great experience for our employees and their families who have joined in this activity. By doing this together under the name of Lucent Technologies, they really feel proud of what we stand for.[15]

Lucent Technologies China Co. Ltd is helping the Chinese government achieve its social, economic, and technology goals for China. No wonder Jiang Zemin was so supportive of the company, which achieved profitability and profound alliances quickly in China.

But it is also very important, we would emphasize, to focus on the profound power of Lucent's support of Project Hope's educational outreach contribution to underprivileged children in a village that otherwise would not have the resources of Lucent. The Chinese government and people are profoundly touched by sincere, sustained gestures like Lucent's Project Hope. There is, in our view, absolutely no substitute for such gestures' sincerity and power to win friends and influence people in China. Such projects must be major ingredients in *all* American companies' China strategies.

Authors' Postscript

This book was written to assist Americans and Mainland Chinese in making choices that will define their relationship with their very different traditions, cultures, and histories but a shared need for prosperity and peace. These authors' postscripts illustrate the adventure of understanding and accepting others, which success in The China Game requires.

John Milligan-Whyte

Only a relatively tiny number of the 300 million Americans and 1.3 billion Mainland Chinese have ever interacted with each other personally. The change in mindsets that China is making and America must now make can be seen in the experiences of individuals born in Mainland China who are now living in the American civilization.

We understand very slowly, if at all, things that are outside our personal experiences. In 1958, I was told to eat my Brussels sprouts: "because children in China are starving." In 1968, I read Harrison Salisbury's *China* and Mao's *Little Red Book* and in 1978, I saw some of the first Mainland Chinese students dressed in their blue pajama-like uniforms arrive in the West. I am only beginning to realize how far these students' leaps between civilizations were. I now understand that children, including my co-authors-to-be really were starving in China, and that at least 800 million Chinese still wait to fully participate in China's success. After writing this book in 2006, my leap between civilizations is merely beginning.

In 1993, at CORE Capital Ltd, I worked with Andy Yang, a Mainland Chinese with one of the most unusual resumes I have ever seen. He had been educated in China as an engineer, and worked on the design of the engine for China's fighter jet and then in policy formation in the State Council, China's equivalent of the White House. He next earned statistics, computer science, and economics graduate degrees at Princeton, and joined the Hudson Institute, an American think tank. At the bottom of his resume in small print, the fact was mentioned that Andy had stood first among all of China's university graduates in 1984. I learned that China ranked its university graduates nationally. As we became friends, Andy shared one of his greatest concerns. His eight-year-old daughter, who had grown up in America, was refusing to speak Chinese.

In 1997, I began to see China and America through Dai Min's eyes. She asked me to speak to a delegation from the China State Council For Economic Restructuring. I met the delegation at the U.S. Secretary of Transportation's office in Washington, D.C. and traveled with them in a van to the office of the President of NASDAQ. I asked the head of the delegation how many times he had been to America. "Eight times" his translator said. That seemed like very few visits to me, but I learned that to a Mainland Chinese, it was an extraordinary number of visits to America. It seemed incongruous that such an important official in admitting foreign joint ventures to China had so little experience of Americans outside of China. It revealed the solitudes of China and America, which remain strangers to each other today. The leader of the delegation was the director of the division at the State Council for Economic Restructuring Committee that approved 256,000 joint ventures investing US$256 billion dollars in China between 1990 and 1994.

In 2002 at Milligan-Whyte & Smith, I worked on the first international acquisition by a Chinese state-owned company. China Netcom was "going global" by acquiring, through a Bermuda subsidiary, 19,000 kilometers of fiber optic cable throughout Asia from Global Crossing Ltd. Seeing the different worlds Chinese and American executives came from, Dai Min and I established the China Bermuda Society in 2003 and then the America-China Partnership Foundation in 2006 to provide a forum for the leaders of Chinese and non-Chinese companies creating joint ventures. Chinese companies are learning to be multinational and non-Chinese companies are learning to do business with China and must learn to align their China strategies with China's economic development strategy.

I have met thousands of Mainland Chinese involved in nation building in many roles, from a Tiananmen Square leader who is now a Wall Street veteran, leading business to government officials, scientists, scholars, artists, workers, and farmers. One of the most memorable was a very elderly Chinese lady who insisted on helping me carry one of the too many suitcases I was struggling with in the Tokyo airport. They all remind me of an article by Kowak, May & Sigmund, "The Arithmetics Of Mutual Help," published in *Scientific American* in June 1995, and of *The Family Of Man*, published in 1958, which celebrated the shared nature of human beings in diverse societies.

Seeing the Chinese and American people I met, first through my own eyes and gradually through their eyes, brought opportunities to empathize with them. Their character, courage, and determination assure me that human beings will grow and understand each other. But one must try very, very hard and persevere to succeed in beginning to understand others. Perhaps this experience will convey what I mean. While driving one day in 2004, Dai Min asked me to stop the car. She got out and began pulling up grass and feeding a charming but noisy goat.

The goat belonged to a farmer and Dai Min was trespassing on his land. I expected the farmer to appear and not be as friendly as the goat. I asked and then insisted that she stop because the goat was on private property. She instead began feeding a second goat baying loudly right by the farmer's door. I angrily said, "That is the problem with you Chinese, you do not respect other people's property!" This expressed a fundamental concern I had been harboring about the moral character of Mainland Chinese. She pulled up another tuft of grass and said, "You have to remember, where I grew up in China, there is no private property." Suddenly I began, at that tipping point of mindset change, to see the contrasting mindsets of those brought up in Rights and Permission Societies. Americans and Mainland Chinese still live in fundamentally different societies and mindsets. Understanding that is a key to "us" understanding each other. Accepting that is the key to prosperity and peace in the Age Of Species Lethal Weapons and to the continuing success of The Human Experiment. *john.milliganwhyte@gmail.com*

Mannie Manhong Liu

I hope that a description of my upbringing in the Cultural Revolution in the desperate poverty of rural China, and of returning 30 years later to the village people who safeguarded me then, helps American readers understand what China's economic and social reforms mean to 1.3 billion Chinese.

As a result of the kindness I have found in both Chinese and Americans, I have evolved as a teacher in a rural school and as a student at Remnin University in China, the University of Oklahoma, Cornell and Harvard, and devoted my life as a professor to learning and teaching about the venture capital businesses in America and China. I hope that this book helps in China's emergence from poverty and assists Americans in understanding the nation-building that is going on in China and in understanding the hearts of Chinese people. We admire America, and very, very much want Americans and Chinese to be real friends and partners in building a better world. Here is the story of my return with three childhood friends after 30 years back to the village that we were sent to during the Cultural Revolution.

On a hot summer Saturday, I drove my new car, together with Lishi, Jun and Xiaozho, to a small village in Shanxi Province where we lived as "re-educated youth" for many years. As we drove, we became more anxious and filled with mixed feelings. Everything seemed so familiar yet remote. The scattered trees and crops, the yellow earth; our land was not fertile or as prosperous as we had been taught in our elementary school textbooks. Nevertheless, it is our motherland.

Jun is retired and a full-time mother and wife. Xiaozho is retired, too, but runs a small business in his town. Lishi and I are still teaching at colleges. Since we left the village 30 years ago, we had not had time to be together again. Each of us has had a different course in life. Life has taken remarkable turns for me. I know life as a farmer, a village schoolteacher, and a factory accountant. Then I passed the first college entry exam given after the Cultural Revolution and became a student in China and America, worked at Harvard, and returned to China among the "sea turtles."

The six and a half years living in the small village always remains my most memorable time. All four of us share the same feelings. In most of the stories, movies, television shows, and novels, the life of those village days is described as hard, dark, and unbearable. Life was very harsh indeed, but the villagers took care of us like we were part of their families and treated us kindly. I could not hold back my tears as we entered the village again with feelings of warmness, homecoming, appreciation, and, somehow, sorrow.

The village is located 250 kilometers west of Beijing. It was very poor then and more than 30 years later, it is still among the poorest in the nation. We parked the car at the turn of a small road, not far from where our old home was located, and went directly into its yard. I held my breath. It is different. The yard was split into two parts; the well we used to fetch water from was gone. The small garden where we grew our vegetables had become a small storage room. Yes, it was our home some 30 years ago, before

"Going home and finding I had never left and must take my neighbors with me in China's good fortune."

I went to college, before I stepped on the beautiful land of America, and before I returned to China.

A lady came from behind us and grabbed Jun's hand. "Jun," she shouted. Jun was astonished. "You still remember my name after thirty years!" he said. The villagers all came. "Yes, we still remember you, all of you" they said. Even the youngsters knew us. They had heard all about us from their parents. They were happy to see us, with their usual kindness and hospitality, just as 30 years ago.

"Do you have enough to eat?" we asked. "Oh, yes, we can eat whatever we want. We are not hungry any more, not like those days when you were here," they said. I recalled those days when we were there in the village. The hardest thing was for us to find something to fill our stomach. It was not rare if we saw someone suddenly pass away from hunger. Food, that was all we thought about then, food. Whatever food was? Now, the village is still poor, but we were so pleased to know they were no longer hungry any more. We were invited to home after home and fed with watermelons, apples, and dry apricots.

Americans may have a hard time understanding that having enough to eat had been such a dream for the Chinese people and such an enormous task for the Chinese government. For hundreds of years, China has been struggling to feed its people. The most popular greeting in China was "Have you eaten?" Only in recent years have the Chinese people changed their greeting to "How are you?" when they meet.

I remember we were working in the field under the sun. I used a hoe to remove all the weeds around the crops. It was hot, and the day was long. I had never worked so hard under such harsh conditions. I remember vividly that after work we needed to pick some fresh grass for the rabbits we raised, but we were so tired and completely out of strength. My hands were bloody and my back ached. But we needed some fresh grass, so we all crawled on the ground and grabbed some greenery. It was painful, but we somehow felt funny at the same time, and laughed with each other. Some young villagers came over and helped us, as they always did. We were very fortunate. We heard that some other re-educated youth like us were treated badly, but we were always taken care of by the villagers.

I was born prematurely and raised by my grandma. I was weak and vulnerable when I was little. She never let me do any housework. My grandpa was a successful businessman and left some real estate in Beijing when he passed away. I had a nice childhood. We were not wealthy, but affluent. I remember each month, our neighbors would come and borrow some money from my grandma, and they would always repay it early next month when they received their salary. I had never worked at home during the Cultural Revolution; I suffered as most Chinese did. My parents, who were underground communists as college students before 1949, were accused as spies and sent to a concentration camp. I had no idea how the family survived. But I am glad we did—not just my family. The Chinese people and China survived and triumphed.

In the center of the village was the old school where I taught for four years. The new school had just been built, and the teachers and students had moved into it. The old school became the village office. Lishi said to me, "We Chinese always pay attention to education." The villagers would always leave the newest and best housing in the village to students. "Remember when you started teaching here thirty years ago, this yard was the new school and the village office moved to the old school buildings?' Yes, I remembered. It was like yesterday.

I remembered one cold winter night the village head was giving a speech to all farmers including us about revolutionary discipline. Everyone felt sleepy. Suddenly he turned to me: "You, you look so thin and fragile, how can you work on the farm? I opened my mouth, tried to find some words, but failed. "Our school needs a teacher" he continued, "maybe you can teach there."

I started teaching the second grade in a middle school when I was barely finished *my* second grade in middle school. I read and studied during the night and taught what I had just learned. Several days after I started my teaching career, a farmer came to me with obvious anger. He handed me a long wooden stick. "You are not a good teacher," he said. "A good teacher has to beat the students. We do not mind your beating them. If you don't, how can you make them study?" He turned to his son, "Kneel down," he said. The young boy got on his knees. The farmer turned to me, ordering, "Spank him!" I was astonished. I could not. *manniemm@sfruc.edu.cn*

Howard H. Jiang

Everyone has a few intimate memories in life. I was sent to the countryside to till the land during the Cultural Revolution at the age of seventeen. There I experienced the extremes of physical exhaustion as well as the freedom from the urban madness of the Cultural Revolution. The farmers were down-to-earth people focused on making a living. They were largely kind and hard working. There I realized the folly of the so-called revolution and that the ordinary folks were more rational than the educated elite. There were different groups of city youth living in the area. There were all kinds of conflicts and fights, some very bloody, often for no meaningful reasons at all. We were young and hormones were dictating our behavior, rather than reason. Those fights were often started by the most cowardly members of the group using the strength of the group as a backup. Often the whole group suffers the consequences for no good reasons. As a result, nobody dared to approach any other group nor went to their territory. One night, on my long walk back from the head office of the commune that covered a vast region, I was so exhausted that I had to seek help from a hostile Youth Point. Help was readily and generously given, to my great relief and surprise. *Howard.Jiang@bakernet.com*

Dai Min

My experiences illustrate the profound changes in China as it emerges from solitude. My grandfather was General Dai Fengxiang, one of the earliest high-ranking generals of the Republic of China honored before and after the 1949 Chinese Revolution for supporting Sun Ya-Sun, the founding father of the Republic of China, in the overthrow of the Qing Dynasty. After growing up in rural China during the Cultural Revolution, I won the first national competition in the performing arts in 1978, and was a leading lyric soprano with the National Opera and Dance Company of China and performed for government officials at state events for visiting foreign dignitaries, and in tours throughout China. In 1988, I left China speaking only Mandarin to study in Germany, England, and America.

In my business career, I sold real estate in South America to Asian investors, worked at the United Nations Headquarters coordinating the visits of Chinese government and business leaders, and was a currency trader on Wall Street and a television producer in New York. I founded a consulting firm advising clients including ABB of Switzerland, BASF and Obermeyers of Germany, the American firm Dectert, and Chinese government entities and companies. Now I am President of CORE Capital Ltd. and China International Strategies, Ltd. , as well as the American-China Partnership Foundation and Forum. This career path was only possible because of the changing history of modern China. I love America and China and know they must be, and therefore will be, successful partners. *daiminusa@gmail.com*

Endnotes

Chapter 1: Mindset Change as a Competitive Advantage for American Companies

1. "Behind the mask," *The Economist*, March 18, 2004.

2. See Julia Lovell, *The Great Wall: China Against The World 1000 BC–AD 2000*, Grove Press, 2006.

3. "Political Minds," *Foreign Policy*, March/April 2006, p. 19.

4. Kishore Mahbubani, *Beyond The Age Of Innocence*, BBS Public Affairs, 2005, pp. 17–9.

5. The American Chamber of Commerce in China reports that 75% of its 254 members are profitable and 50% said their margins were higher than their worldwide margins.

6. A "win-win mindset" focuses on finding a solution that produces sustainably compelling rewards for all key participants sufficient to achieve the objectives of all key participants.

7. C.K. Prahalad & Kenneth Lieberthal, "The End Of Corporate Imperialism," *Harvard Business Review*, August 2003, pp. 2–11.

8. Ibid.

9. In 2005, the five most popular (affordable and sizable) are:

   • Joint EMBA degree from Zhongshan University and the Minnesota University
   • Shanghai Jianotong University and Nanyang Technological University of Singapore
   • University of International Business and Economics and Robert H. Smith School of Business
   • Sino-Dutch International Business Center of Nanjing University
   • University of Science and Technology Beijing and Texas University at Arlington

The top five EMBA degrees with the best schools' reputation (joint programs with degree given by top Chinese universities) and their annual graduates are:

   • Tshinghua University   (100)

- Beijing University   (152)
- FuDan University   (120)
- Shanghai Jiaotong University (240)
- Xiamen University   (230)

In the next five years, the market for EMBA degrees in China is estimated to be at least 1 billion RMB. A Fortune Magazine (China) 2005 China Management Education Survey on a sample of 15,000 executives in China reported that 67.6 were satisfied with the Sino-Foreign Joint MBA and EMBA programs and only 9.2% were satisfied with the Chinese domestic MBA and EMBA programs.

The Ministry of Education indicates that the normal fee for an MBA program is 200,00 RMB, but fees vary from 50,000 to 660,000 RMB. Fees for short training programs by Sino-Foreign joint venture educational institutions range from 2000 to 3000 RMB per day. The Fortune Magazine (China) survey indicated in response to the questions:

What do you think would be the appropriate fee for EMBA programs?

- 100,000 to 150,000 RMB: 51.0%
- 150,000 to 200,000 RMB: 25.0%
- 200,000 to 250,000 RMB: 9.8%
- 250,000 to 300,000 RMB: 2.1%
- 300,000 RMB plus: 1.7%

What do you think about the fees for 2-day training programs?

- 2000 to 4000 RMB: 49.6%
- 4000 to 6000 RMB: 15.0%

10. Haley, Haley & Tan, *The Tao Of Chinese Business*, John Wiley & Sons (Asia) Pte Ltd, 2004, p. 216.

11. Ibid.

12. Ibid., pp. 213–16.

13. Peter Marsh, "Companies from emerging markets setting the pace", *Financial Times*, May 24, 2006, p. 17.

14. Harvard Business School Press, 2005.

15. George T. Haley, Usha C. V. Haley, Chin Tiong Tan, *The Chinese Tao Of Business: The Logic Of Successful Business Strategy*, John Wiley & Sons (Asia) Pte Ltd, 2004.

16. Ibid., p. 82.

17. Harold Chee & Chris West, Myths About Doing Business in China, Palgrave MacMillan, 2004, p. 104.

18. This analysis is based upon and summarizes Peggy Kenna & Sondra Lacey, *Business China: A Practical Guide To Understanding Chinese Business Culture*,

Passport Books, 1994. See also Richard Nisbett, *The Geography Of Thought*, Free Press, a division of Simon & Schuster, 2003.

19. Mark Daniel, "China In A World Of Risk," Braham ed., *China's Century: The Awakening Of The Next Economic Powerhouse*, Laurence Brahm ed, John Wiley & Sons, 2001, p. 105.

20. Ibid., p. 101.

21. Ibid., p. 102.

22. *See Document Of The 16th National Congress Of The Communist Party Of China*, Foreign Language Press, 2002, pp. 169–246.

23. Ibid.

24. Ibid., pp. 104–5.

25. Haley, Haley & Tan, ibid., pp. 258–59.

26. Haley, Haley & Tan, ibid., pp. 266–97.

27. Peter Kreef, *What Would Socrates Do? A History Of Moral Thought And Ethics*, Barnes & Noble Audio Books.

28. Haley, Haley & Tan, ibid., p. 13.

29. Kenneth Hammond, *From Yao to Mao: 5000 Years of Chinese History*, The Teaching Company, 2004.

30. Fritjof Capra, *The Tao Of Physics*, Shambhala, Boston, 2000 pp. 101–02.

31. Ibid., 105–06.

32. Ibid., p. 121.

Chapter 2: Creating Successful Genuine Global Joint Ventures Between American and Chinese Companies

1. Jack and Susan Welch, *Winning*, Harper Business, 2005, pp. 341.

2. Ibid., pp. 341–5.

3. Ibid., pp. 341–5.

4. See Donald N. Sull, *Made In China: What Western Managers Can Learn From Trailblazing Chinese Entrepreneurs*, Harvard Business School Press, 2005.

5. Private conversations of Howard Jiang with State Council officials indicate that they have a completely open mind to free market competition.

6. See Yashang Huang, *Selling China*, Cambridge University Press, 2003.

7. John Stuttard, *The New Silk Road*, ibid., p. 78.

8. Paul Thurrott, "IBM PC division: no profit for more than 3 years," January 3, 2005, *Windows IY Pro. www.windowsitpro.com.*

9. Ibid., pp. 254–55.

10. Haley, Haley & Tan, ibid.

11. Friedman, *The World is Flat, A Brief History of the 21st Century*, Farrus Straus & Giroux, 2005., p. 210.

12. William Buckley, "IBM Profit Rises 22% but Revenue Shows Drop," *Wall Street Journal*, April 19, 2006, p. A3.

13. "Liu Chuanzhi: "The man who acquired IBM PC," China View, *www.chinaview.cn*, September 1, 2005.

14. Clyde Prestowitz, *Three Billion New Capitalists The Great Shift Of Wealth And Power To The East*, Basic Books, 2005, pp. 211–13.

15. Jon Ogden, "Seeking a Peek at the New Lenovo," *Wall Street Journal Online*, August 9, 2005.

16. Evan Ramstad, "Lenovo's Net Profit Rises 6% Revenue Falls at Former IBM Unit," *Wall Street Journal Online*, August 10, 2005.

17. Ibid.

18. Evan Ramstad, "Has Lenovo Group Really Spun Gold Out Of IBM's Chaff?" *Wall Street Journal Online*, August 24, 2005.

19. Ibid.

20. Ibid.

21. See President of Legend China statements at 2004 http//biz.mlogger.cn/lenovo/archive/1112204.aspx.

22. Paul Thurrott, "IBM PC division: no profit for more than 3 years," January 3, 2005, *Windows IY Pro. www.windowsitpro.com.*

23. "Lenovo Group Ltd.: Acquired IBM Unit May Post Profit Earlier Than Expected", *Wall Street Journal Online*, June 15, 2005.

24. Peter Lewis, "The new, improved notebook: Lenovo refines a classic with its first crop of Think Pad portables, successfully combining superior performance, useful new features and darn good looks," *Fortune*, October 31, 2005, p. 201.

25. Evan Ramstad, "Lenovo's Profit Misses Expectations, CEO Amelio Touts China Operations," January 26, 2006, *Wall Street Journal Online*.

26. Ibid.

27. Michael Phillips, "Lenovo Contract May Get Review By Washington," March, 2006, *Wall Street Journal Online*.

28. Ramstad, ibid.

29. Ramstad, ibid.

30. Ramstad, ibid.

31. Ramstad, ibid.

32. Financial Times, May 20, 2006.

33. Donald N. Sull, *Made In China: What Western Managers Can Learn From Trailblazing Chinese Entrepreneurs*, Harvard Business School, 2005, pp. 75–83.

34. Peter Engardio, "Emerging Giants," *Business Week*, July 31, 2006, p. 49.

35. Ibid.

36. Ibid.

37. Donald N. Sull, *Made In China: What Western Managers Can Learn From Trailblazing Chinese Entrepreneurs*, Harvard University Press, 2005, pp. 98–107.

38. Chee & West, *Myths About Doing Business In China*, Palgrave Macmillan, 2004, p. 97.

39. Haley, Haley & Tan, *The Tao Of Chinese Business*, John Wiley & Sons, 2004 p. 250.

40. Ibid., p. 249.

41. Oded Shenkar, *The Chinese Century*, Wharton School Publishing 2005, p. 154.

42. Kenichi Ohmae, *The Next Global Stage*, Wharton School Publishing, 2005, p. 139.

43. Oded Shenkar, ibid., pp. 149–150.

44. Julius Bar, *Tempted by the dragon—Swiss companies in China*.

45. Ibid., p. 99.

46. Ibid.

47. Ibid., p. 108.

48. Dow Jones Newswires, "China's 2005 Computer Product Exports Hit $ 140.85 billion," *The Wall Street Journal Online* January 28, 2006.

49. David Thirlwill, Lowy Institute.

50. *Business Week*, August 22/29, 2005.

51. Julius Bar, ibid., p. 107.

52. Ibid., p. 166.

53. Oded Shenkar, ibid., p. 165.

54. Laurie J. Flynn, "Trying to Halt A.M.D., Intel Plays to Business Market," *The New York Times*, April 24, 2006, p. C5.

55. Fred Vogelstein, "How Intel Got Inside" *Fortune*, October 4, 2004, p. 127, 132.

56. Peter Engardio, "Emerging Giants," *Business Week*, July 31, 2006, p. 49.

57. Ibid.

58. "Fabs" are factories that make silicon chips.

59. Julius Bar, ibid., p. 103.

60. Julius Bar, ibid., p. 99.

61. Ibid., p. 104.

62. Ibid., p. 108.

63. Ibid., p. 103.

64. Julius Bar, ibid., p. 100.

65. Oded Shenkar, ibid., pp. 102–103.

66. Ibid., p. 116.

Chapter 3: Advanced Strategies Aligning American Companies and The Chinese Government and Chinese Companies' Goals

1. Michael J. Moser, "The Role of Arbitrations in resolving Chinese-Foreign Business Disputes: Past, Present and Future," Laurence Brahm, *China's Century*, John Wiley & Sons (Asia) PTE LTD, 2001, pp. 245–49.

2. Ibid.

3. For accounts of litigation in China, see Tim Clissold, *Mr. China*, Harper Business, 2005.

4. Kovak, May & Sigmund, ibid.

5. For good primers, see Carolyn Blackman, Negotiating China XX XXX and John L. Graham & N. Mark Lam, "The Chinese Negotiation," *Harvard Business Review*, October 2003, p. 82.

6. Gongmeng Chen, "A Smart and Sustainable Growth Model for China's Economy in the Following 20 Years: Innovation and Venture Capital," presentation at World Economic Forum's China Summit 2004.

7. Chi Fulin, ibid., p. 24.

8. *The Economist*, "The Myth of China Inc," September 3rd–9th, 2005, p. 54.

9. Oded Shenkar, *The Chinese Century*, Wharton School Publishing, 2005, p. 135.

10. "Building the nation," *The Economist*, June 24, 2006, p. 47.

11. Ibid.

12. Ibid.

13. Ibid.

14. Ibid., p. 89.

15. Kenichi Ohmae, ibid., p. 89.

16. *Ibid., pp. 211–12.*

17. The Economist, March 18, 2005.

18. Jeffrey D. Sachs, ibid.

19. Dow Jones News Wire, "Volkswagen Aims To Slash Production Costs At China Ops," *Wall Street Journal Online*, October 17, 2005.

20. Oded Shenkar, *The Chinese Century*, ibid., p. 45.

21. Gordon Fairclough and Shai Oster, "As China's Auto Market Booms, Leaders Clash Over Heavy Toll," *Wall Street Journal*, June 13, 2006, p. A1.

22. Alvsha Webb and Gail Kachadourian, "China's New Heavy Hitter," *Automotive News*, June 12, 2006.

23. Darren Dahl, "Would you buy a Chinese car from this man?," *Inc*, July 2005, pp. 69–74.

24. Oded Shenkar, ibid., pp. 44–45.

25. Ibid., p. 46.

26. Non-Chinese cultures do not feel a duty to pay royalties for Chinese inventions such as paper, the cross bow, gun powder, cannons, rockets, porcelain, the number zero and negative numbers and all the other intellectual property that has formed the basis of their economic development.

27. Rober Buderi and Gregory Huang, *Guanxi: Microsoft, China, And Bill Gates' Plan to Win the Road Ahead*, Simon & Schuster, 2006.

28. Peter Schwartz and Rita Koselka, " Quantum Leap," *Fortune*, August 7, 2006., p. 76.

29. Stephanie Mehta, "Behold The Server Farm! Glorious Temple Of The Information Age," *Fortune*, August 7, 2006, p. 69.

Chapter 4: An Advanced Structure for American and Chinese Global Joint Ventures

1. "The Dragon Tucks In," *The Economist*, July 2nd–8th, 2005, pp. 54–56.

2. Henry Sender, "Meet China Inc.: Topping Japan Inc. of 1980's," *Wall Street Journal Online*, June 24, 2005.

3. *Fortune*, August 1, 2005.

4. Bill Gates, *Business At The Speed Of Thought*, Warner Books, 1999.

Chapter 5: Traditional Structures, Strategies and Best Practices Used by Companies Investing or Joint Venturing in China in the 20th Century

1. Charts prepared by Baker McKenzie.

2. Ibid.

3. Ibid.

4. Ibid.

5. Haley, Haley & Tan, ibid., p. 91.

6. Ibid., p. 34.

7. Ibid.

8. Harold Chee and Chris West, *Myths About Doing Business In China*, Pargrave Macmillan, 2004, p. 31.

9. William M. Bulkeley, "Kodak Posts Loss As Film Sales Erode," *Wall Street Journal Online*, July 20, 2005.

10. Kenichi Ohmae, ibid.

11. Ibid.

12. "For Ailing Kodak The Picture Dims," *Barron's*, August 7, 2006, p. 14.

13. Wilfred Vanhonacker, "A Better Way To Crack China," *Harvard Business Review*, March–April 2000, pp. 2–3.

14. Ibid.

15. Ted Fishman, *China Inc*, Simon & Schuster, 2005, 214–16.

16 Ibid., p. 216.

17. Dexster Roberts & Michael Arndt, "It's Getting Hotter In The East," *Business Week*, August 22/29, 2005, p. 78.

18. Christopher Rhoads, "Handset Sales Help Motorola Return to Profit," *Wall Street Journal Online*, July 20, 2005.

19. Christopher Rhoads & Rebecca Buckman, "A Chinese Telecom Powerhouse Stumbles on Road to U.S.," *Wall Street Journal Online*, July 28, 2005.

20. Pete Engardio, "Emerging Giants," *Business Week*, July 31, 2006, pp. 42–3.

21. Ibid.

22. Ibid.

Chapter 6: Traditional Structures and Strategies and the Global Joint Venture Model's Advantages

1. John B. Stuttard, *The New Silk Road*, John Wiley & Sons, Inc, 2000.
2. Ibid., pp. 42–3.
3. Ibid., pp. 43–4.
4. Ibid., p. 47.
5. Ibid., pp. 45–6.
6. Haley, Haley & Tan, ibid., pp. 257–8.
7. Stuttard, ibid.
8. Stuttard, ibid., p. 65.
9. Ibid., pp. 65–6.
10. Ibid., pp. 63–4.
11. Ibid., p. 65.
12. Stuttard., ibid., pp. 121–2.
13. Stuttard, ibid., pp. 122–3.
14. Ibid.
15. Stuttard, ibid., p. 52.
16. Stuttard, ibid., p. 51.
17. Stuttard, ibid., pp. 52–3.
18. Stuttard, ibid., p. 56.
19. Stuttard, ibid., p. 49.
20. See Chee & West, ibid, pp. 85–89 and Carolyn Blackman, Negotiating China, ibid.
21. Stuttard, ibid.
22. Stuttard, ibid., p. 80.
23. Stuttard, ibid., p. 77.
24. Stuttard, ibid., pp. 78–9.
25. Suttard, ibid., p. 80.
26. Ibid.
27. Stuttard, ibid., pp. 98–9.
28. Ibid.

Chapter 7: China's Permission Society Enters the World Trade Organization

1. Julius Bar, ibid., p. 16.

2. Lester Thurow, *Fortune Favors The Bold*, Harper Business, 2003, pp. 202–03.

3. Ming Zeng and Peter J. Williamson, "The Hidden Dragons," *Harvard Business Review*, October 2003, pp. 32–40.

4. Kenneth Lieberthal & Geoffrey Lieberthal, "The Great Transition," *Harvard Business Review*, October 2003, pp. 4–16.

5. Ibid.

6. Ibid.

7. Stuttard, ibid., pp. 38–9.

8. See Laurence Brahm, ibid.

9. Hank M. Paulson and Fred Hu, "Banking Reform in China: Mission Critical," Mar & Richter, *China Enabling A New Era Of Changes*, ibid., pp. 49–50.

10. Ibid., pp. 53–6.

11. Peter D Sutherland, "China: The Long March To Capital Market Reform," Brahm, ibid., p. 286.

12. Hank M. Paulson and Fred Hu, "Banking Reform in China: Mission Critical," in Pamela C.M. Mar and Frank-Jurgen Richter, *China Enabling A New Era Of Changes*, John Wiley & Sons (Asia) Pte Ltd, 2003 at p. 59.

13. Krishna Guha, "Paulson approved as new Treasury Secretary," *Financial Times*, June 29, 2006, p. 3.

14. Ibid.

15. "China's Chenming Scraps Sale Of Stake To Citigroup Venture," *Wall Street Journal*, July 31, 2006, p. C5.

16. Mure Dickie, "Chenming paper group scraps deal with foreign equity fund," *The Economist*, July 31, 2006, p. 20.

17. June Kronholz, "China Tests U.S. Immigration Plan," *Wall Street Journal*, July 31, 2006, p. A4.

18. Rick Carew, "Insurer Ping An Set to Branch Out With China Deals," *Wall Street Journal*, July 31, 2006, p. C5.

19. Julius Bar, ibid., p. 13.

20. See for example "Biggest state bank transforms into joint-stock company," *China View*, October 28, 2005, *www.chinaview.cn*.

21. See for example James Areddy, "ICBC to Unveil Goldman Pact," *Wall Street Journal Online*, March 2006.

22. See for example Justine Lau, "Confidence soars in IPOs from China," *Financial Times*, May 24, 2006, p. 14 and Justine Lau, "Bank of China IPO raises $9.7 bn," *Financial Times*, May 25, 2006, p. 19., and Lex, "Bank of China IPO," *Financial Times*, May 25, 2006, p. 12.

23. Kate Linegaugh & Mary Kissel, "China's Banks See Fresh Wave Of Foreign Investment," *Wall Street Journal Online*, August 31, 2005.

24. James Areddy, "Bank of China Offers Mandate To Handle IPO to Three Banks," *Wall Street Journal Online*, August 30, 2005.

25. Ibid.

26. James Areddy, "China's Economic Boom Masks Financing Limits of Big Firms", *Wall Street Journal Online*, October 13, 2005.

27. Ibid.

28. Ibid.

29. Ibid.

30. See Yasheng Huang, *Selling China*, Cambridge University Press, 2003.

Chapter 8: Aligning American Companies' China Strategies with China's Financial Services Development Strategies

1. See Chi Fulin, *China The New Stage Of Reform*, Foreign Languages Press, Beijing, p. 9.

2. To further attract foreign investors, the Chinese government has established a series of favorable policies, including reduced taxation and duty. In the "economic development zones" or "high-tech development zones," for instance, foreign investors are required to pay no taxes for the first three years, with the extra benefit of reduced taxes for an additional three years. Foreign investors are provided with reduced fees for office space and in some instances free rent. In addition, land, equipment, and manufacturing facilities are available at minimal cost to the investors. In Shenzhen, the local government offered a remarkable 70% off land-leasing fees for foreign investors.

3. Chi Fulin, ibid.

4. Chi Fulin, ibid., p. 15.

5. Hope & Lau, ibid., p. 19.

6. China Ministry of Finance Final Account Statistics, *Xinhau*, Beijing June 4, 2003.

7. Richard McGregor, "Private Sector In Control of China Economy", *Financial Times*, September 13, 2005, p. 2.

8. For an article reflecting the development of the academic literature see Tarun Kanna, Krishna Palepu & Jayant Sinha, "Strategies That Fit Emerging Markets," *Harvard Business Review*, June 2005, which attempts to fine-tune zero-sum-game approach to the issue.

9. Ibid.

Chapter 9: Aligning American Companies with China's Banking Industry Goals

1. *Business Week*, "Resorting the balance."

2. *The Economist*, "The Frugal Giant," September 24th–30th, 2005, p. 14.

3. "Foreign banks take 19% market share," *China View, www.chinaview.cn*, October 11, 2005.

4. For a comprehensive summary, see China Online.

5. A. Browne, "China's small firms turn to 'curb' banks: Shoe magnate's saga illustrates why growing concerns seeking capital from private sources," *Wall Street Journal (Eastern Edition)* August 3, 2004.

6. Bodie & Liu, 2000.

7. Martin Haemming, *The Globalization Of Venture Capital*, Haupt Verlag.

8. Future Growth, Future Risks: Opening Up the Financial Services Industry, China Business Summit, 2004.

9. Ibid.

10. Ibid.

11. See Laurence J. Brahm, "Zhu Rongji's 'Managed Marketization' of the Chinese Economy," Mar & Richter, *China Enabling A New Era Of Change*, 2003 pp. 71–84.

12. Ibid., pp. 71–2.

Chapter 10: Aligning American Companies with China's Insurance Reinsurance and Industry Goals

1. Walter B. Kielholtz, "China's Insurance Industry—Facing A New Era Of Opportunities And Challenges," Laurence Brahm, *China's Century*, John Wiley & Sons (Asia) PTE Ltd, 2001, p. 300.

2. Ibid.

3. Future Growth; Future Risks: Opening Up the Financial Services Industry, China Business Summit 2004.

4. Ibid.

5. *Asia Times Special Report*, February 16, 2001.

6. Rick Carew, "Insurer Pin An Set to Branch Out With China Deals," *Wall Street Journal*, July 31, 2006, p. C5.

7. China Life had its IPO on the New York and Hong Kong Stock Exchanges on February 17 and 18, 2003.

8. Ping An Life had its IPO on the Hong Kong Stock Exchange on June 24, 2004.

9. "XL Capital sponsors Chinese Executive training scheme," *Bermuda Royal Gazette*, March 13, 2006, p. 14.

10. ACE Ltd Press Release, May 28, 2002.

11. Julius Bar, *Tempted by the dragon*, pp. 51–7.

12. Ibid.

Chapter 11 China's Stock Markets

1. 2001 mid-year number from China Securities Regulatory Commission.

2. AWJ 5/10/2001.

3. AWJ 4/29/02.

4. China Legal Change Webpage Publication.

5. Andrew Browne, "UBS Clears a Key Hurdle in China," *Wall Street Journal*, June 21, 2006, p. C13.

6. *China Daily*, August 13, 2001.

7. Florian Gimbel, "China Loss for Credit Suisse," *Financial Times*, April 20, 2006.

8. CD December 19, 2001.

9. For a complete English-language summary, see the China Legal Change Webpage.

10. CD February 14, 2001.

11. CD November 16, 2001.

12. AWSJ September 4, 2001.

13. AWSJ February 28, 2002.

Chapter 12: Aligning American Companies with Chinese Companies in China's Venture Capital Sector

1. Robert A. Theleen, Private Equity In China, *China's Century: The Awakening Of The Next Economic Powerhouse*, Laurence Brahm ed., John Wiley & Sons (Asia) Ltd, 2001, p. 155.

2. Huang, ibid.

3. Andrew Tan & John Grobowski, "China," *Global Counsel Handbooks Private Equity Handbook* 2004/05, Practical Law Company, www.practicallaw.com/pehandbook.

4. Ibid.

5. B. Batjargal & M. M. Liu, "Entrepreneurs' access to private equity in China: The role of social capital," *Organization Science*, April 2004.

6. Ibid.

7. For example, see Wright and Robbie, 1998; and Bruton and Ahlstrom, 2003.

8. Gompers and Lerner, ibid., 2004.

9. J. Laurenceson & J.C.H. Chai, "State banks and economic development in China," *Journal of International Development*, March 2003, p. 211.

10. Ibid.

11. Robert Theleen, "Private Equity In China," *China's Century: The Awakening Of A New Economic Powerhouse*, John Wiley & Sons (Asia) Pte Ltd, 2001, p. 163.

12. Ibid., p. 159.

13. This overview comes from IBM's presentation "Partnering with a Multinational Corporation" at *China Update 2005, Mergers & Acquisitions-Making It Happen, Making It Work*, Baker McKenzie and China Institute, June 7, 2005.

14. Robert Theleen, ibid., pp. 156–8.

15. Zero2 IPO (2004).

16. In recent years, researchers, academia as well as practitioners express more and more interest in the Chinese venture capital business. Wright and Robbie (1998), and White, Gao, and Zhang (2002) noted that it is important to investigate venture capital activities within the context: the particular set of economic, political and cultural environment in which venture capital business is developed and operated. Batjargal and Liu (2004) indicated that the context may also include social capital and the role "guanxi" plays in the investment decision-making process.

17. Black and Gilson (1998).

18. Bruton and Ahlstrom, 2003.

19. (2002).

20. Theleen, ibid., pp. 162–3.

Chapter 13: *Alignment Opportunities for American Companies with China's Educational Challenges*

1. Dow Jones Newswire, "Chinese Prs, PM Use New Year To Vow To Help Rural Poor," *Wall Street Journal Online*, January 29, 2006.
2. Ibid.
3. Ibid.
4. Bruce Einhorn, "No Peasant Left Behind," *Business Week*, August 22–29, 2005, p. 102.
5. "Chaos in the classrooms," *The Economist*, August 12, 2006, pp. 32–3.
6. Ibid.
7. Ibid.
8. Robert A. Theleen, "Private Equity In China," *China's Century: The Awakening Of An Economic Powerhouse*, Laurence Brahm, ed., John Wiley & Sons, 2001, p. 160.
9. Speech by Chinese President Hu Jintao at Yale University, April 21, 2006, pp. 1–2.
10. Ibid., pp. 13–4.
11. Bruce Einhorn, "A Whole New School Of Thought," *Business Week*, August 22/29, 2005, p. 106.
12. Stuttard, ibid., pp. 71–2.
13. Stuttard, ibid., pp. 72–3.
14. Ibid., p. 73.
15. Ibid., pp. 73–4.